Merely Players

Edward Wagenknecht

A great actor becomes the second author of his
parts by his accents and his physiognomy.

MADAME DE STAËL

UNIVERSITY OF OKLAHOMA PRESS : NORMAN

Some other books by Edward Wagenknecht

Cavalcade of the American Novel, 1952; *Cavalcade of the English Novel*, 1943; *Chaucer: Modern Essays in Criticism* (edited), 1959; *Chicago*, 1964; *Dickens and the Scandalmongers*, 1965; *Edgar Allan Poe: The Man Behind the Legend*, 1963; *The Fireside Book of Christmas Stories* (edited), 1945; *Harriet Beecher Stowe, The Known and the Unknown*, 1965; *Henry Wadsworth Longfellow: Portrait of an American Humanist*, 1966; *An Introduction to Dickens* (edited), 1952; *The Man Charles Dickens: A Victorian Portrait*, 1966; *Mark Twain, The Man and his Work*, 1961; *The Movies in the Age of Innocence*, 1962; *Mrs. Longfellow: Selected Letters and Journals*, 1956; *Nathaniel Hawthorne, Man and Writer*, 1961; *A Preface to Literature*, 1954; *Seven Daughters of the Theater*, 1964; *The Seven Worlds of Theodore Roosevelt*, 1958; *Stories of Christ and Christmas* (edited), 1963; *Washington Irving: Moderation Displayed*, 1962

Library of Congress Catalog Card Number: 66–22715

Copyright 1966 by the University of Oklahoma Press, Publishing Division of the University. Composed and printed at Norman, Oklahoma, U.S.A., by the University of Oklahoma Press. First edition.

In Memory of
E. H. SOTHERN
(1859–1933)
The Perfect Actor

Preface

Merely Players is a kind of masculine counterpart to my *Seven Daughters of the Theater*, but there are important differences between the two books. While the *Daughters* concerned, besides three actresses of the legitimate stage, two opera singers, a dancer, and a film star, *Merely Players* confines itself entirely to "the legit" and mainly to the nineteenth century. (The opening portrait, that of David Garrick, is an exception, of course; here, for the first time, I have gone back to the eighteenth century.) Another influence toward unity proceeded from the fact that all my players except Joseph Jefferson were considerably preoccupied with Shakespeare, Richard Mansfield less so than the others. Perhaps I should also mention the fact that this time I am writing about eight actors none of whom I myself ever saw. Other things being equal, I should expect a gain here in disinterestedness and a loss of intimacy. Finally, I take it as axiomatic that no man can write about another man in quite the same spirit that he writes of a woman.

For me the book has a special interest in that though it has all been written in 1965 and 1966, it was conceived more than forty years ago. In 1922 or 1923 I took Robert Herrick's "English 5" at the University of Chicago. Though I had made up my mind that I was going to be a writer when I read *The Wizard of Oz* at the age of six, and had at once begun to practice, I had got no help from my freshman composition course and not much direct training in writing from the English courses I took in high school. Herrick's course, however, was very important to me; so was David Allan Robertson's "English 4," which I had taken just before it. Neither of these men tried to teach me how to write, for they were both much too intelligent not to know that writing cannot be taught. But they put me to work writing, and they read what I had written and encouraged me, and this was very important to me. Though my relations with Robertson were much the closer, Herrick's encouragement was particularly important, both because he was then at the height of his reputation as a novelist, and because he was not considered to be in the habit of scattering praise indiscriminately over the Chicago terrain.

The second paper I wrote for him was a portrait of Richard Mansfield, and this was my very first essay in psychography. He liked it well enough so that I was encouraged to send it to Gamaliel Bradford, together with a letter in which I tried to tell him how much his books meant to me. Bradford might very well have been offended, for my imitation had been slavish. Instead, he was wonderfully kind and generous, even telling me that I should probably be able to carry psychography on from the place where he would have to drop it, and this was the beginning of a close friendship which ended only with his death.

My paper on Richard Mansfield was published in *The Sewanee Review*, Vol. XXXVIII (1930), 149–60, where it served at least one good purpose: it greatly pleased Mrs. Mansfield. It is not, however, the Mansfield paper which appears between these covers. This is entirely new.

The interesting thing that all this is leading up to is that having done the Mansfield, I immediately saw it as part of a collection of psychographs of great actors which should pass under the title of "Merely Players." And this time Herrick discouraged me.

He did not, he said, think any publisher would take a chance on such a book by an unknown writer.

I do not know whether he was right or wrong, for I took his word for it, and did not try any publisher out. But now, these many years and many books later, I am at last publishing *Merely Players.* All of which, I suppose, shows that everything comes to him who waits—if he lives long enough—or, as John Burroughs put it:

> *Serene I fold my hands and wait,*
> *Nor care for wind nor tide nor sea;*
> *I rave no more gainst time or fate,*
> *For lo! my own shall come to me.*

One thing more. In these days, when every high school boy who reads one book, one magazine article, and one newspaper item for his "term paper" imagines himself to be doing "research," I know that it is dangerous to state openly that the eight portraits in this volume are not researched to the extent that I hope some of the books I have devoted to single figures deserve to be so described. I have, however, once again made delighted use of the rich resources of the Harvard Theatre Collection, and I acknowledge gladly, as always, the kind and generous co-operation I have enjoyed from Miss Helen D. Willard, its curator, and her assistant, Miss Penelope Hull.

EDWARD WAGENKNECHT

West Newton, Mass.
March 1, 1966

Contents

Illustrations

Merely Players

1

David Garrick
(1717–1779)

D AVID GARRICK is the most famous of all English actors. Thomas Gray did not admire him, nor Horace Walpole either, and Dr. Johnson's admiration was mean and grudging, as if to suggest that he was jealous of the old pupil who, coming to London with him, had somehow managed to corral more wealth and fame in a less intellectual pursuit than his own. But Edmund Burke said of him that "he raised the character of his profession to the rank of a liberal art," and the actress Kitty Clive once exclaimed, less elegantly, "Damn him, he could act a gridiron." Certainly he was one of the representative men of his time, and he associated on terms of equality with those commonly accepted as the leaders of the age outside the theater to an extent which none of his successors have equalled.

It may seem odd and ironical, therefore, that Garrick's very greatness as an actor should have conspired with his virtues as a man to make it more difficult to paint a vivid portrait of him than is the case with others who were probably less gifted than he. If he did not act a gridiron, he did enact practically everything else. Grimm said of him that he tried to "*be* the thing he represented," and the German traveler Lichtenberg recorded

3

that "when he turns to some one with a bow, it is not merely that the head, the shoulders, the feet and arms, are engaged in this exercise, but that each member helps with great propriety to produce the demeanor most pleasing and appropriate to the occasion." How completely he entered into his characters may be inferred from his criticism of Preville on the occasion when he and the French actor tried playing drunk together; Garrick criticized Preville's performance because, as he said, his legs were not drunk. In short, he seems to have been one of those rare actors who really can disappear into their roles, so that when he came on the stage one night as a country bumpkin, his wife did not recognize him, though his dog Biddy did and signalized his entrance by a joyful tail-thumping. Moreover, the firm eighteenth-century legitimate commitment to what present-day film fans speak of as "double" or "triple" bills made it possible for him to display his astonishing versatility in the most effective possible way, by portraying, say, King Lear and a loutish school-boy on the same evening.

Whether this really is the ideal in acting need not be debated here, but it should be understood that the subject is not closed. There is the famous story of the Lichfield grocer who, coming to London with a letter from Garrick's brother, failed to present it after seeing him in his greatest comic role, that of Abel Drugger in Ben Jonson's *The Alchemist*, because he desired no contact whatever with such a shabby, mean, pitiful hound as he had seen on the stage, and if this seems too much like Partridge in *Tom Jones*, who preferred the King to Hamlet because he made more noise, it is still true that many lovers of the theater wish to be conscious of the artist as well as the character (and of the interplay between the two), and that most of those who are remembered in theatrical history have survived because their contemporaries found their personalities as memorable as their art. It is certainly an aesthetic achievement to lose oneself in a character, yet one cannot but remember that there are personalities too great for submergence, just as there are said to be persons

4

so far removed from mediumistic sensibility that they cannot be hypnotized. Many good judges consider mimicry the lowest of the actor's gifts. For Garrick, on stage and off, mimicry was as easy as breathing; he was always ready to mimic anything or anybody at the drop of a hat, and though nobody would be so foolish as to pretend that his art ended here, one may still wonder whether this extraordinary gift helped or hindered the development of his higher powers. When we pass from the actor to the man, the power declines and the gift of accommodation remains. Garrick was a good man; he was delightful, charming, companionable; but except when he was in control of a situation, as in his relationship to his company, he did not dominate in either the good sense or the bad; and though he had faults, they were too petty to be called interesting faults, and they added no color to his personality.

It is interesting too that England's greatest actor should have had so little English in him. He was born at the Angel Inn, Hereford, on February 19, 1717, and grew up in Lichfield. His father was a minor army officer of French Huguenot stock, and his mother was half-Irish. The family was a large one, and there was very little money.

He was sent to Lichfield Grammar School, where he studied under a cruel master who had oppressed his fellow-townsman Samuel Johnson before him, and was later (1736) one of Johnson's own pupils at Edial Hall, where he amused his classmates by peeping through the keyhole of their bedroom door at Johnson and his grotesque wife and mimicking what he saw. In between, he had been apprenticed briefly to his Uncle David in the wine business at Lisbon, which did not work out, and had had his interest in the theater fired by a troupe of strolling players, and had himself appeared at the Bishop's Palace in an amateur performance of Farquhar's *The Recruiting Officer.*

In 1737 he and Johnson came to London together, and he was entered as a student at Lincoln's Inn. This did not get him far, and he did not do much better in a return to the wine trade, managing the London end while his older brother Peter looked after the home office in Lichfield. Possibly the Covent Garden area was too near to permit him to concentrate all his energies upon business. In March, 1741, he substituted for another actor at Goodman's Fields, and in the summer the manager Giffard took him to Ipswich, where he appeared as Aboan in Southerne's dramatization of Mrs. Behn's *Oroonoko* and in other roles. He did not venture actually to commit himself to acting until after his mother's death, and even then his brother Peter, the proper wine merchant, seems to have gone through a series of fits that would have done credit to the principal of a Victorian young ladies' seminary.

As "a Gentleman who never appeared on any stage," Garrick "arrived" in the theater when he acted Richard III at Goodman's Fields on October 19, 1741. The *Daily Post* declared that his reception was "the most extraordinary and great that was ever known on such an occasion"; later his clear, sweet, harmonious voice and his graceful mien and gait were praised. "When three or four are on the stage with him, he is attentive to whatever is spoke, and never drops his character when he has finished a speech." It was at once recognized that he had declared war upon the stately, beplumed chanters, with stereotyped costumes and gestures, who had been holding the stage in tragedy, so that their leader James Quin himself remarked that "if the young fellow is right, I and all the rest of the players have been all wrong." Garrick went on to *The Orphan, The Rehearsal,* his own play *The Lying Valet,* and much more before the end of the season, first using his own name when he appeared as Lothario in *The Fair Penitent* on December 2, and his success was so great that the Licensing Act of 1737, confining the performance of the legitimate drama to Drury Lane and Covent Garden (hitherto more honored in the breach than in the observance), was invoked against Goodman's Fields, and Garrick found himself engaged by the Lane for the coming season.

He spent the summer acting in Dublin and appeared at the

6

Lane on October 5, 1742, in *The Orphan*. *The Rehearsal, The Recruiting Officer, The Beaux Stratagem, The Alchemist, Richard III, King Lear, Hamlet,* and others followed. On January 7, 1744, he made a great point of restoring Shakespeare's *Macbeth* to the stage but failed to clear out all D'Avenant's rubbish. Partly because his short stature, black face, and turban reminded spectators of the little Negro Pompey in Hogarth's *The Harlot's Progress*, he was less successful as Othello (March 7, 1745), but he triumphed again as Sir John Brute in *The Provoked Wife*.

In 1747 he and James Lacy secured control of Drury Lane, whose artistic affairs he thereafter controlled. His first production was a revival of *The Merchant of Venice*, with Charles Macklin as Shylock, and with Garrick speaking Johnson's Prologue—

> *The drama's laws, the drama's patrons give,*
> *For we that live to please, must please to live.*

This might perhaps have been taken as a warning of what happened at Christmastime 1750, when Garrick staged the pantomime *Queen Mab*, attempting to dethrone his rival, John Rich, as "Pantomime King" at Covent Garden,[1] and in 1755 he brought the great Jean-Georges Noverre to London and introduced French ballet.[2] Meanwhile, among many other plays, he produced *Much Ado About Nothing*, in November, 1748, with Mrs. Cibber and himself, and in September, 1750, he participated in a *Romeo and Juliet* war with George Anne Bellamy and himself playing against Barry and Mrs. Cibber at the Garden. On February 6, 1749, he put on Johnson's *Irene*, and in 1753 he appeared as Beverley in Edward Moore's protest against one of the reigning vices of the time, in *The Gamester*.[3]

[1] Margaret Barton believes that "the effectiveness of Rich's miming" may well have "brought home to Garrick the sterility of the classical style of acting," and that "he owed much of his power of expressing thought by gesture and byplay to the inspiration of Harlequin." *Garrick*, 113–14.

[2] Because of current anti-French feeling in England, the immediate result was a disastrous riot, but Noverre's great period opened with this engagement.

[3] According to George M. Kahrl, the average Drury Lane season embraced

On June 22, 1749, Garrick married the Austrian opera dancer, Mlle Violette (Eva Maria Veigel). In 1751 he made a trip to Paris with her, and in 1754 he established her and himself in a beautiful estate at Hampton, on the bank of the Thames, which caused Johnson to remark that it was leaving such places that made death terrible. Waning popularity was ingeniously re-stimulated by an absence from the stage between 1763 and 1765, followed by an arranged return by royal command in *Much Ado*, on November 14, 1765. In 1769 he ran the first Shakespeare Jubilee at Stratford, and in 1772 he moved his town residence to the new architectural wonder created by the Adam brothers, Adelphi Terrace.

In 1775, Garrick sold his Drury Lane patent to Richard Brins-ley Sheridan, and on March 7, 1776, he announced his retire-ment. Between then and June 10 he took leave of his public in all his leading roles. Garrick's retirement drew spectators from all over Europe; it may well have been the most impressive event in theatrical history. His last appearance on the stage was as Don Felix in Mrs. Centlivre's *The Wonder! a Woman Keeps a Secret*. He died on January 20, 1779, and was buried in the Poet's Corner at the Abbey, leaving Eva to linger on, cherishing the memory of her "Davy," until 1822, when she had nearly but not quite rounded out a century.

II

Dr. Johnson was less rough than he seemed when he told Gibbon that Garrick acting felt about as much passion as Punch, for he added: "Ask Reynolds whether he felt the distress of Count Ugolino when he drew it," and he showed a true under-standing of his old pupil when he said that he "left nothing to

---

180–90 days and included fifty plays, of which an average of less than five were new. Nine performances was a long "run," and few plays were acted more than fifteen times during the season. *The Letters of David Garrick*, ed. by Little and Kahrl, I, xlviii–ix. See, further, in *PMLA*, Vol. LXXIV (1959), 225–32, Fred L. Bergmann's account of "Garrick's *Zara*," which he put on for twenty-three con-secutive seasons.

chance. Every gesture, every expression of countenance and variation of voice, was settled in the closet before he set his foot upon the stage." For Garrick himself told young Edward Cape Everard that he would never be an actor if he could not "give a speech, or make love to a table, chair, or marble slab, as well as to the finest woman in the world."

This would seem to be quite the opposite of what is called "Method" acting today, but it should be understood that Garrick was too intelligent not to use impulse or even accident when they could serve his needs. Sometimes he went to the Old Bailey to study the emotions displayed by the unfortunates there, and his Lear was importantly influenced by his observation of a man he met who had accidentally killed his child by dropping her out the window and who, having lost his mind in consequence, would reproduce the experience in pantomime upon demand.[4] He believed that "the greatest strokes of genius have been unknown to the actor himself, till circumstances and the warmth of the scene, has sprung the mine as it were, as much to his own surprise as that of the audience. Thus I make a great difference between a great genius and a good actor. The first will always realize the feelings of his character, and be transported beyond himself." And he criticized the great French actress Clairon because he thought she lacked those "instantaneous feelings . . . that keen sensitivity that bursts at once from genius, and, like electrical fire, shoots through the veins, marrow, and bones and all of every spectator."

Garrick advised young William Powell and other actors to develop their minds and culture beyond immediate theatrical requirements and to avoid dissipation. He himself had much more culture and scholarship than could reasonably have been expected under the circumstances of his life. Like Shakespeare in the eyes of another Jonson, he may have had "small Latin and less Greek," but he had some of both. Davies says: "He was a

---

[4] Garrick's own reproduction of this action as a parlor piece seems more than a little heartless to modern taste.

master of the French language, and spoke it fluently; he understood Italian, but could not long maintain a conversation in it; Spanish he could read, but I believe, with some difficulty."

He seems to have been considerably more sensitive to nature than some of us might have expected of a pre-Romantic; when in 1763 he saw the snow-capped Savoy Mountains with the cultivated fields and the winding rivers below, he thought the sight ample compensation for the fatigue of the journey he had undertaken, even if no other loveliness should uncover itself. He did not get very far with music, but he had the sound eighteenth-century taste in architecture, and he was an indefatigable collector (and inspirer) of pictures and *objets d'art*, with a sufficiently catholic taste to be enthusiastic about both Rubens and his friend Hogarth. He had a magnificent library, yet I cannot think of him as a very bookish person; Davies rings true when he writes:

> A mind like his was continually improving from the company by which he was constantly surrounded. His house was a rendezvous for excellence of every kind; for
>
> *Lights of the church and guardians of the laws;*
>
> for the learned, the elegant, the polite, and the accomplished in all arts and sciences; so that he was continually drawing from the great fountains of wisdom and knowledge. . . .[5]

Except that he lacked height (he was only five foot, four),

[5] Garrick was, of course, himself a prolific writer, but the analysis and evaluation of his plays and verses does not fall within my province here. There is a detailed study of *David Garrick, Dramatist* by Elizabeth P. Stein (Modern Language Association of America, 1938), who finds in him "an extensive and thorough acquaintance with the drama of France, of Italy, and of England from Elizabeth's day through that of his own" and a Shakespearean readiness to borrow what he needed. He was classical in his preference for keeping tragedy and comedy apart, and his acting versions of Shakespeare's plays never restored any comic matter that had been expunged. He preferred "humor and kindly ridicule" to "the pathos and sympathy of sentimental comedy." See, further, the chapters on Garrick as dramatist and poet in F. A. Hedgcock, *David Garrick and His French Friends*, and Dougald MacMillan, "David Garrick as Critic," *Studies in Philology*, Vol. XXXI (1934), 69–83.

Garrick had about all the natural qualifications the actor needs. When he was playing Romeo against Barry, a current epigram ran:

> *So reversed are the notions of Capulet's daughters,*
> *One loves a whole length, the other three-quarters.*

And when the malevolent Samuel Foote was asked whether his puppets were to be as large as life, he replied cruelly, "Oh, no, not much larger than Garrick."

He lost his voice halfway through his first Richard III but restored himself by sucking oranges; except that he always had to be careful not to strain it, it seems thereafter to have met the demands he placed upon it, but it is never spoken of as of extraordinary beauty. His eyes were his really extraordinary, apparently almost hypnotic, feature. Even during his last season, they terrified young Mrs. Siddons when he glanced at her sharply upon her forgetting some of her business in *Richard III,* and once when, as Macbeth, he whispered, "There's blood upon thy face" to the First Murderer, the actor wiped himself involuntarily and cried, "Is there, by God?" Diderot speaks of *"un jeu prodigieux dans les yeux,"* and goes on to credit Garrick with much *"esprit"* and *"finesse."*

The *esprit,* as least, has never been doubted. Until his health finally broke,[6] Garrick had tremendous energy; he was never still. On the stage this was largely deliberate; he wanted a more "natural" movement and delivery than had been in vogue, and when he went to Paris in 1851, he professed himself, at the outset, unable to judge the actors, both their speaking and their acting

[6] One of Edmund Kean's biographers declares loftily that Garrick "never in his lifetime knew a single day of suffering," but was nevertheless (though I do not see the connection) "a vain and petty tyrant." There was never a better illustration than this of the truth of the saying that ignorance never settled a question. For his sake, one can only hope that the lofty gentleman will never be called upon to endure the agonies of gout and kidney stone which plagued Garrick's later years. When a postmortem examination was made, it was found that Garrick had never had but one kidney, and when it became diseased he was done for. The immediate causes of his death were uremia and inflammation of the bladder.

being so different from what he was accustomed to, "and I think not agreeable to their own or any nature." So when Quin, glancing at the new Methodist movement, called Garrick "the Whitefield of the stage," and prophesied that people would come back "to church" after the novelty had worn off, Garrick replied cleverly that

> *When Doctrines meet with gen'ral approbation,*
> *It is not* Heresy, *but* Reformation.

His facial expression varied constantly; he once mischievously baffled Reynolds trying to paint his portrait by putting on a new face every time the painter glanced at him, and when, late in life, he was accused of looking older than his years, Johnson said it was no wonder, his face having experienced so much more wear and tear than those of other men. He knew every trick in the book. When he returned to the stage after having murdered Duncan, his clothes were disarranged and his wig hanging crooked, and he had taken the trouble to wipe the make-up off his face so as to suggest pallor. He enlisted the aid of his hairdresser to cause his hair or his wig to stand on end when Hamlet sees the Ghost. His readings, too, kept his audiences continually on their toes, and it was said of him that "no man ever did, nor possibly ever will, speak . . . broken sentences, and make transitions with such penetrating effect."

Naturally not everybody found all this pother equally attractive. When *Irene* was in preparation, Johnson declined to make some changes Garrick desired, because "the fellow wants me to make Mohomet run mad, that he may have an opportunity of tossing his hands and kicking his heels." Though this was probably unfair, it was not determined entirely by an author's sensitive vanity, for Johnson also told Boswell that he hoped he would not behave like Garrick in *Hamlet* if he himself were to see a ghost: "If I did, I should frighten the ghost." Even Macklin, Garrick's only important immediate predecessor in "natural" acting, and an influence upon him, objected to his "bustle," his "squeezing his hat, thumping his breast, strutting up and down the stage, and pawing the characters [*sic*] that he acted with." Some thought his Hamlet, as first enacted, "a hot, testy fellow, for ever flying into a passion," and Othello's speech to the Senate was criticized for "too many gestures, which were inconsistent with the natural modesty and dignity of the situation." He does not seem to have had much ear for the rhythm of blank verse. He was not famous for his reading of any sustained passages, and some readings have been recorded which are so bad as to cause one to wonder whether he had any understanding of what he was saying.[7] It has been charged that he did not like enterprises which had been suggested by others, but he did not "create" many of his greatest roles, and he was always willing to modify an interpretation even when it was a perfect stranger who had pointed out his error to him.[8] He had difficulty with lovers and with "gentlemen," and he was painfully sensitive to his audiences and always capable of being thrown off when something went wrong, either in the auditorium or on the stage. When Lord March fell asleep during a private reading, he was so greatly disturbed that he told his hostess she must never ask him to read again when March was of the company. Apparently acting was a great strain for Garrick. He never appeared every night, as modern actors do; during his later years he cut his appearances drastically, and though he was only in his fifties when he retired, he had already lost the power to learn new roles. It is part of his greatness that it has never been decided whether he was greater in tragedy or in comedy, but Johnson was not alone in the view that he was primarily a comedian. To support this, Garrick's own statement to Charles Bannister, when he was thinking of giving up tragedy for comedy, is often cited: "No, no, you may humbug

[7] For an extreme statement of this point of view, see C. B. Cooper, "Captain Thomas Morris on Garrick," *Modern Language Notes*, Vol. XXXII (1917), 504–505. "Garrick and verse were not made to agree." No one ever differed more from Shakespeare: "Shakespeare wrote from his heart; Garrick played from his head."

[8] See *Letters of David Garrick*, ed. by Little and Kahrl. I, 350 ff.

the town some time longer as a tragedian, but comedy is a serious thing." But if this means anything more than that Garrick did not think Bannister suited for comedy, it would seem to suggest that he himself found it the more difficult mode of expression of the two.

III

In twenty years at Drury Lane, Garrick put on 1,448 performances of twenty-eight of Shakespeare's plays, himself appearing in eighteen different roles. His contemporaries equated him with both Shakespeare and nature, and often appealed to him for the elucidation of difficult passages. Diderot dubbed him "David Shakespeare," and the poem on his memorial in the Abbey, which so infuriated Lamb, ends:

> *Shakespeare and Garrick like twin stars shall shine,*
> *And earth irradiate with a beam divine.*

Modesty would have prevented Garrick from going quite that far himself, but he had no doubts concerning his own devotion to "the God of my Idolatry—Shakespeare!—*Him him! He is the Him!*—there is no Other." He thought of Drury Lane as the "House of Shakespeare." "I am afraid my madness about Shakespeare is become very troublesome," he once wrote a correspondent, "for I question whether I have written a single letter, without bringing him in, head and shoulders." He made an important collection of Shakespeare books, and the relics he gathered together were no less sincere a testimonial to his affection for being a little absurd. The great Stratford Jubilee—"that foolish hobby horse of mine," as he called it, looking back upon it—had its absurd side too, and this not only because it was crippled by the Avon choosing to overflow its banks just as it was being apostrophized, but, even more, because no work of Shakespeare's was either acted or read during the festivities, yet here again there can be no doubt of Garrick's complete sincerity.[9] When he went to Paris, the French regarded him almost as Shakespeare's personal representative, and he apparently avoided meeting Voltaire because he could not stomach his attitude toward Shakespeare. He certainly encouraged, though he did not inaugurate, the Shakespeare revival then going on in France, and it would seem reasonable to credit him with considerable influence upon Shakespeare criticism in England also. " 'Tis my chief wish," so ends his Prologue to his acting version of *The Winter's Tale:*

> *'Tis my chief wish, my joy, my only plan*
> *To lose no drop of that immortal man!*

But there's the rub! Garrick imposed what the eighteenth century considered unity upon *The Winters Tale* itself by beginning with Act IV, summarizing the earlier events meagerly, and blowing out the rest of the play with his own songs and verses. On the same night he reduced *The Taming of the Shrew* to the proportions of an afterpiece as *Katherine and Petruchio. A Midsummer Night's Dream*, as Theophilus Cibber sarcastically put it, was

[9] Few subjects have been more overinvestigated during recent years than the Jubilee. The year 1964 produced three books on the subject: Christian Deelman, *The Great Shakespeare Jubilee* (Michael Joseph); Johanne M. Stochholm, *Garrick's Folly: The Shakespeare Jubilee of 1769 at Stratford and Drury Lane* (Methuen); Martha Winburn England, *Garrick's Jubilee* (Ohio State University Press). Deelman calls the "Ode" which Garrick read "a wonderful jumble of lines from all the poetry he knew; an actor's poem, a cento of tags, images, and dog-ends, so constructed as to allow him to interpret half a dozen aspects of Shakespeare's art. Its tone was one of outright idolatry, blended with heavy infusions of patriotism. There was no uniting theme; it moved from one idea to another with a momentum sustained only by the rhapsodic tone of the whole." But he agrees with the *Gentleman's Magazine* that it served the occasion well: "It was not meant to be read; it was meant to be heard, and heard through the medium of the voice for which it had been written." It is noticeable that all the immediate reports praise its poetic merits. It *sounded* superb." And Deelman himself calls Garrick's reading "the greatest performance of his life. . . . Alone, without costume or make-up, with no text apart from the inept patchwork of his own construction, aided only by that mysterious spell which music can cast upon the spoken word, Garrick lived up to his reputation." There is a briefer account of the Jubilee by Martha England in her *Garrick and Stratford* (New York Public Library, 1962), and Lily B. Campbell antedated all these studies in "Shakespeare's Vagary," in *Shakespeare Studies by Members of the Department of English at the University of Wisconsin* (University of Wisconsin, 1916).

"minced and fricasseed into a thing called *The Fairies*," and *The Tempest* "castrated into an opera." Garrick's *King Lear* came closer to Shakespeare than what his predecessors had been presenting, but he did not restore either the Fool or the tragic ending. In *Macbeth*, only Hecate was allowed to fly, but the witches still danced and sang, the drunken porter was sobered up and the murder of Lady Macduff omitted, and Macbeth's dying agonies were prolonged through the addition of a new speech of Garrick's own composing. *Hamlet* lost the gravediggers, the fencing match, the deaths of Rosencrantz and Guildenstern and the Queen, the advice to the players, and the soliloquy on finding the King at prayer. *Romeo and Juliet* was subjected to senseless emendation, the Rosaline episode dropped out, and Juliet awakened after Romeo had taken poison but before he died, so that the lovers might have a dying scene together, compounded of Otway, Congreve, and Garrick himself. When Garrick revived *Antony and Cleopatra* in 1759, for the first time since the Restoration, he made some cuts but otherwise left the text unaltered. But this was the exception, not the rule, and unfortunately *Antony and Cleopatra* was not of his successes.

But none of this, bad as it seems to us, can be judged by twentieth-century standards. A "rage for retouching" was characteristic of the time, and not even the Shakespeare scholars objected to it. Warburton "read the reformed *Winter's Tale* with great pleasure," and Steevens described the butchery of *Hamlet* as "a circumstance in favor of the poet." Dr. Johnson certainly was quite exceptional when he wondered whether Garrick had ever read a Shakespearean play through in the original. But the idea that Shakespeare is actable as he stands seems to be peculiar to his time and to ours. Garrick's *Romeo and Juliet* still held the stage when Percy Fitzgerald published his *Life of Garrick* in 1868, and Fitzgerald still regarded its superiority to the original as axiomatic. I am happy to say that I have seen the Garrick-type ending only in Gounod's opera (where the operatic form and conventions make it inevitable), but I never saw the whole of the last scene performed before Katharine Cornell's production; even Sothern and Marlowe dropped the curtain on the death of the lovers. As for Cibber's version of *Richard III*, Robert Mantell used it as long as he performed the play, and I must admit that he made it more thrilling than any *Richard III* I have seen since, though this was probably because he was Mantell and not because he was mouthing Cibber.[10]

Little can be charged against Garrick as a producer. In twenty-nine years he produced seventy-five new plays. Sometimes he missed a play that he ought to have taken. Home's *Douglas* and Goldsmith's *The Goodnatured Man* are the two most frequently cited examples, but *Douglas* was not in actable condition when it was presented to him. He did produce Home later, and greatly overpraised him: "You have written some passages . . . more like Shakespeare than any other author ever did." He also produced much trash—as George M. Kahrl points out, "barely half a dozen of his ninety or more roles, exclusive of Shakespeare, are ever revived"—but he could not have kept the house open without this. His principal fault was that he some-

10 George Winchester Stone, Jr.'s Harvard (1938) dissertation, "Garrick's Handling of Shakespeare's Plays and his Influence upon the Changed Attitude of Shakespearean Criticism during the Eighteenth Century," has not been published, but see his valuable articles: "Garrick's Long Lost Alteration of *Hamlet*," *PMLA*, Vol. XLIX (1934), 890–921, which includes the full text of Act V, as performed by Garrick; "Garrick's Presentation of *Antony and Cleopatra*," *Review of English Studies*, Vol. XIII (1937), 20–38; "*A Midsummer Night's Dream* in the Hands of Garrick and Colman," *PMLA*, Vol. LIV (1939), 467–82; "Garrick and an Unknown Operatic Version of *Love's Labour's Lost*," *Review of English Studies*, Vol. XV (1939), 323–28; "Garrick's Handling of *Macbeth*," *Studies in Philology*, Vol. XXXVIII (1941), 609–28; "Garrick's Production of *King Lear*: A Study in the Temper of the Eighteenth-Century Mind," *Studies in Philology*, Vol. XLV (1948), 89–103; "The God of His Idolatry: Garrick's Theory of Acting and Dramatic Composition with Especial Reference to Shakespeare," in James G. McManaway *et al.*, eds., *Joseph Quincy Adams Memorial Studies* (The Folger Shakespeare Library, 1948); "David Garrick's Significance in the History of Shakespearean Criticism," *PMLA*, Vol. LXV (1950), 183–97; "Shakespeare's *Tempest* at Drury Lane During Garrick's Management," *Shakespeare Quarterly*, Vol. VII (1956), 1–7; "*Romeo and Juliet*: The Source of its Modern Stage Career," *Shakespeare Quarterly*, Vol. XV (1964), 191–206. The conclusions which emerge from Stone's careful and exhaustive studies are very favorable to Garrick and have considerably increased his stature.

times allowed influential persons to pressure him into producing plays that he knew were not worth producing, but here again allowance must be made for the conditions under which he had to work.

"Direction" in the modern sense did not exist in Garrick's time, when modern ideas of ensemble playing had not yet been born, and actors of force and independent spirit were more or less allowed to "gang their ain gait." Yet Garrick came much closer to directing than his predecessors had come. His rehearsals were frequent and prolonged for his time, and he was quite capable of disciplining players who failed to attend by fining them or leaving them out of his casts. In 1763 he discharged his future biographer Thomas Davies for breach of playhouse discipline. He often devoted three to eight weeks to getting a new play ready, and one play was in preparation for a year. "From the very outset he conveyed his concept of the characters and their interpretations by acting out all the roles [male and female] with appropriate facial expressions."[11] During the summer, young players were sometimes invited to his house at Hampton, to be instructed there. "I have seen you," wrote Kitty Clive, "with your magical hammer in your hand, endeavoring to beat your ideas into the heads of creatures who had none of their own. I have seen you, with lamb-like patience, endeavoring to make them comprehend you; and I have seen you when it could not be done. I have seen your lamb turned into a lion." Yet he was not tyrannical about such things, and was quite capable of accepting the interpretation of another actor even when it conflicted with his own.

Persons who feel sure that manners have deteriorated during the twentieth century might find a useful antidote to pessimism

11 Kalmin A. Burnim, *David Garrick, Director* (University of Pittsburgh Press, 1961), an authoritative study, upon which this paragraph is based. See, further, Dougald MacMillan's introduction to his *Drury Lane Calendar 1747–1776* (Oxford University Press, 1938) and his article, "David Garrick, Manager: Notes on the Theatre as a Cultural Institution in England in the Eighteenth Century," *Studies in Philology*, Vol. XLV (1948), 630–46.

in studying the behavior of Garrick's audiences.[12] Garrick faced riots all through his career; once his dear public even rioted in the King's presence. (His Majesty, having inquired the cause, discreetly withdrew!) Sometimes such disturbances were caused by the manager's attempt to reform abuses—like abolishing sitting on the stage or keeping the rakes out of the dressing rooms—and sometimes they were deliberately worked up to satisfy private grudges. Once, having wrecked the theater, the "gentlemen" repaired to the manager's house and broke the windows. Garrick was never craven on such occasions; once he cowed the mob by threatening to quit the theater forever. But the snake was never more than scotched, not killed, and there were times, too, when he submitted to indignities which seem inconceivable in our less vocal age.

Garrick's relations with other actors cannot be summed up in a word. Davies' statement that he never spoke warmly "in the commendation of any actor, living or dead" is obviously untrue, for evidence exists to the contrary, but he does seem to have been more at ease with the French, who could not loom up as potential rivals, than he was with the English. When William Powell filled Drury Lane during his absence in Europe, he appears to have rejoiced in the excellent business and at the same time to have felt a little uneasy lest he might be supplanted. He was never friends with Quin until after Quin had retired.

One thing is certain, however: Garrick surrounded himself with the finest company available, and he allowed them ample opportunity to exercise their gifts. Genest's statement that he rejected Home's *Douglas* and Dodsley's *Cleone* because they gave Mrs. Cibber better roles than they afforded him seems worse than doubtful, and young Mrs. Siddons' impression that he was surrounded by "fulsome adulation" during his last year on the stage is not worth much. It is true that he assigned leading roles to himself, and sometimes even fattened his roles—he could

[12] See Harry William Pedicord, *The Theatrical Public in the Time of Garrick* (King's Crown Press, 1954).

not have pleased his public otherwise—but he produced many plays in whose cast he did not appear at all, and, as Burnim has pointed out, he did not take on one new role in the thirty-eight new main pieces produced after 1763. He had trouble from time to time with Wilkinson, Woodward, and others, and there was nearly always some lady who was not being treated right. He once said of Kitty Clive that it was a pity she was not "as rational off the stage as she is meritorious on it," and he told Frances Abington that he had never seen her "theatrically happy" for a week at a time. In his most famous quarrel—with Charles Macklin—he was technically in the wrong, but practically he was right.[13]

Yet it would be idle to claim that other actors greatly liked Garrick, and I think it would be disingenuous to pretend that this was altogether their fault. No doubt they were jealous of him, but this does not completely cover the case. To begin with, he was a snob, who made no secret of his contempt for the "poor, unedifying, commonplace gabble" of his fellow mummers, and wanted nothing to do with them socially. I do not doubt Garrick's sincere affection for "my best of Ladies," Georgiana Countess Spencer (he elevates her almost to the Shakespearean level when he calls her "the Goddess of my Idolatry"), but there are many passages in his letters to her which justify the comment of the editors that "he could never be entirely natural," and she herself once exercised a great lady's privilege by writing him:

[13] Garrick and Macklin organized a kind of actor's strike at Goodman's Fields, and after many negotiations found themselves in a position where the situation could not be resolved without leaving Macklin out of the settlement. Garrick used every possible means of avoiding this, even to the extent of being willing to sacrifice considerable income himself, but without avail, not yielding until his other colleagues pointed out that he must choose between sacrificing Macklin and sacrificing all of them, including Macklin. Though Garrick opened his management at Drury Lane with a play in which Macklin enacted the leading role, it may be doubted that the latter ever forgave him. No doubt he honestly believed that Garrick had betrayed him, and theoretically an excellent case can be made for this view. But Macklin seems to have been quite unable to perceive that when he insisted that Garrick and the others should sacrifice themselves for him, he was not himself manifesting any overwhelming or ennobling spirit of selflessness.

"I have no great partiality for studied letters, nor do I much admire those you have sent." It was not bad that he should be a strict, even sometimes a severe manager, but apparently he could also be superior, rude, overbearing, sometimes even coarse or profane, and this was resented all the more because his victims knew they were under his thumb and had no real redress. Very likely a feeling of inadequacy on his own part was at the root of such behavior.

He had even more trouble with aspiring playwrights, and it has been the fashion to ascribe this to his indecisiveness. We are told that he did not like to say no, that consequently he often half promised what he ought to have denied, and that therefore when the time came that he could not deliver, there were hurt feelings all around. But the publication of the letters in the Little-Kahrl collection now makes it extremely difficult to justify this view.

I have no doubt that Garrick was a master hemmer and hawer. But in spite of all his near stammering when he was embarrassed, his promises to talk the matter over with Mrs. Garrick, and all the rest of it, there is abundant evidence that he was capable of direct dealing. He himself once wrote Lady Spencer that he was "of a very warm, hasty disposition, and in pain somewhat inclined to be peevish." Again and again, he not only gives a definite answer but takes the trouble to defend his position rationally and at great length. The playwrights, on the other hand, nearly always took up the position that it was Garrick's obligation to produce the play because they happened to want it produced. What could you do with a man like Thomas Ryder, who wrote, "The Drama you reject has been approved by some of the first people of the kingdom for learning and ability! Were I to make use of my power and influence, you must act it." Here, as in his private life—if he can be said to have had a private life—the real trouble was not that he was indecisive but that he spent about half his time explaining himself. It did no good, of course, because it never does, for the simple reason that those capable of understanding have no need of the explanation, while the others could not or would not believe, "though one rose from the dead."

In general, I should say, Garrick was fairer toward actors and playwrights than he was toward other managers, or, in a sense, the public. There were no holds barred in the rivalry between Drury Lane and Covent Garden. They raided each other's talent whenever the opportunity came (which was whenever an actor was jealous or disgruntled, that is, nearly all the time), and tried to ruin each other's first nights with rival productions. Once, when, in ignorance of the French law, Garrick tried to extend such tactics into France, he seems very narrowly to have escaped serious trouble. We have already glanced at the *Romeo and Juliet* war. Garrick also took care to put on Hugh Kelly's *False Delicacy* the same night the *Good-Natured Man* went on at the Garden, and there were other manipulations even less edifying. It is not necessary to take Mrs. Garrick literally when she asked Kean why he did not write his own notices, adding "David always did." But he certainly tried to control the press so far as his influence might extend, and Pope himself was not more addicted to the eighteenth-century habit of rushing into print to attack anybody who had attacked you, in verse if possible, or, still better, to anticipate their attack, or blunt the point of their satire by attacking yourself first. Garrick did all these things, and the least that can be said of them is that frequently they were undignified. If he did not advertise his "milk baths," as Anna Held was to do in the twentieth century, we may be sure that he would have done so if he had been an alluring Frenchwoman. The "publicity" he sought was somewhat different in kind from that which was to be sought by Anna Held—or Sarah Bernhardt—or Mary Garden—but he knew just about as much about "public relations" as any one of them was to learn.

IV

Socially, and away from the theater, Garrick was one of the sprightliest of men. If he detested balls, as he once said, he certainly did not detest human contact, and it has been said of him that he had more friends than any other man of his time. It is true that Dr. Johnson never discovered in his conversation "any intellectual energy, any wide grasp of thought, any extensive comprehension of mind, or that he possessed any of those powers to which *great* could, with any degree of propriety, be applied." But then, Johnson, who frequently blew both hot and cold on Garrick, also said that he was "lively, entertaining, quick in discerning the ridicule of life, and as ready in representing it; and on graver subjects there were few topics in which he could not bear his part."

He was fond of practical jokes, but this seems to have been merely another outlet for his histrionic energy; I have heard no cruel practical jokes recorded of him.[14] He was never more charming than with children, and the fact that he had no child of his own was certainly the great deprivation of his life. Once, as a guest at a country house, he disappeared from the company, and when sought was found imitating a cock for the benefit of a little Negro servant boy in the back yard: "Massa Garrick do so make me laugh! I shall die with laughing!" But he was capable of more sophisticated social intercourse also, and it is not strange that he was such a social success in France, where he associated with the Encyclopedists and others and created a legend which endured for many years. Perhaps his French background and heritage came in here, though he was completely Anglicized in his moral outlook, and all his judgments were English enough.[15]

[14] Perhaps the cleverest was the trick he played on the coachman who refused to start until he had three other passengers. Three times Garrick went off and returned in altered aspect, and after his third entry into the coach, it drove off.

[15] George M. Kahrl believes that his visit to Paris "made Garrick aware that he had a mind for something other than business" and thus contributed to his development as an artist (*Letters*, ed. by Little and Kahrl, I, xliii). It certainly did not incline him in the direction of French classicism, however, and he once wrote a correspondent that "Politisse" had so standardized the French "that when you have seen half a dozen French Men and Women you have seen the whole" (II, 634–35). But he was much harder on the Dutch, whom he considered so "warp'd to traffick" as to be incapable of either "the politer Arts" or friendship and affection" (III, 1178).

Unlike many players, he loved to perform socially, the reason perhaps being that Garrick was born acting, and could not have stopped acting if he had tried. Wherever he was entertained, he would give his impersonations, the dagger scene from Macbeth in dumbshow, as a study in facial expression, being one of his favorites, and Sir Joshua Reynolds, who detested him, said that "he was so artificial that he could break away in the midst of the highest festivity, merely in order to secure the impression he had made."

His social faults were an exaggerated concern with the impression he was making—or what was being said about him (Arthur Murphy was quite right when he said Garrick "lived in a whispering gallery"), and a certain officiousness. One does not think of him as a quarrelsome person, yet he was involved in many quarrels. The eighteenth century was a quarrelsome age, and perhaps people made more of an art of quarreling than they do today. Yet Garrick generally gives me the impression of honesty, even in his touchiest letters, and though he certainly might have avoided many of his quarrels, he was in the right much more often than his opponents.

Garrick's admirers have frequently pointed out that however often he may have quarreled, he rarely refused an overture toward reconciliation. This is true, and as far as it goes, it certainly is to his credit. I would only add that while a willingness to be reconciled may be Christlike, it may also be craven. I do not find much that is Christlike in Garrick, and while I certainly should not call him a coward, there were times when he behaved in a cowardly fashion; sometimes he even stooped to buy off an adversary to save wear and tear. Whether it was the great and formidable Junius whom he had the misfortune to offend or the obscure blackmailer who, apparently without anything to go on, was deviling him when he was taken with his final illness, Garrick rarely confronted the situation as a really strong man would have done. And certainly he treated such people as Foote and Churchill with more consideration than they deserved.

But if there is a trace of meanness here, there is none to be discerned in the area where Garrick has been constantly accused of it—that is, in money matters. Garrick's stinginess was as much a legend in his lifetime as, more playfully, that of a certain well-known comedian is today. There was nothing to it except that, having been brought up in poverty and being a prudent man, he did not waste his money, as so many of his more bohemian colleagues did.

That Garrick left a fortune of about £120,000 when he died would alone suffice to show that he knew how to take care of his money. He did not have the habit of carrying money about with him in his pockets, and this may sometimes have created the impression that he wished to have other people pay for him. As a paymaster he was fair but not lavish, as Sir Henry Irving was. But where there was need, he gave. Johnson does him justice here, for Johnson says he gave away more money than any other man of his time. He would lend small sums or large ones, with security or without security; indeed I have found no record of his ever refusing anybody. He even lent or gave money to people who hated him and of whose hatred he was well aware. When Clairon was in trouble with the French government, he offered her five hundred louis, which, as Voltaire pointed out, was more than a duke or a marquis would have done. It is true that he left it to Covent Garden to organize an actors pension fund, but he did not allow the chagrin he manifested upon their taking the initiative to prevent him from co-operating and making a princely contribution of his own. Moreover, Garrick showed love, as well as a sense of responsibility, by doing little things that require thought and care for all sorts of people, and if he had connections that might be of value to others in need, he would work them for all they were worth. Once, in his own carriage, he came to Hannah More's lodgings with hot minced chicken and a canister of her favorite tea—surely unusual behavior for a man.

Though Garrick finally became a churchwarden, I cannot think of him as a devout man. But he had respect for all sincere forms of religion. He lived happily with a Roman Catholic wife, though he could not resist teasing her about her religion, as when he read Robertson's *History of Scotland*, which is anything but a Catholic book, aloud to her. One Christmas Day he sent George Colman some verses he had composed in church during the sermon! He seems also to have respected the Methodists, whom it was the fashion in his circle to ridicule, himself going to hear Whitefield preach.

There is little fault to be found with his morals. He did not gamble. He was considered a most moderate drinker, but it should be understood that this was by eighteenth-century standards. He was not a nighthawk but a morning lark, and he always warned young actors against the bottle. Once in his life, and once only, having dined with unwonted elaboration before a performance, he found that he could not control his tongue on the stage; this thoroughly frightened him, and he made up his mind that it would never happen again. Yet when he was abroad in 1763–64 he himself records that he ate and drank himself sick, and in 1771 he writes to a reverend correspondent that he cannot do without "Peck and Booze," and that "if the Devil appears to me in the shape of turbot and claret, my crutches are forgot," but five months later he is on castor oil, honey, and barley-water. I would guess that the gout which plagued him during his later years came from its usual cause.

As for morals in the sexual sense, Garrick thought Beaumont and Fletcher's *Philaster* "very indecent." Twentieth-century taste (where there is any) finds certain passages in his own writings coarse, and apparently there was coarseness in his talk at times, but compared to the Restoration comedians, he certainly moved with the age toward decency.[16] When he went to

[16] What is to be made of young Garrick's smart-alecky comment to his father when the latter returned home after a long absence at Gibraltar: "I daresay I have now a good many brothers and sisters at Gibraltar," I do not know; I let the query stand. But Davy did not recognize his own bad taste until he saw his mother's eyes fill with tears.

Paris in 1751, he thought Frenchwomen in general "very ugly and most disagreeably painted," but he also thought them "very easy, well shaped and genteel—they tread better than our ladies and their legs (from their shape and neatness) are more worth seeing than anything else about them." When, during a single walk, he encountered "two *very pretty French women*" unpainted, he found it "a greater curiosity than any I have yet seen in Paris." When, late in life, he caught his niece in a flirtation with a Frenchman whom she had met on the stairs, and whose intentions were so far from being dishonorable that he wished to marry her, Garrick went into moral hysterics and put the poor girl through ridiculously and cruelly humiliating apologies.

Early in his career, Garrick seems himself to have had a liaison with Peg Woffington.[17] Even then he was seriously in love; he wished to marry Peg, and would probably have done so if she had been capable of fidelity. Once he had satisfied himself that she was not, he broke with her completely, and, says Letitia Hawkins, "to have recalled to his mind the time of his early passion (and I have never heard of more than one) would have been, I suppose, to have forfeited his friendship for ever." And she adds that "he was a great instance of the entire change of conduct which so many plead as impossible." He was friendly with Mrs. Cibber, but there is no known foundation for insinuations that they had an affair. Toward the end of his life, both he and his wife were very close to young Hannah More. He also acquired a number of female correspondents, but the only one who calls for special mention is the French actress-novelist, Marie Jeanne Riccoboni. Madame Riccoboni obviously possessed considerable force of mind and character, but Garrick's letters to her suggest that she also enjoyed playing the rattle. She called him "the dearling of her heart," and he himself would

[17] The story that Garrick and Peg Woffington maintained a common household with Macklin seems to be merely a persistent legend, due to the bad habit of biographers in copying unsubstantiated statements from each other.

begin a letter "Thou dear, wild, agreeable Devil!" But the tone is always playful, not passionate, and he hardly ever fails to inform her that Mrs. Garrick is by his side as he writes.

Except for Eva Maria herself, that seems to have been all. The beginning was more like a storybook than real life. She was herself a distinguished artist (if opera dancing is an art), and she came to England disguised as a boy, bearing letters of recommendation, so the story goes, from the Empress Maria Theresa. Under the patronage of Lord and Lady Burlington she became the toast of the town, but the evidence intended to support contemporary gossip that she was Burlington's natural daughter collapses completely upon examination. According to the story, she fell so desperately in love with Garrick from seeing him on the stage that Lady Burlington, who had desired a higher connection for her, was forced to accommodate her.

If this is what really happened, it constitutes a grand combination of eighteenth-century practicality with the idealism of the mediaeval love romances; after the marriage the practicality remains, and the romanticism settles down into an idyll. Lady Spencer once wrote Garrick concerning his wife: "You, I am sure, can neither hear, see, nor understand without her," and she herself said in her old age: "He never was a husband to me; during the thirty years of our marriage, he was always my lover!" No letters passed between them, for he never spent a night away from her. Because "I'll speak to Mrs. Garrick" was ever on his lips, there were those who thought he was henpecked. But this was obviously a Spenlow and Jorkins kind of arrangement, and if Garrick was under his wife's thumb that was just where he wanted to be. He also said, playfully, that he kept his ill-humors for her, and he loved to tease her—about her religion, her broken English, and everything else that amused him. He wrote Lady Spencer that his wife had "crown fadder than a Big," and he has one letter, purportedly from her, which approximates a kind of Katzenjammer Kids dialect. Yet he consulted her judgment on everything; before Wilkinson was engaged for Drury Lane, he was invited to give the manager a taste of his quality, and it was not until Mrs. Garrick laughed out behind the screen which concealed her that he realized he was auditioning for the manager's wife also. Except that there were no children (there was at least one time when Garrick had hopes), it seems to have been about as close to a perfect marriage as any on record; I am only puzzled by his will, which hedged her about with restrictions, instead of leaving everything to her outright, as I should have thought he would have done. Years before he had painted her portrait:

'Tis not, my friend, her speaking face,
Her shape, her youth, her winning grace,
Have reach'd my heart; the fair one's mind,
Quick as her eyes, yet soft and kind.
A gaiety with innocence;
A soft address, with manly sense.
Ravishing manners, void of art,
A cheerful, firm, yet feeling heart.
Beauty that charms all public gaze,
And humble amid pomp and praise.

"Sweet Mrs. Garrick," as everybody who knew her called her, deserved every word of it, but not all the deserving find. Burke said she gained the hearts of all who knew her, and Laurence Sterne thought she could "annihilate" all the beauties of the Tuileries. Fortunate in much, the Garricks were supremely fortunate in each other, and who can doubt that the sensitive, nervous genius of England's greatest actor owed much to the peace and quiet that Eva Maria always created for him to come home to?

2

Edmund Kean

(1787?–1833)

K EAN WAS THE GREAT ACTOR of the Romantic movement. Specifically he may be said to have incarnated Romanticism on its passionate, rebellious, "natural," spontaneous (or, to sum it all up, its Byronic) side. *Chambers's Encyclopaedia* said he was among actors what Byron was among poets and Napoleon among generals. Richard Henry Dana I went further still: he thought Kean stood to other actors much like Shakespeare to other dramatists. "He seems . . . to have possessed himself of Shakespeare's imagination, and to have given it body and form."[1] When the hundredth anniversary of his death was celebrated at Drury Lane in 1933, Sir Frank Benson called him "perhaps the greatest actor who ever lived."

Interestingly enough, Byron, who wrecked his own life through faults and errors closely resembling Kean's, and who is said to have been thrown into a convulsive fit by Edmund's power as Sir Giles Overreach in Massinger's play *A New Way to Pay Old Debts*, understood the actor's weaknesses and temptations as well as anybody did and acted like a good friend toward

[1] Richard Henry Dana, *Poems and Prose Writings* (Marshall, Clark & Co., 1833).

him, attempting vainly to save him from himself. Alone among the persons considered in this book, Kean represents the stock caricature of the dissipated, profligate actor whose power carries within itself the seeds of its own ruin. If a novelist or playwright had written his story, nobody would have believed it. Only life is allowed completely unashamed melodrama.

He was of illegitimate birth, and neither the date nor the names of his parents can be stated other than conjecturally. Two birth dates are given in the old records—November 4, 1787, and March 17, 1789. H. N. Hillebrand, the only really scholarly biographer Kean has ever drawn, favored the earlier date, though he added frankly that "there is no reason to suppose that either is correct." More recently Giles Playfair has reargued the case for 1789.[2] I should say it has been reasonably well established that his mother was a very minor actress, peddler, and drab named Ann Carey, daughter of George Saville Carey and granddaughter of the Henry Carey who wrote *Sally in Our Alley* and to whom *God Save the King* has also sometimes been attributed. The father was probably Edmund Kean, though his brother Moses has also been nominated. The actor's Semitic cast of features, and the use of the names Moses and Aaron in the family, has led to the suggestion that the Keans were Jews and that the name was originally Cohen, but there is no positive corroboration for this.

Kean's mother paid as little attention to him as possible, except when he could earn money for her by his talents (all of which, he says, she took from him), and insofar as he was brought up at all, the job was performed by another minor actress, Charlotte Tidswell, Moses Kean's mistress, who, according to her own account, was present when he was born. Kean himself seems to have believed, or wished to believe, at times that Charlotte was his mother by the Duke of Norfolk, with whom she apparently had a connection ("Why did Miss Tidswell take such good care of me if she was not my mother?"), and he gave both his sons

[2] *Kean*, "Preface."

Norfolk names—Howard and Charles—but this need not have been anything more than an attempt to stake out a noble pedigree for himself. When the question was put to the Duke himself, he is supposed to have replied that he would have been proud to claim Kean as his son if the story had been true. Certainly Ann Carey called herself his mother; he supported her; and, at the end of his life, when she was down on her luck, he gave her a home. Actually Kean did not need the Duke of Norfolk to supply him with a pedigree, for Henry Carey was the reputed natural son of the Marquis of Halifax. Unfortunately, however, blue blood was not the actor's only inheritance. If there was talent on both sides of the family (several of his immediate forebears were in the theater, and Moses Kean earned considerable reputation with his one-man shows), there was recklessness and lack of control also and very likely a sprinkling of madness and melancholy. Both Henry Carey and the elder Edmund Kean committed suicide, the latter in his early twenties.

It would be impossible to exaggerate the misery and penury of Kean's early years, nor could there be any point in attempting to enumerate the endless engagements he filled from early childhood on. It was in no Pickwickian sense that he was a rogue and a vagabond. The greatest tragedian of his time sang, danced, made faces in farces, and jumped through a hoop of fire as Harlequin until comparatively late in his career.[3] There were sections of his public that preferred his Harlequin to his Hamlet, and he was a famous man when his wife found him turning somersaults one day, and upon asking why he was doing it was told that he wished to be ready if he had to go back to it. His

[3] Cf. T. C. Grattan on one performance he witnessed at Waterford: "After the tragedy [Hannah More's *Percy*], Kean gave a specimen of tight-rope dancing, and another of sparring, with a professional pugilist. He then played the leading part in a musical interlude; and finished with Chimpanzee, or some such name, the monkey in the melodramatic pantomime of *La Perouse*." It is recorded that he once came home in the Chimpanzee costume, which was made of skins and evil smelling, and insisted on sleeping in it, driving his wife to the sofa. He may not have enjoyed playing the monkey on the stage but he often undertook it in private life.

earliest instruction in acting probably came from Miss Tidswell; at any rate, she took him with her behind the scenes at Drury Lane, and what his eyes and ears taught him there constituted the most important part of his education. Because of injury or neglect, he at one time had to wear irons on his legs. At one time, too, he was befriended by a lady of social position named Mrs. Clarke, but this did not work out altogether happily.

The old story that he appeared as Cupid in an opera called *Cymon* in 1791 has now been exploded by Hillebrand, and we cannot be sure that he appeared as a goblin in the caldron scene of *Macbeth* when John Philip Kemble and his sister, Mrs. Siddons, reopened Drury Lane on April 21, 1794, nor that he incurred Kemble's wrath by upsetting the other goblins. The earliest certain reference we have seems to be that signalizing his appearance as Robin in *The Merry Wives of Windsor* at Drury Lane on June 8, 1796. Around 1800 we hear of him giving recitations as "the infant prodigy, Master Carey," and we know that he recited at Covent Garden, between the comedy and the farce, on May 18, 1802. He toured fairs with a showman named Richardson, and he became a circus performer under a Mr. Saunders. The legend that he spent the years 1803–1806 at Eton is no longer taken seriously, though it is still possible to believe that he appeared before King George III at Windsor. In 1804 he was playing George Barnwell, Rolla (in Sheridan's *Pizarro*), and other leading roles with Samuel Jerrold's company at Sheerness, at a salary of fifteen shillings a week; in 1805 he played with Mrs. Siddons in Belfast; and in 1806 he was working for an illiterate but uncommonly kind-hearted manager named Mrs. Baker, who controlled a string of provincial theaters.

On July 17, 1808, he married Mary Chambers, an Irish actress, several years his senior, whom he had met at Gloucester, and tradition says that they made a 180-mile journey on foot from Birmingham to Swansea in southern Wales when Mary was six months gone with her first child, the beautiful and promising Howard, whom both his parents so passionately loved, and whose death, on the very eve of his father's first London success, was such a terrible sorrow to both. Howard was born at Swansea, and Charles, eighteen months later, at Waterford, in Ireland.

In 1813, Kean was at last engaged for Drury Lane, but his debut was delayed because of contractual confusion. At this time, Drury Lane and Covent Garden still had a monopoly during the season of the legitimate drama in London, and an actor who appeared at a minor theater not only automatically debarred himself from the major roles but also made his subsequent engagement at either of the major theaters highly unlikely. In his desperation and destitution, Kean had allowed himself to incur a commitment to Robert William Elliston, then the manager of the Olympic Pavilion, and when the crisis came, he found himself engaged to appear at two theaters, with each management refusing to put him on until the difficulty was adjusted and meanwhile enjoining him from appearing at the other! Elliston was anything but generous, and Samuel Arnold's behavior at Drury Lane strongly suggests that he may have collaborated with him to punish Kean as much as possible. Between them they came within an inch of killing him, and if it had not been for the charity of two maiden ladies with whom they lodged, it is hard to see how the whole family could have escaped starvation.[4]

The great night of January 26, 1814, came at last, and with it Kean's first appearance at Drury Lane as Shylock. But it should be understood that he appeared as a *pis aller*. Everybody else had been tried and found wanting, and the financial condition of the theater was desperate. Even so, he got no help from anybody. He went on, without advance puffing, on a snowy night, before a poor house; the stage manager had told him that his interpretation was all wrong, and the other actors shunned him and regarded him as a joke. What could be made of a Shylock who wore a black wig instead of a red one, who wore neat, clean clothes, and who, though malignant, was a believable, compre-

---

[4] "My God! If I should succeed now, in London? If I *should*, I think that it would drive me mad."

hensible human being in the circumstances presented? "I could scarcely draw my breath," Dr. Drury told Kean afterwards, "when you first came upon the stage. But directly you took your position and leaned upon your cane, I saw that all was right." As the performance proceeded, the people back stage began to wonder how so small a house could make such a racket. "His style of acting," wrote William Hazlitt in the *Morning Chronicle*, "is . . . more significant, more pregnant with meaning, more varied and alive in every part, than any we have almost ever witnessed." And Kean rushed home to his lodging in Cecil Street and cried, "Mary, you shall ride in your carriage, and Charley shall go to Eton."[5]

He had insisted upon Shylock for his trial run because though it afforded him excellent opportunities, it was a brief role, and it gave him a chance to conceal his unimpressive figure under a gaberdine. Full-scale testing was reserved for February 12 with *Richard III*. On March 12 came *Hamlet*, which was less suited to his temperament, yet Hazlitt thought his returning to kiss Ophelia's hand at the end of the "nunnery" scene the finest bit of Shakespearean commentary he had ever witnessed,[6] and on May 5 he appeared as Othello, followed shortly thereafter by Iago.

Now every lickspittle in London was at Kean's feet. In those days, when the repertory system prevailed, plays did not have "runs"; they went into the repertoire, and an actor continued to appear in his successful roles, from time to time, as Kean did, as long as he lived. Nor were the returns large, judged by modern standards, and Kean did not always fill the house. But he saved Drury Lane and brought to his family and himself such prosperity as they had never dreamed of.

[5] Truman Joseph Spencer and Capitola Harrison Spencer, *"Here He Comes . . . in the Likeness of a Jew"* (Truman Joseph Spencer, 1898) tells the story of the first night at Drury Lane in the form of a rather sentimental short story.

[6] Ludwig Tieck thought Kean's Hamlet brilliant "in all the playful, humorous speeches, all the bitter cutting passages." But "he could not touch the tragic side of the character."

As soon as the season was over, he embarked, against Drury Lane advices, upon a provincial tour. Kean never abandoned the provinces, and in spite of his dissipation he remained a phenomenal worker to the end. There were ten new roles during the second season, beginning with Macbeth on November 5, 1814. On January 5, 1815, he made an ill-advised appearance as Romeo, prompted, no doubt, by the great success of Miss O'Neill in the same play at Covent Garden. He was not much better suited to Richard II, on March 9, whom he made entirely too robust. Indeed he did not have another really first-rate triumph until January 12, 1816, when he did his first Sir Giles Overreach, "without doubt the most terrific exhibition of human passion that has been witnessed upon the modern stage." It may indeed have been the greatest of his roles.

On February 20, 1817, Kean as Othello acted young Junius Brutus Booth as Iago, then generally regarded as his imitator, off the stage, and Booth, disdaining further comparison, returned penitent to Covent Garden, where he had made his debut on February 12 as Richard III, and sued for peace.[7] The other Shakespearean roles in which Kean appeared were Timon of Athens, King John, Hotspur in *King Henry IV, Part I*, which he did only twice, Coriolanus and Cardinal Wolsey in *King Henry VIII*, each of which got four performances, King Lear, Posthumus in *Cymbeline*, and, in his decline, King Henry V, in which he failed egregiously, on March 8, 1830, because he could not remember his lines. The only triumph among these was the King Lear, which he acted first on April 24, 1820, and which got twenty-eight performances before the end of the season. But he kept to the Tate ending until 1823, and even then Shakespeare's ending was apparently used at only three performances.

[7] It is generally assumed that Kean invited Booth to play with him with malicious intent, planning to show him up, and that the courtesy with which he treated him on the night of their joint appearance was hypocritical. This may be so, but there is no hint of it in Edwin Booth's warmhearted tribute to Kean in the piece he wrote about him for the Mathews-Hutton *Actors and Actresses* nor any suggestion that his father ever cherished resentment.

On December 22, 1817, Kean appeared in *Richard, Duke of York*, which had been arranged by J. H. Merivale from the three parts of Shakespeare's *King Henry VI*, and on July 19, 1830, he appeared at the King's Theater in the Haymarket in a bill comprising *Richard III*, Act IV; *The Merchant of Venice*, Act IV; *A New Way to Pay Old Debts*, Act V; *Macbeth*, Act II; and *Othello*, Act III, which would be a herculean feat for any actor, and which, for a man in his state of health, could only be described as bordering upon the miraculous.

Kean was not notably successful in Paris, though he made a friend of Talma, but he roused great enthusiasm in America, where he made his debut, as Richard III, at the Anthony Street Theater, New York, on November 29, 1820, and where the demand for tickets was so great that they were sold at auction, with the excess donated to charity. The star seems to have been on his best behavior in America, and all went well until spring, when, after the close of the regular theatrical season, he insisted upon returning to Boston, and walked out on a slim audience the third night of his engagement, an insult for which he was made to pay, on his second visit, out of all proportion to the offense.

Meanwhile there had intervened the terrible Kean-Cox scandal, which ruined the actor's career. In January, 1825, Alderman Robert Albion Cox sued Kean for alienating his wife's affections and was awarded damages of eight hundred pounds. Charlotte Cox was a woman of no character and, in other eyes than Kean's, of no attractions (T. C. Grattan, who had often seen her before the scandal broke, could not even remember what she looked like). Though there is no defending Kean's conduct, there is grave doubt about the justice of the verdict, for Cox, who had almost thrust his wife into the actor's arms, was either a completely complaisant husband or else the most egregious ass on record, and the most likely guess is that the whole thing was a put-up job engineered in the hope of financial gain.[8] The pack

[8] The Kean-Cox scandal inspired a good many contemporary publications which may be found in great theater collections but which need not be listed

of wolves that came down upon Kean were led by the editor of the London *Times*, himself known to be living in adultery, and their notion of upholding the moral code was to cause a riot when Kean reappeared at Drury Lane on January 24, 1825.

Other cities in the British Isles scorned to be thought less moral than London, and when Kean reappeared in New York on November 14, Americans were exhorted by the *Daily Advertiser* to do their "duty just like London and Edinburgh"! New York did just that, and some, though not all, of the other cities in which Kean appeared were equally faithful, the most disgraceful exhibition being reserved for the Hub, which had its own score to settle. Here, on December 21, the riot act had to be read, and Kean, having "wept like a child" in the green room, literally fled from Boston to save his life.

Though Kean continued to appear in his great Shakespearean roles as long as he was able to stand on the stage, and frequently when he was not, he was by no means exclusively a Shakespearean actor. He appeared in Marlowe's *The Jew of Malta*, Massigner's *The Roman Actor* and *The Duke of Milan*, Rowe's *Tamerlane*, Jonson's *Every Man in His Humor*, Southerne's *Oroonoko*, Maturin's *Bertram*, Colman's *The Iron Chest*, Ambrose Phillips' *The Distrest Mother*, M. G. Lewis' *The Castle Spectre*, and many more. Most of these are only names to us today, and some are not even that. On October 1, 1828, he appeared in Glasgow with his son Charles in John Howard Payne's *Brutus*, and his last great achievement was his appearance as Virginius in Sheridan Knowles's tragedy of that title, on December 15, 1828, he having taken on the play to prove that he was still capable of learning a new role, in spite of the breakdown he had suffered in Thomas Colley Grattan's *Ben Nazir* in the spring of 1827.

In 1831 he acquired a small theater of his own at Richmond,

---

here. There is a brief popular account in Horace Wyndham, *The Mayfair Calendar* (Hutchinson, n.d.). Kean's letters to Mrs. Cox are in the Harvard Theatre Collection.

where he now lived. He had wished to become lessee of Drury Lane, where at one time he had been compelled to work under his old enemy Elliston, but he had not been able to achieve this. The Richmond theater was not a financial success, and he was compelled to act elsewhere to recoup his losses. Even in his decline he was still a "draw" that no manager could refuse; when he was offended with the Lane, he would go to the Garden, and when the Garden displeased him more, he would return to the Lane. It was at the Garden, however, that he appeared on the stage for the last time, on March 25, 1833, as Othello to his son's Iago. He had warned Charles that he did not believe he would be able to kneel but that if he did, Charles must help him up. He got as far as "Villain, be sure thou prove my love a whore," then fell into his son's arms with "Oh God! I'm dying . . . speak to them for me," and was carried off the stage. Removed to Richmond, he rallied, and was even able to go out, but early in May he took to his bed for the last time. He died on May 15 and was buried in the parish churchyard.

II

Probably the most famous critical observation ever made about any actor is Coleridge's remark that to see Kean act was like reading Shakespeare by flashes of lightning. It is not, of course, wholly complimentary to him, for if it suggests brilliance and penetration, it also suggests unevenness. It was Hillebrand's opinion that Kean "lacked sustaining power," and this may well have been true. One would hardly expect a man like him to be able to sustain a career, but there are suggestions that individual performances were uneven also. According to Sir Arthur Wing Pinero, Hannah Brown Meredith, the friend and companion of the Baroness Burdett Coutts, told Sir Henry Irving that Kean "had moments of passion and intensity that almost lifted you out of your seat," and that "the rest of the time, he was like a stroller in a booth." This seems somewhat intemperate however. George Henry Lewes says that he did not begin to show power in *Othello* until the third act, but Shakespeare did not give Othello much to do before the third act. When Leigh Hunt first saw him, he judged him "only a first-rate actor of the ordinary, stagy class," with occasional "passages of truth and originality," but he admitted that in some of these he surpassed all other actors, and in 1818 he was "suspended and heart-stricken" by Kean's Othello, beyond anything even Mrs. Siddons had been able to achieve. It is a pleasure, both for Kean's sake and for her own, to record the generous judgment of Mrs. Siddons' niece Fanny Kemble, who had not been brought up in an atmosphere very friendly to Kean, and who was not herself treated very generously by him when her star was rising as his was going down, that "he possessed those rare gifts of nature without which art alone is a dead body. If he was irregular and unartist-like in his performances, so is Niagara to be compared with the water-works of Versailles." It was Fanny's uncle, John Philip Kemble, of course, who was always in supreme command of the waterworks; the painter Haydon said of him that he "came into a part with stately dignity, as if he disdained to listen to nature, however she might whisper, until he had examined and weighed the value of her counsel."

Kean's biographer, F. W. Hawkins, calls George Frederick Cooke "the first actor who dared to introduce the familiarities of daily life into tragedy." All such terms are relative. As we have seen, Garrick was a "natural" actor in his time, though his naturalism had certainly not descended to Kemble. It seems unlikely that Cooke or Kean or Garrick himself would be considered at all "natural" today, but there can be no doubt as to Kean's reverence for Cooke. When he was in New York, he erected a monument over his grave, and carried one of his fingerbones back to England, where he deposited it on the mantel like the relic of a saint, until Mrs. Kean, who did not share his reverence for it, is said finally to have taken it upon herself to see that it got "lost."

Like Garrick, Kean greatly impressed spectators by his energy.

"The character never stands still," said Hazlitt; "there is no vacant pause in the action; the eye is never silent." He was "always on full stretch—never relaxed," and this sometimes seemed a fault. Yet "if Shakespeare had written marginal directions to the players, in the manner of the German dramatists, he would often have directed them to do what Mr. Kean does."[9] As Zanga in Edward Young's play, *The Revenge*, or so Crabb Robinson reports, Kean "rushed on the stage . . . as a wild beast may be supposed to enter a new den to which his keepers have transferred him." One pittite exclaimed, "By God! he looks like the devil!" and Byron, who elsewhere hailed him as "the sun's bright child," was not far from this when he cited a passage in Canto I of *The Corsair* as expressing his feeling about Kean's Richard III:

> *There was a laughing devil in his sneer*
> *That raised emotions both of rage and fear,*
> *And where his frown of hatred darkly fell,*
> *Hope withering fled, and mercy sigh'd farewell!*

But such impressions can at best indicate only one side of Kean's gift, and at least one paper, the *Theatrical Inquisitor*, thought him wasted in roles like Zanga:

> The very excellence of his system destroyed the part, for it showed, in glaring lights, its absurdity; his action and utterance were those of a human being: but Zanga is not a human being, and no better mode could have been devised to make that fact evident to common comprehension than that of natural acting.

Kean was, in the ordinary sense at least, no ranter; for one thing, his voice lacked the power to make the rafters ring. Indeed, his methods were better adapted to the small theaters of today than to the great barns in which he was compelled to act, and his wonderful pantomime would have made him an incom-

---

[9] "Old Playgoer" (William Robson) called Kean's Othello "a little vixenish black girl in short petticoats." John Philip Kemble said that "if the justness of Kean's conception had been equal to the brilliancy of its execution it would have been perfect. But the whole thing is a mistake, the fact being that the Moor was a slow man."

parable film actor. Benjamin West said "he had never seen so much expression in any human face" as in Kean's as Macbeth, and that it haunted him through the night, and Hazlitt was never sure that it was mere snobbery which caused the boxes to regard him with less enthusiasm than the pit, for the pit was closer to him and saw him better. "We do not hesitate to say that those who have only seen him at a distance, have not seen him at all. The expression of his face is quite lost, and only the harsh and grating tones of his voice produce their full effect on the ear."

Often it was the quiet, tender touches in Kean's performances that his admirers remembered best. Mention has already been made of his kissing Ophelia's hand after the "nunnery" scene. His enunciation of "father" in "I'll call thee king, father, royal Dane" was heartbreaking; he was far gentler toward his mother in the closet scene than his predecessors had been; and he showed his good taste and sensitive feeling in Act I by pointing his sword at his friends to prevent their restraining him from following the Ghost, and not at the Ghost himself, as had been the custom. Hotspur's scene with his wife was playful, not brutal; he was restrained too in the wooing scene of *Richard III*; and though nothing could have been more evil than his Iago, there was no melodramatic horror about it. Some of us had to wait for Henry James to teach us that evil is most dangerous when it does not smell of the pit but wears instead a perfect air of worldly bonhomie, but Kean did not need anybody but Shakespeare to teach him that. Hazlitt thought Othello's "tranquil mind" speech and the scene following the killing of Duncan in *Macbeth* his finest achievements.

The former was the highest and most perfect effort of his art. To inquire whether his manner in the latter scene was that of a king who commits a murder or that of a man who commits a murder to become a king, would be "to consider too curiously." But, as a lesson of common humanity, it was heartrending. The hesitation, the bewildered look, the coming to himself when he sees his hands bloody; the manner in which his voice clung to his throat, and

42

choked his utterance, his agony and tears, the force of nature overcome by passion—beggared description. It was a scene which no one who saw it can ever efface from his recollection.

Charlotte Tidswell is said to have taught Kean to read Hamlet's "Alas, poor Yorick!" by reminding him of Moses Kean, who had lost a leg, and having him say "Alas, poor Uncle!" instead. This gives her high rank among the pioneers of "Method" acting. But Kean as a mature artist did not work thus; neither did he depend upon "inspiration." Like Garrick's, his spontaneity was a prepared spontaneity, his art the art that conceals art. Sometimes, and again as with Garrick, a flash of perception did come while he was on the stage, and then he was flexible enough to be able to make use of it: "I felt that what I did was right. Before I was only rehearsing." But he had far too much sense to depend on such things. "Because my style is easy and natural . . . [people] think I don't study, and talk about the 'sudden impulse of genius.' There is no such thing as impulsive acting; all is premeditated and studied beforehand."

One who was close to him reported that "he used to mope for hours, walking miles and miles alone, with his hands in his pockets, thinking intensely on his characters. No one could get a word from him. He studied and slaved beyond any actor I ever knew." Often he rehearsed alone, late at night, in his own house, with a mirror and props; in the morning he would perhaps try what he had worked out on his wife. He visited insane asylums while preparing his Lear, as many actors have done, and he depicted the death of Romeo from poison, and again that of Hamlet, with minute and perhaps repulsive realism. Once he saw a friend so enraged after a farmer had thrashed him as a trespasser that he tore his collar to shreds; Kean reproduced the action in the last act of *A New Way to Pay Old Debts*. And once he himself fainted upon receiving a wound in fencing; when he came to, his first question was "How did I fall?" Having got a performance fixed the way he wanted it, he never changed it for variety's sake, though it might be affected by his particular condition while he performed, and his characterization might improve or deteriorate over the course of the years.

He had not, in all respects, been generously endowed by nature. "He was a little man with an inharmonious voice, and no very great dignity or elegance of manner," says Hazlitt. His lack of inches was not the worst of it. A man does not need to be a giant to express tragic passion. But there was something common about Kean which was less easy to get over.[10] Like Garrick, however, he did possess wonderful eyes, whose power even Mrs. Siddons recognized, though she does not make them seem very attractive when she essays an excursion into unnatural natural history to try to explain them: "His eyes are marvellous, having a sort of fascination, like that attributed to the snake."[11]

Kean seems to have valued his musical gifts; when his aged admirer, Mrs. David Garrick, pointed out his deficiencies as compared to her late husband, he asked, "Could David sing?" and when she replied in the negative, he said, "Well, I can." Barry Cornwall says that he was quite ignorant of written music but that he could perform very acceptably by ear and even fit verses to tunes of his own devising. There can be no question that singing meant much to him as a form of self-expression, for he sang and played for his own amusement, and sometimes that of his friends, even in his later broken years, and there were times when some of them were profoundly moved. But Hazlitt did not care for either his singing or his dancing, declaring that he himself could do either just about as well, and Mrs. Merivale says that he attempted music which was too difficult for him.

More important was the speaking voice, and enough has been said already to establish the fact that Kean had his limitations here. Hawkins says that though the voice was harsh in the upper register, it was sweet and melodious in the lower. As I have al-

[10] There are some good illustrations of how this operated in Hazlitt's account of Kean's performance as Coriolanus; see *Hazlitt on Theatre*, 186–88.

[11] The Harvard Theatre Collection has two locks of Kean's hair, still a beautiful brown in color, and of exquisite texture.

ready said, it was not suited to great outbursts of passion, in which it often became screechy or incoherent or both. Sometimes, as in Overreach's outbursts, the harshness itself was part of the picture. He seems to have paid little or no attention to the tempo of blank verse, and Hazlitt complained that he made every sentence "an alternation of dead pauses and rapid transitions." Ordinary level passages seem to have bored him, and sustained declamation was too stately for his nervous, erratic style. He spoke greatly only in brief passages which inflamed his imagination, and George Vandenhoff says he gave his reading of Othello's "Farewell" speech as if he were speaking it from score. "And what beautiful, what thrilling music it was! the music of a broken heart—the cry of a despairing soul!" Junius Brutus Booth, too, carried this passage in his memory across a lifetime, from his not too endearing contact with Kean, and told Edwin that "no mortal man could equal Kean in his rendering of Othello's despair and rage; and that above all, his not very melodious voice in many passages, notably that ending with 'Farewell, Othello's occupation's gone,' sounded like the moan of ocean or the soughing of wind through cedars." But Booth also said that Kean's "peculiar lingering on the letter 'l' often marred his delivery," and Sir Theodore Martin thought that, as time went on, he stylized even his pathos. He seems to have been capable of carelessness when he was getting tired of a role, and though he declared that he could not forget Shakespeare's lines and could not remember those of poor writers, he does not always seem to have been letter-perfect. W. B. Wood noticed that in *Othello* he always read

> *Are there no stones in heaven*
> *But what serves for the thunder?*

as

> *Are there no stones in heaven?*
> *For what then serves the thunder?*

and that when his attention was called to the discrepancy, he said, "I believe I have always read it so."

Kean had no more difficulty with the outer adjustments which the actor is constantly compelled to make than one might have expected in the conditions under which he functioned. He did not, in the usual sense, suffer from stage fright, though he is reported to have said before his first Drury Lane Richard III that he was so frightened he expected to be obliged to act in dumb show. He also once declared that he played better in the provinces than in London, and Barry Cornwall attributes this to his dread of London criticism; Grattan, on the other hand, thought him always at his best in response to the Drury Lane challenge. Great art is created from within, and advice from others is not, in the last analysis, worth much to any artist, but Kean does not seem to have been pig-headed toward those who had anything to say that was worth hearing; he seems, for example, to have been very tractable toward Mrs. Garrick, who thought him inferior only to her late, great husband and tried to bring him up to the mark where he fell short of it! He prized Richard Henry Dana's piece about him because "that man understands me," which is not too common an experience, as any actor can tell you. Kean had superb self-confidence, but he was not vain or conceited. Hawkins says he inclined to regard Hamlet as his greatest accomplishment; Barry Cornwall says that he thought well of himself in Macbeth's murder and death scenes but considered John Philip Kemble his superior in the banquet scene. He was sometimes compelled to kowtow to his boisterous audiences in what modern actors would consider a shameful fashion, and he sometimes insulted his audiences as nobody except John Barrymore, who in some ways resembled him, has ventured to insult them in our time, but in general it may be said that he treated them quite as well as they deserved.

In his relations with other actors, his record is somewhat uneven.

46

Mrs. W. West has frequently stated that even when professional troubles pressed heavily upon him, she, in common with every member of the company, invariably experienced at his hands the utmost kindness and consideration; that no traces of ill-temper were ever visible when he spoke to his actresses, and that he always treated them in the most gentle and reassuring manner.

As we have seen, he worshiped the memory of George Frederick Cooke as only a great Romantic could worship anything, and he certainly admired Mrs. Siddons and Miss O'Neill. Testimony is contradictory concerning his attitude toward the great French actor Talma. According to Hawkins, he reproached his wife for her failure to appreciate him, then when she was kindled to enthusiasm, became angry and declared that he thought he could do better, but this may not be accurately reported. W. B. Wood says he called Talma a third-rater, but T. W. Clarke says that he wept at the news of his death. Being what he was, Kean may well have done both.

One thing is certain, however: Kean had no use for any actor who got in his light. He would not be billed second to anybody else; neither would he enact what he regarded as an inferior role. "Damme," he told his wife, "I won't play second to any man living except John Philip Kemble." He received "the character of Joseph Surface" from the Drury Lane committee "with surprise and mortification," and returned it the same day, reminding them of his services to the theater, and declaring that he would "never insult the judgment of the British public by appearing before them in any other station but the important one to which they have raised him." In his youth he was jealous of Master Betty, whose powers he quite rightly judged inferior to his own; as a mature artist, he showed the same touchiness toward Charles Young and Macready. Despite Mrs. West's testimony, there are ugly stories about his blocking the advancement of actresses at Drury Lane because they were too good and he did not care to see two suns in the sky. Perhaps he was kindest to those who were no danger to him; when the young Edwin Forrest waited upon him at Albany to receive his instructions, he told him pleasantly enough that he did not care what he did so long as he always kept before him and kept out of his way. Few of us are at our best when proclaiming our own dignity, and Kean was no exception. "The Throne is mine," he wrote Elliston, when Young was the bone of contention. "I will maintain it even at the expense of expatriation—go where I will I shall always bear it with me—and even if I sail to another quarter of the globe, no man, in this profession, can rob me of the character of the first English actor." And again, "You must forgive my being jealous of my hard earned laurels. I know how brittle is the ground I stand upon and how transient is public favor." That, no doubt, was the explanation. He had borne all but the pangs of hell to climb to the peak he occupied, and he was prepared to defy hell itself to avoid being pushed from it. He knew that he could never be sure of his public, but that was not the worst of it: he could not be sure of himself either.

Kean may have shown jealousy even toward his son. It is possible that at the outset he opposed Charles's theatrical ambitions because he wished to spare him the agonies that he himself knew only too well (when the boy was born, he intended him for the navy!), but it is said that he told his wife that there was going to be only one Kean in the theater, and that the name must die with him. We cannot be sure that he really said this, but he was anything but generous toward the boy when the latter refused to fall in with his plans and made demands concerning his mother which Kean did not choose to grant. Ironically enough, the inevitable result of this was to force Charles into the theater to earn his living, thus thwarting his father's wishes in the most effective possible way. Later, as we have already seen, they were reconciled and played together, and Kean seems to have been pleased. Charles Kean did not inherit much of his father's genius, but he did inherit his mother's character, and he had an honorable and useful career in the theater and out of it, being especially distinguished for the dignified productions of Shakespeare's plays in which he appeared with his wife, Ellen Tree.

Looking back over his theater-going lifetime from the vantage point of his later years, George Eliot's common law husband, George Henry Lewes, tried calmly to evaluate Kean. He knew that the giant that had enthralled his youth had had "many and serious defects." He was "small and insignificant in figure," though "he could at times become impressively commanding by the lion-like power and grace of his bearing." Gaiety he had none. He was limited as a mime, and his style was tricky and flashy. His performances were uneven at best, and his elocution impressive only in highly emotional passages. "He had tenderness, wrath, agony, and sarcasm at command. But he could not be calmly dignified; nor could he represent the intellectual side of heroism." Yet, take him all in all, he was "incomparably the greatest actor I have seen." "He stirred the general heart with . . . a rush of mighty power." Only Rachel could touch him.[12]

III

How much was there to Kean besides his genius and his thirst? How much one admires—and forgives—him (and he was a man who cannot be admired except by those who are able to forgive much) will depend largely upon how one feels about the Romantic temperament, with its grandiloquence, its aspiration, and its melancholy—perhaps, even, its inbuilt tendency toward self-destruction. As his contemporaries perceived, Kean was "terribly in earnest," and he had tremendous courage and endurance.[13] He came literally out of the gutter, the sufferings and

---

[12] George Henry Lewes, *On Actors and the Art of Acting* (Smith, Elder, 1875).

[13] His temperament and his family history being what they were, one cannot but wonder how Kean managed to escape suicide. It is said that he came very close while waiting for his chance at Drury Lane. T. W. Clarke says that he "talked . . . quite jocularly of . . . cutting his own throat" when he was in America in 1825, and there is a story about his having moved toward jumping off the roof of an American insane asylum he had visited with Dr. Francis, and thus making the same end as his father. But he may not have been serious. Possibly he used alcohol to dull his sense of reality. On the other hand, the fact that the real Romantic enjoys melancholy even while he sucks the last drop of poison from it may have helped to save him.

privations of his early life are indescribable, and he cannot be fairly judged except by those who have suffered something comparable. By the time he achieved success, much that he needed to sustain it had been destroyed in him.

It was Hillebrand's feeling that almost nobody liked Kean personally, and that he paid for this when he got into trouble.

> He was never able, as some have been, to draw people to his defense by the attraction of his personality; he held them, precariously, by art alone. When the howling mob let loose upon him, men did indeed rally to his support, not from love, however, but from pity and a British sense of fair play.

Yet the American manager W. B. Wood found him modest, gentlemanly, and well behaved in every way, and Dr. Francis writes:

> He won my feelings and admiration from the moment of my first interview with him. Association and observation convinced me that he added to a mind of various culture the resources of original intellect; that he was frank and open-hearted, often too much so, to tally with worldly wisdom.[14]

Kean himself was always painfully conscious of both his social and his intellectual liabilities, and he suffered terribly from what we should now call an inferiority complex; as he himself said, he could see a sneer across Salisbury Plain. He had no education to speak of, and it is easy to make fun of the absurd tags of learning with which he decked out his letters, as when he wrote to Drury Lane's Samuel Arnold:

> Be assured, sir, I shall treasure the admonitions it [Arnold's letter] contains *memoria in aeterna*; the *verbum* from you is alone sufficient to create a *sapientia* in the object that may have been insensible before.

T. W. Clarke says he never saw Kean with a playbook in his

14 John W. Francis, *Old New York* . . . (Charles Roe, 1858).

hands but that he would have works of history, philosophy, and general literature strewn over his bed, and that he was particularly fond of criticism. Of course one may have books strewn over the bed, one may even enjoy having books strewn over the bed for their own sake, without reading them, and we know that Kean, in Baltimore, once denied himself to callers on the ground that he was engaged in the study of Gibbon and could not be disturbed! For all that, he did read and study and learn, and one wonders how much better those who laugh at this kind of thing would have done if they had found themselves in his place.[15]

On the whole, he seems to have wrestled with books more successfully than with men. "Society" wooed him when he became the toast of the town, and we see how sensitive he was about it in his cautioning his wife to dress simply for fear of being thought to be wearing stage finery. T. W. Clarke says that "his address was perfectly easy and graceful," and that "he was diffident and retiring in his manners," but Hobhouse says he ate with his knife. For that matter, even Clarke must qualify: "his intercourse was not uniformly agreeable; on the contrary, there was much in it to excite pity, surprise, and disgust." One cannot blame him for refusing to perform for those who had invited him to their houses "not as a gentleman—scarcely as a man of talent—but as a wild beast to be stared at," but it was not good for him that his scorn for the aristocracy (the Romantic movement had its radical side) should develop into an inverted form of snobbery. Because he could not behave the way they did (which, in many of its aspects, he secretly admired), he chose to behave outrageously; so he kept a pet lion (which seems to have been a mild pussycat indeed), and made scenes, and tore off on wild rides through the night, and insulted Byron himself by taking French leave from one of his dinners, to take himself off to some low tavern, where he could associate with harlots and "boozers" and pugilists who brought out all the worst in him but who

---

[15] See Hillebrand, 59–60, and the plate facing page 60, for Kean's attempts at self-culture.

looked up to him and flattered him, and with whom he did not need to be careful.

We do not hear much about the harlots; there may not have been many of them. Kean was not enslaved to all vices; he abhorred gambling, for example, and would have nothing to do with it, and drinking on the scale he practiced it comes close enough to being a full-time occupation so as to leave little time for drabbing. But except for his wife, his taste in women seems to have been deplorable. There is nothing to be said for Charlotte Cox—"Little Breeches" was perhaps the most absurd pet name in the history of adultery, but it was right for her—and there is nothing to be said for Kean in his connection with her except that, vulgar as his passion was, it was genuine, and that, even when he was at his worst, there were lengths beyond which he would not go. "After my duty to my family, I am all in all yours forever." It was a considerable exception. "I will dare the worst . . . with the exception of making them miserable whom I am bound to protect." Toward the end of his life, Kean was entangled with an even worse woman than Charlotte Cox, an Irish-Jewish virago named Ophelia Benjamin, whose memory can still make his friends shudder after more than a hundred years. "The villainy of the Irish strumpet Ophelia Benjamin has undone me, and though I despise her, I feel life totally valueless without her. I leave her my curses."

It will be replied, no doubt, that Kean must have had peculiar ideas about marital loyalty, but it was not that so much as that he was a man whose passions were too strong for his principles. Giles Playfair's attack on Mrs. Kean, in his biography of her husband, is ridiculous, and it shows how desperate his case is that he should be driven to citing Charlotte Tidswell's testimony as evidence against her. Through Charlotte Tidswell, Mary Kean learned that a woman may experience "mother-in-law trouble" without a mother-in-law, and the fact that Miss Tidswell was willing to act as a go-between in Kean's affair with Mrs. Cox shows what her judgment was worth in such a connection. Of course Mary had her limitations. She was a human being. But except for his genius, she was the best thing that ever came into her husband's life, and he knew it, and it was to her that he turned back at the end. The best of him had never stopped loving her. In a sense he had been faithful to Cynara in his fashion, perhaps the only fashion of which he was capable.

There was a large intermixture of the child in Kean's temperament. His hardships did everything for him except one thing—they never brought him to an emotional maturity. Nor did he ever really know women—bad women at any rate; if he had known them, he could not have been taken in by them as he was. Perhaps the best illustration of this curious childlikeness, in its more harmless manifestations, came when, during his second visit to America, he was made a Huron Indian chief and given the name of Alanienonideh.[16] He exhibited himself in his new regalia after returning to England and sometimes even w)re it for his own pleasure when he was alone. Moreover, he had himself painted in it, and his calling card was engraved with "Mr. Kean" on one side and "Alanienonideh" on the other, with an Indian head, a tomahawk, and a bow and arrow.

None of this was greatly out of character. Kean himself was like an Indian, or like the stock, conventional notion of the Indian at any rate: he could not manage liquor, and he could not forget or overlook either a kindness or an injury. Those who had helped him in the smallest way possible when he was starving found the bread they had cast upon the waters returning to them manifold in later days. As for those who had slighted him, he could not resist them either if they were in real need when they applied to him, but when one of them presumed upon his kindness to claim friendship with him, he told him publicly that he was helping him not as a friend but as "a fallen man." Perhaps Kean is most winning with his inferiors, and perhaps it flattered his

[16] In the biographies, Kean's Indian name is given as Alanienouidet, but the two specimens of his calling card in the Harvard Theatre Collection read Alanienonideh (see Picture 6 in this volume), though a *t* seems to have been added with a pen after the final *h* on one of them.

ego to play Lord Bountiful. Certainly his charity was as "unwise" and impulsive as everything else about him, but the memory of his good deeds at Richmond remained a tradition for many, many years after his death. And even when he was a wreck who could only totter on and off the stage fortified by brandy, he could still inflame the imagination of sensitive people. Young Helena Faucit has recorded how kind he was to her when she met him one day, an old man in his forties, swathed in many wrappings. His eyes were so large, "so piercing, so absorbing that I could see no other feature," and his voice seemed to come from "a long, long way behind him," but she never forgot him.

It is usually believed that Kean drank himself to death. Certainly he drank enough to kill a man; at the end he was virtually living on brandy. It may be that, like Poe's, his toleration for alcohol was low, but unlike Poe he was a tavern roisterer. Yet the common assumption is, to say the least of it, inaccurate, for the man was spitting blood as early as the time of his first successes at Drury Lane; the only wonder is that he should have lasted as long as he did. Giles Playfair is no more than just when he remarks that "it was Edmund's real tragedy that he had a soul which belied his coarse behavior." After his public disgrace over Caroline Cox, he faced the mob with superb courage, but he was never the same man again, for he had lost his self-respect. He believed in God, and he never pretended that his sins were virtues; T. W. Clarke once heard him read the Lord's Prayer "with a devotional fervor which I have never heard equalled." When complete and utter disillusionment had been piled on top of the always seductive Romantic melancholy, the die was pretty well cast. It was his tragedy not so much that the gods made scourges of his pleasant vices as that his virtues conspired with them to destroy him.

3

William Charles Macready
(1793–1873)

Edward robins says wittily that Macready "suggested an unfortunate man who had gotten into prison, and was always explaining to visitors that he was infinitely superior to his surroundings."[1] England's greatest early Victorian actor never wanted to act; he would much have preferred being a barrister or a schoolmaster or a clergyman. It was not that he failed to appreciate the drama in its higher aspects. Nobody could have believed in it more than he. It absorbed almost all the interest and passion he had left over from his devoted home life. He was sure that acting achieved a less fallible interpretation of great poetry than criticism, for which, with a few exceptions, like the work of Goethe and Coleridge, he had little respect, and once when somebody wondering aloud why Scott had not become a dramatist, said, "I suppose he did not choose," Macready replied, "Choose! it's no matter of choice. If he had had the true dramatic fire, he couldn't have suppressed it." Macready swept out the corruptions of Tate, Cibber, Dryden, and Aaron Hill and restored Shakespeare's text to the stage. When he was an old man, long retired, he still knew "every word" of *Hamlet* by heart, and

[1] *Twelve Great Actors* (Putnam, 1900).

"every pause; and the very pauses have eloquence," and at the very end he was greatly excited by some new ideas he had conceived about Iago, though he no longer had the power of speech to communicate them.

But if he loved the drama he hated the theater. Temperamentally Macready was the Perfect Victorian Gentleman raised to the nth power, and he had all the faults and virtues of an almost mythical type. He was a lofty-minded idealist, but he could also be an unconscionable prig. He was a passionate democrat, but he was also what a costermonger would have called a "bloody" snob. It distressed him that actors should be regarded as rogues and vagabonds, yet in his heart of hearts he himself thought of most of them as just that, "wretched biped beasts" with whom he felt nothing in common, "the lowest human animal," the most degraded class outside the penitentiary. He sometimes doubted that a lady could be an actress, and he once persuaded a young man to adopt a mercantile pursuit instead of the stage. Nor would he allow his own children to see him act.

It is only fair to Macready to admit that many of his colleagues were just what he called them. He could not have been what he was at his best without finding the atmosphere of the green room quite as incompatible as he did. But he certainly made the situation much worse than it needed to be. For all his tenderness toward those he loved, he had a fiery temper and an irascible disposition. As director and manager, he never learned—he hardly even tried—to conceal the contempt he felt for others, and it is not surprising that many cordially hated him in return.

William Charles Macready was born in London, March 3, 1793. His father, the son of a Dublin upholsterer, was an actor who had become a manager of provincial theaters, a fiery Irishman with a temper worse than his son's. His mother, who had also been an actress, was a Derbyshire woman, and died at twenty-eight.

The boy was sent to Rugby, where he made an excellent record and also first manifested his dramatic flair. But in 1808 his father's losses at Manchester made it impossible for him to carry out his plans for further study; so he went into the theater instead and loyally fought in the family battle to stave off financial disaster. He made his debut, under his father's management, as Romeo, at Birmingham, on July 7, 1810, and apparently enjoyed himself greatly. "I feel," he said to one of the other actors when he had finished, "as if I should like to act it all over again." At Newcastle he played with Mrs. Siddons, who was wonderfully kind and encouraging and at Leicester with Dora Jordan. It has been conjectured that Macready's lack of sympathy for actors in minor roles was due to his never having been one. This may be true, but he did not always get the roles he wanted; even after he had established himself at Covent Garden, he was condemned to work his way through a long line of melodramatic villains, whom he detested.

His debut at the Garden was as Orestes in *The Distrest Mother*, by Ambrose Philips, on September 16, 1816. Kean applauded generously, and Macready was engaged for five years. He alternated with Charles Mayne Young as Othello and Iago, showed his Romeo opposite the Juliet of the beautiful Irish actress, Miss O'Neill, then at the height of her brief but brilliant career, and created Rob Roy in Isaac Pocock's dramatization of Scott's novel. On October 19, 1819, he was forced, against his will, to undertake Richard III, thus daring a direct comparison with Kean. The result was a triumph, and he became the first actor to be called before the curtain at Covent Garden. Coriolanus, Hamlet, and Macbeth all followed, and King Henry IV, in the second part of the play which bears his name, which was mounted as a coronation spectacle for George IV in 1821. In May, 1820, Macready had one of his great non-Shakespearean triumphs in *Virginius*.

In the fall of 1823 he left the Garden, which had fallen upon evil days, for the Lane, where he was to play all his old roles and many new ones. On January 5, 1825, he had a great success as Romont in Massinger's *The Fatal Dowry*, and on December 15,

1830, he first enacted Byron's *Werner*, which perhaps gave him the very best opportunity he ever found to demonstrate his grasp of Romantic *Weltschmerz* and melancholy. In 1832 he played ten Iagos to Kean's Othello, near the melancholy end of the latter's career. The association brought no pleasure to either. To Macready, Kean was "that low man," and what Kean called Macready was not considered printable. He won success in America, where he toured for nearly a year in 1826–27, and in Paris, where he was compared to Talma. On May 23, 1834, London first saw his Lear.

When Alfred Bunn secured control of Drury Lane, however, Macready's peace of mind at that house was destroyed, for this theatrical speculator not only outraged his idealism but bruised his *amour propre* at every turn. Bunn needed Macready as the outstanding exponent of the classical drama in England, but he did not really care for the classical drama, and he would probably himself have preferred less intellectual fare even if it had not earned more money for him. He kept Macready inactive, therefore, or subordinated him to inferior artists, or placed him in inferior and undignified positions. On April 16, 1836, the leading tragedian of Drury Lane was required to act William Tell *in the afterpiece*, and on the twenty-ninth he was cast in *the first three acts* of *Richard III* on a triple bill.[2] After much agitated soul-searching, Macready accepted both assignments, but as he passed the open door of Bunn's office after leaving the stage as Richard III, his pent-up sense of wrong overcame his self-control. "You damned scoundrel!" he cried, "how dare you use me in this manner?" and flung himself upon the astonished manager. Macready spent half his life losing his temper and the other half in unavailing and unredemptive remorse, but on no other occasion did he lose it quite so dangerously as here. If Bunn had been a "gentleman," he might well have "called him out." As it was, he

---

[2] In Macready's time, as William Archer conveniently reminds us, "the bill generally consisted of a five-act play and a farce, a three-act drama, or a music piece; sometimes both a farce and an operatta would be given."

preferred to prosecute for assault, and the jury awarded him only £150, not the £1,000 that Macready had expected. As for the public, it frankly enjoyed the excitement and judged Bunn to have got what he had been asking for. The Garden at once made Macready an offer, and when he appeared there, as Macbeth, on May 12, he received an ovation. In his address to the audience, he restated his grievance against Bunn but frankly admitted his own consciousness of guilt for having attacked him. It is the most curious oddity of Macready's otherwise unexceptionable career that the one disreputable thing he ever did should really have contributed to his popularity and advancement.[3]

From 1837 to 1839, Macready himself controlled Covent Garden, and from 1841 to 1843 he was in charge of Drury Lane. From testimonial dinners to tributes from the Laureate, his contemporaries used every means at their disposal to make it clear to him and to the world that they regarded him as having performed a distinguished public service:

> *Thine is it that our drama did not die,*
> *Nor flicker down to brainless pantomime*
> *And those gilt-gauds men-children swarm to see.*

He opened the Garden on September 30, 1837, with a production of *The Winter's Tale* in which his acting as Leontes in the reunion scene was so impressive that Helena Faucit, as Hermione, was almost overcome. "It was the finest burst of passionate, speechless emotion I ever saw," she said, "or could have

[3] Alfred Bunn was undoubtedly a theatrical speculator of the type with whose prostitution of the theater we have become only too familiar since Macready's time, but he was not the worst of his kind, and there is considerable good sense in Sir Edward Parry's defense of him, in his "Bunn v. Macready," *Cornhill Magazine*, N.S., Vol. LIV (1923), 641–52, reprinted in his *Concerning Many Things* (Cassell, 1929). The manager told his side of the story in a three-volume autobiography, *The Stage . . .* (Richard Bentley, 1840). Bunn also had a run-in with Macready's great friend, Jenny Lind, whom he had arranged to bring to England and who broke her contract with him, and I do not see how it can be denied that in this contretemps he was the reasonable party; see my *Seven Daughters of the Theater* (University of Oklahoma Press, 1964), 19–20.

conceived." Among his Shakespearean productions, *Macbeth*, *Lear*, and *Coriolanus* were particularly noteworthy during the first season and *The Tempest* and *Henry V* during the second. The role of Coriolanus favored him, and his handling of the mob seems to have evinced directorial genius. With *Lear* he restored the Fool, though casting a girl, Priscilla Horton, to play him, on the oddly alleged ground that the character should look like "a fragile, hectic, beautiful-faced, half-idiot-looking boy"! In *The Tempest*, Miss Horton as Ariel flew as triumphantly as even Peter Pan was to fly about British theaters in years to come, and the production was so beautiful that it haunted Macready even when he was away from the theater. "To impress more strongly on the auditor, and render more palpable those portions of the story [of *Henry V*] which have not the advantage of action, and still are requisite to the Drama's completeness, the narrative and descriptive poetry spoken by the Chorus . . . [was] accompanied by PICTORIAL ILLUSTRATIONS from the pen of MR. [Clarkson] STANFIELD." In *Romeo and Juliet*, Macready himself, surprisingly, essayed the role of Friar Laurence.

But Macready was not a Shakespearean producer exclusively. Covent Garden mounted many plays like *The Hunchback* and *Venice Preserved*. He encouraged Talfourd, Knowles, and others to produce new plays, and he got two new, resounding successes out of Bulwer-Lytton: *The Lady of Lyons* during the first season and *Richelieu* during the second. As Claude Melnotte in the first of these, Macready seems to have been wonderfully and somewhat unexpectedly successful in suggesting the idealism and high spirits of youth, while Pauline became one of Helena Faucit's very greatest roles, and *Richelieu*, in which he was almost a collaborator, served a whole line of distinguished actors, clear down to Mantell, who died as recently as 1928. More intellectual but less theatrically effective fare was provided by Robert Browning with *Strafford*, but Tennyson's tribute must not lead us to suppose that Macready wholly shunned the "brainless pantomime," if that is the word for it, nor farce nor opera either; if he had tried to do this, he would not have lasted even as long as he did. During his first three months he lost £3,000, but by the end of the season the "brainless pantomime" had helped cut this down to £1,800. And, for all his high moral pretensions, Macready knew how to deal with competitors as well as Garrick or any other manager. When Bunn, at the Garden, announced Balfe's Joan of Arc opera, Macready rushed out with "a grand historical and legendary spectacle" about the same heroine, hastily thrown together for him by T. J. Serle, and when Bunn prepared to revive Rossini's *William Tell*, he was anticipated by Macready's fresh production of the Knowles play, with interpolated music from the same composer.

Between the Garden and the Lane, Macready acted, at £100 a week, for Benjamin Webster at the Haymarket, where his most sensational success was Bulwer's modern play, *Money*, whose contemporary popularity surpassed that of either *The Lady* or *Richelieu*. At the Lane, he opened his first season (December 27, 1841) with a revival of *The Merchant of Venice*, and the second (October 1, 1842) with his very favorite production, the "beautiful pastoral" *As You Like It*, which was followed hard upon (October 24) by an impressive *King John*. On February 24, 1843, he selected *Much Ado About Nothing* for his benefit; critical opinion was divided about his Benedick, but some good judges admired it; except for the triumphant Mr. Oakly in George Colman's *The Jealous Wife*, it seems to have been the only comic role in which anybody ever cared for him. *The Patrician's Daughter*, by Westland Marston, was an interesting attempt at a blank-verse tragedy of modern life, but Browning's *Blot in the 'Scutcheon* was no more successful than *Strafford* had been at Covent Garden, and the production led to a permanent estrangement between poet and actor.[4] But the mounting of

[4] See Joseph W. Reed, "Browning and Macready: The Final Quarrel," *PMLA*, Vol. LXXV (1960), 597–603. Ashley H. Thorndike regarded this quarrel, which left Browning without a theatrical outlet, as one of the most unfortunate things that happened to English dramatic literature during the nineteenth century. See, further, William Lyon Phelps, *Robert Browning*, Revised Edition (Bobbs-Merrill, 1932), ch. XI.

Handel's *Acis and Galatea,* also decorated by Stanfield, on February 5, 1842, seems to have been one of Macready's great achievements.

During the eight years of acting which remained to him after relinquishing Drury Lane, Macready played in Britain (much of the time in the provinces), in Paris again in 1844, and twice more in America—first in the triumphal tour of 1843–44, which netted him £5,500, and then in the disastrous one of 1848–49, which culminated in the riot from which he narrowly escaped with his life. As it was, he fled from New York to New Rochelle, and thence to Boston, where, after his New England admirers had poured oil on his wounds, he sailed for home.[5] His last appearance, as Macbeth, at Drury Lane, on February 26, 1851, was one of the great "farewells" of theatrical history. He may have hated the theater, but he left it in the grand manner, and he had the satisfaction of knowing that at last the British public knew what they had lost.

Macready married Catherine Frances Atkins, an actress, on June 24, 1823, and by her had ten children, only three of whom survived him. Mrs. Macready died, of tuberculosis, September 18, 1852, at the age of forty-six. Eight years later, her husband married Cécile Louise Spencer, who was thirty-four years his junior, and who had never seen a play! "There are, I know, as all the world does, imprudences in marriages, where the ages are disproportionate," he wrote his friend Lady Pollock. "From the many motives that have led on to this, in addition to the primary one of sober affection, I believe this will be found an exception to the general rule." It was, though it produced but one child, a boy, born in 1860, who lived until 1946, and then died, full of years and honors, the son of a father who had been born during the French Revolution![6] Whatever else he may or may not have

[5] For an excellent popular account of Macready's social success in Boston and a warm appreciation of his friendly feeling toward America, see Walter Prichard Eaton, "A Theatrical Lion on Beacon Street," in his *The Actor's Heritage* (Atlantic Monthly Press, 1924).

[6] General the Right Hon. Sir Nevil Macready, first Baronet, P.C. (Ireland), G.C.M.G., K.C.B.

been good at, Macready proved twice that he knew how to choose a wife.

He had twenty-two years of retirement after that last performance at Drury Lane. They began at Sherborne, in Dorset, but at his second marriage he removed to Cheltenham. Sometimes he gave readings and lectures, and he always enjoyed reading to his friends, but most of his outside energies went into the night school for poor children which he established at Sherborne and where he taught. He suffered from asthma and from aphasia, and at the end he could not hold a book nor speak clearly, but his mind was unclouded, and when Helena Faucit visited him again after many years, he reminded her of "a great ship, past its work, but grand in its ruin." Her husband, Sir Theodore Martin, had no reason to love him, but he was moved, in spite of himself, by his "snowy head, and fine form, the eager eyes, and the tender tones of the broken voice," and "the sweet smile of the beautiful mouth, which spoke of the wisdom of a gentle and thoughtful old age." He was making a quiet ending for so violent a man, and he passed away even more quietly, after a brief attack of bronchitis, on April 27, 1873, fully conscious to the end.

II

As an actor, says George Vandenhoff, "Macready's style was an amalgam of John Kemble and Edmund Kean. He tried to blend the classic art of the one with the impulsive intensity of the other; and he overlaid both with an outer plating of his own, highly artificial and elaborately formal." Westland Marston thought no feature of his acting more distinctive than "the sudden, yet natural, infusion into his own heroic vein of some homely touch of truth which gave reality to the scene," but George Henry Lewes often found these touches out of harmony with the exalted level of the performance as a whole. Apparently there was a great deal of this in *King John*, especially in the "surpassingly powerful" naturalistic death scene, whose "mascu-

line and horrible . . . display" seemed to a contemporary critic
to go "beyond the truth required by the poet and the public."

When he made his debut, he was called "the plainest and
most awkwardly-made man that ever trod the stage"; later, age
added dignity to his severe and asymmetrical features, but John
Coleman always found his nose "a mixture of Grecian, Milesian,
and snub, with no power of dilation in the nostrils." His personal
eccentricities did nothing to cover up these deficiencies, and it
was said of him, in effect, as it was later to be said of Irving, that
the foremost actor on the English-speaking stage could neither
walk nor talk. His costuming was often considered odd also, and
he was fond of

> standing in profile, or semi-profile, to the audience, with his
> shoulders thrown very far back, the weight of his body resting on
> one leg, and the other bent forward at a sharp angle.[7]

As for the voice,

> There were rich tones in the middle register; there were deep
> notes employed occasionally with great effect; there was a clear,
> ringing resonance in the excitement of passion, and a peculiar
> capacity for purely intellectual expression. But there was no fine
> mellowness or sweetness; you were more often startled by a
> stacatto than subdued by a melting *sostenuto*; and the higher
> notes were sometimes shrill and habitually tremulous. The musi-
> cal flow of the verse was almost utterly lost, the sense alone di-
> rected the elocution, leading sometimes to abrupt changes of
> intonation that had the effect on the ear of a sudden change of key
> without modulation in a musical composition. On the other hand,
> no false note was ever struck, no shade of meaning was left
> undiscriminated, no measured or monotonous recitation ever
> wearied the ear.[8]

His principal vocal idiosyncrasy was that he was so careful to

[7] William Archer, *William Charles Macready.*

[8] John Foster Kirk, "Shakespeare's Tragedies on the Stage: Remarks and
Reminiscences of a Sexagenarian," *Lippincott's Magazine*, Vol. XXXIII (1884),
604–16.

articulate clearly and to avoid running his words together that his pauses often gave the effect of an "-a" or an "-er." Fanny Kemble, who seems to have disliked him as much as he disliked her, complained that

> he growls and prowls and roams and foams around the stage, in every direction, like a tiger in his cage, so that I never know which side of me he means to be, and keeps up a perpetual snarling and grumbling so that I never feel sure that he *has done* and that it is my turn to speak.

Westland Marston declared of Macready that "if it be granted that one or two tragedians have, in some parts, excelled him in the sudden revelations of passion, it is yet probable that he has never been excelled, if equalled, in the complete and harmonious development of character." George Vandenhoff did not place him that high (he "excelled in executive power and certainty of effect, rather than in imagination, in individualization of character, or poetic feeling"), but the difference seems to be less on what Macready could do than on the value assigned to it, for Marston, too, found the actor "at home in finesse and strategy, and in all that involved gladiatorship, as in Iago and Richelieu. Combatativeness in any aspect had a charm for him," and he sometimes suppressed impulse "by over-elaboration of design."

Macready himself thought his best Shakespearean roles to have been Lear, Hamlet, Iago, and Macbeth. The last named was, of course, his most celebrated part; John Coleman thought it unequalled for "subtlety, intellectuality, and vigor," though he immediately adds that Macready "was the only possible Lear I have seen." The actor himself considered his Othello inferior to the characters named, and there is general agreement on this, but few place his Hamlet so high as he did, though Spedding thought it more intellectual than that of other actors. Lewes found it finicking and lachrymose—"too fond of a cambric pocket handkerchief." (It may well be that when Forrest hissed the "fancy dance" he introduced into the play scene, he was a better critic than gentleman.) To be sure, Lewes criticizes other roles also. In general he thought Macready "irritable where he should have been passionate, querulous where he should have been terrible." In *Macbeth* he was fine in suggesting the struggles of conscience and the weight of superstition, but "he was fretful and impatient under the taunts and provocations of his wife; he was ignoble under the terrors of remorse; he stole into the sleeping chamber of Duncan like a man going to purloin a purse, not like a warrior going to snatch a crown." Lady Pollock thought that "it was in passages of profound sorrow, of concentrated solemn passion, that his great strength lay: the tones of suffering, between resignation and despair, the last utterances of a broken heart, were expressed by him so that the impression they made upon the hearer became a part of his future existence," and she makes it clear that in his private readings he sometimes achieved effects he could not have produced in the theater, as in his powerful reading of Juliet's almost unreadable Potion Speech, where, she says,

> his passion so worked upon the imagination of his hearers that they themselves conceived the whole terror of the successive images before they were shaped by utterance—the mangled Tybalt seemed there in his shroud, while the reader gasped out the words. Then a sound like a stifled scream burst from him, and his hand fell heavily upon his book; and when his aspect of concentrated terror changed with the changing thought, and love profound and holy passed into his face while he spoke the words, "And die an unstained wife," the relief was exquisite and brought down tears like rain.

Marston agrees that Macready was at his best in tender and in religious passages, though he also thought him better as father than as lover.

Macready is generally called an intellectual actor, standing opposed to Kean as an actor of passion. As we shall see, this statement needs modification; such validity as it has, it wins from the

Garrick with the Bust of Shakespeare, by Thomas Gainsborough. Formerly in the Town Hall, Stratford-upon-Avon.

Garrick in Tragedy and Comedy: as Richard III, engraved by S. W. Reynolds, after N. Dance; as Abel Drugger, in Ben Jonson's The Alchemist, *engraved by S. W. Reynolds, after J. Zoffany.*

Garrick's bookplate.

Edmund Kean as Sir Giles Overreach, in Massinger's A New Way to Pay Old Debts.

Kean's calling card, engraved with his Indian name and Indian regalia.

Kean as Richard III.

*William Charles Macready
by Robert Thorburn.*

*Macready
as Macbeth,
from a
contemporary
drawing.*

Macready as Werner in Byron's play, by Daniel Maclise.

Edwin Forrest.

*Forrest as Spartacus,
from a contemporary cartoon.*

Forrest as Macbeth.

fact that he always knew what he wished to do (though he was not always able to do it), and strove for the symmetrical development of an entire play or character, not reserving himself for "electric points." In his early days, he excited ridicule by always *acting* his role at rehearsal, though it was then the custom merely to walk through it, and he never ceased to study his plays and to rehearse his company in them, no matter how often he or they had played them. There was literally no trouble too great for him to take. He would stalk about for hours to get a Roman's "stately tread," practice endlessly with Tell's bow, or learn all the details of piquet for a short scene in *Money*.[9] And when he thought he was becoming too robustious,

> I would lie down on the floor, or stand straight against a wall, or get my arms within a bandage, and, so pinioned or confined, repeat the most violent passages of Othello, Lear, Macbeth, or whatever would require most energy and emotion; I would speak the most passionate bursts of rage under the supposed constraint of *whispering them* in the ear of him or her to whom they were addressed. . . .

Macready's intellectuality failed him, however, in that his performances were always at the mercy of his moods. Many great actors have suffered from stage fright, but Macready was the only actor I know who was so frightened by the sight of his name on the playbills that he would cross the street to avoid encountering it. If we may trust his own comments on his performances, he was one of the most uneven actors who ever lived, and undeserved praise or applause when he thought he was bad displeased him as much as abuse when he thought he was good. Sometimes he even relished a bad review of what he considered a bad performance. "I played only tolerably." "I acted *disgracefully*." And again, rather amusingly, he did not play "like a great actor." Or, on the other hand, "acted Othello—if I have any right to judge in such cases—I should say more finely, more passion-

[9] W. T. Price, *A Life of William Charles Macready*.

ately, more nobly than I have *ever* done before. I care not where the exception may be made." Once, in Dublin, he even acted Hamlet "in a very, very superior manner" before a house that did not appear to have more than ten pounds in it. "I was not well, but I was resolved to show in the first place, that the performance did not merit such utter neglect; and, in the second place, I thought it best so far to profit by the occasion as to use the night for study."

Macready believed that the private character of actors was important for their art. "Meanness and selfishness must affect their sincerity. They cannot express with full power by mere intellect the nobler emotions with which they have no real sympathy." John Foster Kirk calls him "the only actor I have ever seen who was always under the apparent influence of the emotion he was depicting, and never gave the impression that he was seeking to represent what, at the time, at least, he was not actually feeling."

In other words, he was what we now call a "Method" actor and therefore necessarily subject to all the cruel demands which that most wasteful and self-centered of all thespian ideals exerts upon the performer. "I cannot act Macbeth without *being Macbeth*, which I must have time to prepare my mind for." He could not act anybody else without becoming him either; once he writes, "I could only try to say those things well which alluded to the desperate condition of my own affairs." Before going on as the impassioned Shylock in the third-act street scene of *The Merchant of Venice* he would deliberately whip himself up into a passion of his own in the wings. Of one performance as Virginius he writes, "Much I did well—in the betrothment of Virginia the thought of my own beloved wife and child flashed across me, and I spoke from my soul—the tears came from the heart." On another occasion, he "gored his own thoughts" for the same character, "for my own Katie was in my mind, as in one part the tears streamed down my cheeks; and in another she who is among the Blest, beloved one!" And Lady Pollock says that he habitually achieved the Ghost scenes in *Hamlet* by recalling an extraordinary dream of his youth, in which a dead friend had appeared before him with words of admonition.

Nobody denies Macready his due meed of praise for "restoring" the authentic Shakespearean text to the stage, and if he did not go far enough, he doubtless went as far as it was possible to go in his time.[10] "My hope and my intention was, if my abilities had kept pace with them, to have left in our theater the complete series of Shakespeare's acting plays, his text purified from the gross interpolations that disfigure it and distort his characters, and the system of re-arrangement so perfected throughout them that our stage would have presented as it ought, one of the best illustrated editions of the poet's works." But it was not ability that ran out; it was time and money and public support.

The elaborate staging which he introduced, and which was developed beyond him by Charles Kean, Sir Henry Irving, Sir Herbert Beerbohm Tree, and others is a more controversial matter; even in his own time there were those who felt that he was smothering Shakespeare himself under a blanket of *décor*. Such am not I, but Macready himself had his doubts before the end and expressed them to Lady Pollock:

> I, in my endeavor to give to Shakespeare all his attributes, to enrich his poetry with scenes worthy of its interpretation, to give to his tragedies their due magnificence, and to his comedies their entire brilliancy, have set an example which is accompanied with great peril, for the public is willing to have the magnificence without the tragedy, and the poet is swallowed up in display. . . . Did *I* hold the torch? Did *I* point out the path?

Just what he did may best be seen by reference to Professor

---

[10] Charles H. Shattuck's remarks on Macready's production of *Comus* apply also to his Shakespeare: "To the Miltonist the ending of Macready's version will seem an almost criminal sacrifice of poetry to spectacle: of Milton's last 110 lines only 26 were sung or spoken. To the theatergoer of 1843, on the other hand, who only the season before had luxuriated in the profusely magical effects of Madame Vestris' so-called *Comus*, it would have seemed either worthily 'classical' or merely 'tame.' " See "Milton's *Comus*: A Prompt-Book Study," *Journal of English and Germanic Philology*, Vol. LX (1961), 731–48.

Shattuck's richly-illustrated editions of his prompt-books for *King John* and *As You Like It*,[11] both of which are designed to enable the reader to come as close to visualizing the production as paper and ink can take him, or, as Shattuck himself more imaginatively expresses it in the case of *As You Like It*, "to dream his way nearly back to the Forest of Arden as it appeared on the stage of Drury Lane Theater over a century ago." The *King John* interiors, incidentally, strongly suggest those which Fritz Lang was to use in *Siegfried* and *Kriemhild's Revenge*, thus reinforcing A. Nicholas Vardac's thesis[12] that the pictorial stage of the nineteenth century anticipated many cinematic ideals and effects.

The only unpleasant aspect of Macready's life in the theater concerns his relations with other actors. He tyrannized over them when they were subject to him and was furiously jealous of them when they were not. He was as hard on the women as he was on the men—when Helena Faucit first encountered him, she felt, despite all her admiration for him as an actor, that he was so "cold," "distant," and "repulsive" in his manner that she could never like him—and even children who played with him were sometimes scolded.

Perhaps the severest indictment is that of George Vandenhoff, who writes:

> . . . Actors were expected, and, as far as in them lay, by his directions, were compelled to lose all thought of giving prominence to their own parts when he was on the stage. They were, in the sight of his tyrannical self-aggrandizement, mere scaffoldings to support his artistic designs; mere machines to aid the working out of his conceptions; lay figures for his pictures, his groupings, his *tableaux vivants*. As for any thing they might have to say, as far

11 *William Charles Macready's* King John: *A Facsimile Prompt-Book* (University of Illinois Press, 1962) and *Mr. Macready Produces* As You Like It: *A Prompt-Book Study* (Beta Phi Mu Chapbook, Number Five-Six, Urbana, 1962).

12 *Stage and Screen: Theatrical Method from Garrick to Griffith* (Harvard University Press, 1949). Vardac mentions Macready only once, in his introduction, where he calls him, oddly, "Charles Macready."

as it was necessary to be said, as a *cue* for his speech, or for the carrying out or explaining the plot in which he was concerned, let them say it; and say it in such a manner as will make best for his reply; otherwise, he would prefer them to be silent.

He adds that when Macready played Othello, "Iago was to be nowhere," but when he played Iago, Othello became "a mere puppet for Iago to play with."[13]

This, to be sure, is another actor's view, but there is considerable supporting evidence, some of it in Macready's own words. Sir Theodore Martin, who married Helena Faucit, has remarked of his published *Diaries* what many other readers have noticed:

> Where his own effects are marred by the incompetency of others . . . Mr. Macready is always ready to note the fact with almost peevish soreness; but in no one instance does he mention any man or woman as having helped him in bringing out the full purpose of the author, or in heightening the effect of his own scenes.

And it is Helena Faucit herself who tells us how *Punch* once remarked that Mr. Macready must be under the impression she had a very beautiful back since he never permitted the audience to see her face.

Macready would have been the last to claim that he was always fair to other actors. "Our interests in this profession come too frequently into collision to ensure, without steady vigilance, that magnanimity which makes the peace of conscience." When Charles Mayne Young dies, he remarks that "for several years we were in rivalry together: disliking, of course . . . ." He speaks sharply of almost all his rivals—once he even shocks himself by realizing that he is pleased to hear bad news of the Kembles!— and when he could despise them for their private lives, as in the case of Edmund Kean, he seems to rejoice to find contempt a kind of duty. He says frankly that he wishes Forrest success in England insofar as he does not endanger his own supremacy,[14]

[13] George Vandenhoff, *Dramatic Reminiscences* . . ., ed. by Henry Seymour Carleton (James W. Cooper & Co., John Camden Hotten, 1860).

[14] Unless his diary is completely mendacious, however (which nobody be-

71

and he was brutally frank to young Samuel Phelps, when the latter complained of the roles that were being assigned to him: "Do you imagine that, after fighting all these years for the throne, I'm going to abdicate for the purpose of putting you or any other man in my place?" He was even patronizing toward his great friend Dickens when the latter took to acting and play production for charity, and it was not until later, when he himself was no longer contending for prizes, that he generously called the fearsome *Oliver Twist* reading "two *Macbeths*." By that time, the only theater that existed for him, really, was his own, as he preserved it in memory; Charles Fechter was the only one of the younger actors that he would have cared to see, and he soon lost his interest in him also.

Macready resented sharing calls with other actors when he thought they did not deserve it, but I fear he sometimes resented it even more when they did. Sometimes he took Helena Faucit out voluntarily; once at least he yielded a call to her. But at other times he insisted upon going out alone, notably in Paris, where for some strange reason he had got it into his head that she was intriguing against him. ("Either Mr. Macready has grown more selfish and exacting, or I am less capable of bearing with such ungenerous conduct.") There is one curious entry in the diary about Charlotte Cushman kissing his hand; he was "only kind" to her because he did not want their relationship to become "more intimate." But only a few days later, she too is "an *intrigante*, I fear, a very double person." Two years later, he would prefer her as leading lady to Faucit but does not wish to say so, but immediately after that he does not like Cushman either, for she is no longer sufficiently tractable. On the whole, it seems to me that though he speaks slightingly of Garrick and hated Junius Brutus Booth, Macready was only generous toward

---

lieves), it does prove that Macready tried to restrain his great friend, the influential critic John Forster, later Dickens' biographer, from attacking Forrest, and that Forster's slashing reviews were written against Macready's advice. Yet I wonder what Macready would have said if his friend had praised Forrest.

the actors whom he knew in his early years or to foreigners like Talma, with whom his later sense of rivalry was only indirect. He labored unselfishly to get Mrs. Siddons her statue in the Abbey, and he speaks kindly of Mrs. Jordan, Miss Stephens, and Miss O'Neill, and even of the juvenile prodigy Master Betty, who was his playmate as a boy and whose decline during his later career he thought not wholly deserved. Though he criticized some of her performances, he was very kind to Rachel when she first came to England, but he dropped her self-righteously as soon as she began to be gossiped about, and he even resented Malibran's carrying off so much English money.[15]

If actors were "beasts" in Macready's eyes, critics were "vermin," and when two reviewers whom he especially disliked went to their reward, he remarked that he was glad both were "gone where we all must soon follow." He was a little better with

[15] Sometimes an actor got the better of Macready, as in the well-known story about Ellen Tree, who brought him to time by placing upstanding pins in her coiffure to prevent him from rumpling her hair as Virginia after she had several times requested him not to do so, and John Coleman tells another delightful anecdote about a *Werner* rehearsal:

"Sir, will you be good enough to—err—to do me the favor when I say—err-err—to stand—err-err—and don't move hand or foot till I lift my—err-err—You understand me?"

"Not quite, sir."

"Good God! Am I not speaking the English language?"

"Undoubtedly; but if you will kindly tell me once more where I am to stand when you say—err-err—I won't move hand or foot till you lift your—err-err—"

"He looked at me dubiously, and even angrily for a moment, then repeated the direction with clearness and precision" (John Coleman, *Players and Playwrights I Have Known* [Chatto & Windus, 1888].)

But perhaps the best story on Macready comes from the *Diaries* itself. It, too, relates to a performance of *Werner*:

I was inconvenienced and rather annoyed by Ulric looking on the ground, or anywhere but in my face, as he should have done; my displeasure, however, vanished on seeing the tears fast trickling down his cheek, and forgiving his inaccuracy on the score of his sensibility, I continued the scene with augmented energy and feeling, and left it with a very favorable impression of the young man's judgment and warm-heartedness. In the course of the play he accosted me, begging my pardon for his apparent inattention to me, and explaining the cause, viz. that he had painted his face so high on the cheek that the color had got into his eyes, and kept them running during the whole act. What an unfortunate disclosure!

73

authors, for he respected literature, and when Bulwer dedicated a play to him, he was almost overcome. There seems no doubt that the happiest hours of his life, outside those he spent with his family, were passed in the society of his author- and artist-friends. When an author turned playwright, however, there was no question who was master, and though both he and Bulwer show attractively, upon the whole, in the detailed account of their intercourse, with which Shattuck has now supplied us,[16] Macready did not allow either his respect for literature or his contempt for the stage to disturb his conviction that the interests of one particular actor must be supreme. *Richelieu* was revised over and over again, and while it is clear that Macready contributed much to its final success, I think it is also clear that part of his dissatisfaction at the outset was that not enough of the play's burden was thrown upon him. Moreover, though, in 1846, he wrote Bulwer that he had enjoyed playing Richelieu more than any other character in a modern play, he and the author never saw eye to eye in their conception of the leading character, and Bulwer never saw the role played as he had conceived it.

III

Discussions of Macready's temperament generally stop after the second syllable, and there is considerable excuse for this. The *Diaries* are crammed with self-accusations in wearisome iteration. "What would I not do, or give, to cure myself of this injustifiable, dangerous, and unhappy disposition? Regret is no expiation of a vice that injures others and degrades myself." But it was no remedy either, and the universe remained "but an atom before the vastness of one's self!" He was always being slighted. Once he pettishly refused to receive a communication which had

16 In his *Bulwer and Macready: A Chronicle of the Early Victorian Theater* (University of Illinois Press, 1958), which, incidentally, reprints and corrects all the material contained in *Letters of Bulwer-Lytton to Macready*, which Brander Matthews edited for The Carteret Book Club (1911). *Bulwer and Macready* is a remarkablly vivid book, containing probably the most detailed study anywhere extant of an important nineteenth-century writer's dramatic labors and frustrations.

been addressed to "Mr. Macready" instead of "William Charles Macready, Esquire," and on one occasion he glared from the stage at a man who, as he supposed had laughed at him, only to learn afterwards that he had been glaring at the wrong person!

He allowed himself few of the comforts of self-delusion. Theoretically he was quite clear that "we have no right to show anger to any man; it is right only of the tyrant over his slave, and there is first the right of tyranny in the abstract to be established." Though he hated Edinburgh, he granted its "surpassing beauty" and admitted to himself that his attitude was determined by his being "always disregarded here." When Lady Pollock compared his temperament to Dante's, he swept the consolation aside: "Dante was less irritable; and if he chafed, it was about greater things." Like St. Paul, he did what he would not do. "I am not what I would be—God! how far removed from the height of my desires; I would live a life of benevolence, blessing and blest." Such a disposition does not make living easier, and it is not surprising that Macready was sometimes tempted to wish himself dead, and even tried to make himself believe that his family itself would be better off if he were dead.

The prime illustrations of all this comes in connection with Macready's attack on Alfred Bunn and its aftermath. To himself he admitted again and again the indefensibility of his conduct. "Words cannot express the contrition I feel, the shame I endure." "The fair fame of a life has been sullied by a moment's want of self-command." Later he even probes his feelings toward Bunn himself as a skillful confessor might probe them:

> If interrogated on my feelings when thinking on this vile creature, I must admit that I have very much wished his downfall. Did this arise solely from the injury to my art and my own advancement that his continuance in power occasioned? Was it on grounds of sympathy with other sufferers and on abstract points, or was it from personal detestation that I desired his degradation?

But if anybody else criticized him, Macready would tell even his diary that "I simply took that vengeance and inflicted that just punishment which the law would not"! And though he got off much more lightly than he had feared, he never forgave not only Bunn but Frederick Thesiger, who prosecuted the case against him, and Thomas Noon Talfourd, who, in his opinion, conducted a weak defense, and his references to all three in his *Diaries*, even in connections which have nothing to do with his case, are almost hysterical.

In other aspects, Macready shows much more attractively. He was a highly cultured man, and both his reading and the comments he makes on it are more like what one might expect of a writer than an actor. He never allowed his Latin to fall into disrepair, and though he had no German, he was well versed in both French and Italian. His range was not confined to belles-lettres, nor to those aspects of literature which border upon the drama. He took an intelligent interest in music and the plastic arts also; if a professional prejudice shows anywhere, it is in his scorn for the opera, which in his time was a formidable rival to the classical drama to which his heart was given. So *Norma* is "nonsense"; *Fidelio*, "though short," strikes an Englishman as "rather heavy"; *La Sonnambula* is, quite vulgarly, "the very excrement of trash." Yet he could always be counted upon to recognize a great artist, even here: Wilhelmine Schröder-Devrient, Adelaide Kemble, Malibran, Jenny Lind. Taglioni, too, who danced in the opera, was "a creature of genius" or "a realization of some young poet's dream whose amorous fancy offered to his slumbers beside some stream or fountain the nymph whose divine beauty consecrated the natural beauty of the scene," though, for some reason, he thought her rival, Fanny Ellsler, "exceedingly vulgar." Jenny Lind was, even upon his first view of her, "the most charming singer and actress I have ever in my life seen. . . . I was enchanted with her." When they met, she was as much attracted to him as he to her, and whether they knew it or not, they had very much the same failings in natural amiability.

In English literature he ranged far and wide. His best commentary on Shakespeare was his acting, but he once considered an edition of Shakespeare, and Bradbury and Evans did publish his expurgated Pope for young readers. He was not incapable of a penetrating summary, as when he calls *Timon of Athens* "only an incident with comments on it."

He loved Chaucer, whom he found "delightful, humorous, animated, various, graphic, and abounding in character most broadly, nicely and distinctly marked," and his friends seem to have found his readings in Milton very impressive.

He could not read the *Arcadia*, and he did not read *Clarissa* until 1852. It cannot be said that he failed to appreciate its art, but he preferred Miss Howe to Clarissa herself, whom he could not forgive for her interest in Lovelace, a character he found more detestable than Iago. He thought Fielding's *Amelia* inferior to *Tom Jones*, but *Tom Jones* itself was inferior to Scott. He was something of a Scott connoisseur, yet he describes Abbotsford as "the most disagreeable exhibition I have almost ever seen, itself the suicidal instrument of his fate, and monument of his vanity and indiscretion."

Jane Austen was not didactic enough to suit him, and too much preoccupied with the surfaces of life; it is significant that he valued Wordsworth because he "makes me anxious to be virtuous, and strengthens my resolution to try to be so." He had similar experiences with such different novels as George Sand's *Consuelo*, which drove unworthy thoughts out of his mind, and Harriet Martineau's *Deerbrook*, from which he rose "much benefited by the confirmation of good aspiration and intention that has feebly existed within me."

When he was in Italy in 1822 he hoped to meet Byron, but this hope was not realized. He does not seem to have cared much for Tennyson, and his brilliant comment on *The Princess*—"such *determined* poetry"—certainly has a much wider application. He was an enthusiast for Browning from *Paracelsus* days, though considerably less enthusiastic about the plays submitted to him for production, and, as we have already seen, their attempt to work together turned out badly; by *The Return of the Druses* the actor was beginning to fear that the poet's intellect was "not quite clear"!

In Dickens he had a proprietary interest through their close friendship. Though generally enthusiastic and appreciative, he was always faithful to his own ideas, one of them being that Dickens editorialized too much, since a novelist should never thrust himself into a story, which must have been a rather unusual notion for those days. Many Victorians were overwhelmed with grief by the death of Little Nell, and nobody more so than Macready,[17] but in his case we must remember that he had recently lost a daughter. Dickens' great rival Thackeray he approached with a certain prejudice but frankly and generously acknowledged the genius shown in *Vanity Fair*. He admired *Adam Bede* but was surprised when Lady Pollock conjectured it to have been written by a woman.

For politics as such Macready felt only contempt. "Don't let them make you a Cabinet minister," he begs Bulwer in 1841, "or spoil you in any way." He resented public memorials going to soldiers and statesmen while the heroes of peace go uncommemorated, and though he honored his own soldier-brother, he generally thought of a soldier as "an ass or a monkey" who had put on "a fool's jacket." "War! war! That men, the creatures of a God of wisdom and of love, should rush forward in savage delight to mangle and slay each other! Oh, God! oh, God! when will Thy blessed gift of reason be universal in its use among men?"

In 1839 he approved of Daniel O'Connell's activities in Ireland, and though, by the time O'Connell died, he could no longer regard him as a good man, he still thought him a great one. We may gulp down the aggressive egalitarianism of *The*

[17] "Found at home notes from Ransom, and one from Dickens with an onward number of *Master Humphrey's Clock*. I saw one print in it of the dear dead child that gave a dead chill through my blood. I dread to read it, but I must get it over. I have read the two numbers; I never have read printed words that gave me so much pain. I could not weep for some time. Sensation, sufferings have returned to me, that are terrible to awaken; it is real to me; I cannot criticize it."

Lady of Lyons unthinkingly nowadays, but when Macready first appeared in it, the classes were very conscious of this. He was disgusted by those who thought of England and France as "natural" enemies, and he celebrated the Fourth of July because, "as one of the great family of mankind," he had profited by it and could thank God that "the great cause of liberty and improvement" had been advanced by it. Dickens' attack on the United States in *Martin Chuzzlewit* displeased him, and at one time he seriously considered spending his retirement in Cambridge, Massachusetts. A man named Edwin Forrest was ultimately to take care of that idea (one could not voluntarily become the compatriot of such a scoundrel!), but the sight of American slavery and lawlessness had their influence too, and it was before, not after, the Astor Place Riot that he wrote, "A crust in England is better than pampering tables here," and even, a little later, "Let me die in a *ditch* in England, rather than in the Fifth Avenue of New York here—and *no mistake!*" Even then, though his heart had changed, his head was still much the same, and in 1850 he declared, "America *will* become the champion (however unfitted morally) of human freedom."

Macready's republicanism may, as has been suggested, have been influenced by the fierce pride which resented his not himself belonging to the aristocracy (or even being, in the technical sense, a gentleman), but he is perfectly consistent in it. Westland Marston once heard him correct a lady at dinner for speaking of the "lower classes"; he preferred, he said, "the poorer classes." Sometimes he carries his anti-aristocratic principles to amusing extremes, and sometimes he is rude or inhuman. Thus it is not enough to denounce the "barbarity, injustice, and treachery" of King Charles I, and to find "horrid blasphemy" in "the form of prayer on his martyrdom"; the hapless monarch must even be blamed for the sufferings of the Pilgrim Fathers, though he had not even begun to rule when they left England! Macready was disgusted that Bulwer and others should be set up by a compliment from an eighteen-year-old girl just because

79

she happened to be queen of England. When she went to see the lions at Drury Lane, or asked to have the price of her box at Covent Garden reduced, he was disgusted with her too, and when she came to see his Lear, he pointed the appeal for the "poor, naked wretches" in the storm scene directly at her box. It was reasonable enough to feel that England was making too much of a fuss over King William IV in his last illness, but when "the old Dowager Duchess of Salisbury" is burned to death at Hatfield House, and Macready can find nothing better to enter in his diary than that "there are poor enough to engross my pity till these dwellers in palaces can learn to feel for the inmates of the hovels round them," one can only hope that he is not as brutal as he sounds.

Macready sometimes considered himself a solitary man outside the theater as well as in it. "It is not my wish to be proud. I would live a life full of love to all mankind, and redeem the sins of my life by benevolence of thought and deed. Why, then, have I so few companions?" Yet he would seem to have a large number of friends among the distinguished men and women of his time, and sometimes he was even attracted to a person (like George Sand) by whom one might have expected him to be repelled. "His first aspect was perhaps severe," says Lady Pollock, "but what a charm there is in a grave countenance when it breaks into a pleasant smile. . . ."

The dearest of all his friends was, of course, Dickens, who dedicated *Nicholas Nickleby* to him and chose him and Mrs. Macready to take charge of his children when he and Mrs. Dickens went to America in 1842. Lady Pollock writes:

> I think we never visited Sherborne without carrying there some token of the friendship of Dickens—a friendship which, beginning, as our own began, with ardent admiration for the actor, augmented almost daily with the intimate knowledge of the man. Of all friends, Dickens was the truest; he was enthusiastic, and he was stedfast; no work and no trouble of his own impeded him, if he believed that his friend wanted him; he shared trials which to

his sensitive nature were especially painful, and lightened them by his care; he was the last friend (outside the family circle) who saw Catherine (Mrs. Macready) in her sinking condition. The last flush of pleasure that passed over her face was caused by the sight of him; and as he took her hand to say farewell, she, sinking back exhausted in her chair, said feebly and faintly, "Charles Dickens, I had almost embraced you—what a friend you have been!" He stooped and kissed her forehead; and when he was next one of the family circle the mother was no longer there.

In the latter days of Macready's life, when the weight of time and of sorrow pressed him down, Dickens was his most frequent visitor; he cheered him with narratives of bygone days; he poured some of his own abundant warmth into his heart; he led him into his old channels of thought; he gave readings to rouse his interest; he waked him up again, by his vivid descriptions, his sense of humor—he conjured back his smile and his laugh. Charles Dickens was and is to me the ideal of friendship.

Dickens once said that he had never met anybody he could not manage to get along with except one, and she was the woman he married! It was his biographer-to-be, John Forster, who introduced him to Macready, and it says much for the novelist's good disposition that he was able to remain on agreeable terms with two such difficult men, who could not always get along with each other.[18] Nor was Dickens disturbed when Macready refused to produce a play which he had submitted to him. "He returned me an answer," wrote the actor, "which is an honor to him. How truly delightful it is to meet with high-minded and warm-hearted men." Macready may have been right about this play, but he could hardly have been more wrong than he was in his strange notion that *Oliver Twist* was undramatizable.

Macready's charities were not so fantastically generous as Edwin Booth's; neither did they have the wild spontaneity of Forrest's or Mansfield's. There was nothing spontaneous about

---

[18] There was, however, one terrible clash between Dickens and Forster, which Macready records, and at which he functioned as peacemaker. See *Diaries*, II, 74 (August 16, 1840).

him either as an actor or as a man, and I suppose this is the basic cause for a certain lack of charm which one feels in him. It had been strongly impressed upon him that charity was a Christian duty, and he used this touchstone to test the sincerity of religious professions, but he admits that he sometimes gave grudgingly, and he says frankly, "I do not like to expend my money." Once he went to court with a cabman rather than pay what he considered an overcharge (the price asked was two shillings); this was not stinginess but principle, but it is typical of Macready's inflexible kind of man. Once he criticizes Lady Byron for not having given in a case of dire need, then solemnly records his own contribution of ten shillings, and once, having contributed the considerable sum of twenty pounds to buy coals for the poor, he adds, "I do not perceive why, with the sentiments I entertain of this as a religious and moral duty, I should mix myself with persons who have nothing else in common with me."

Yet there is a certain unfairness in setting down these facts. They derive from Macready's own record, and we should remember that many persons have felt the same way without setting down their feelings for posterity to gloat over. He himself was of the opinion that if he had had great means he would have made a "munificent patron," but he is not the only human being to whom that flattering idea has occurred. In December, 1839, he took a financial inventory:

> Arranged my accounts, and found myself possessed of £10,000, a small realization out of such a receipt as mine has been the last twenty years. But I have lost much, given away much, and, I fear, spent much; but what I have lost and what given, would leave me with all my spendings a rich man.

A few days later, he records that his donations to "poor or importunate people" had come to two hundred pounds for the year. When he hears of a widow's mite kind of gift, he finds himself unable "to aspire to such proud virtue; it is really noble. My children make me fearful, and my habits, I believe, make me too selfish." Care for his children—and concern for their future—was certainly a part of it, yet he could be very generous, and sometimes he even gave himself with his gifts. His young second wife, who had heard of him as a kind of ogre, began to love him when she found him, around Sherborne, "in poor men's cottages reading to the sick and relieving want." He was certainly very kind to Mrs. Ternan and her children after her husband's suicide, and when Mrs. Warner (Marie Huddart) died, he divided the responsibility for her children with the wealthy Miss Coutts. Macready's attitude toward his fellow-Thespians being what it was, it is especially pleasant to note that these generosities were extended toward theater people. He once gave up his fee to help a Birmingham manager who had lost money on his engagement, and the story of his generosity to Samuel Phelps may best be told as J. C. Trewin gives it in *Mr. Macready*:

"What right had you to get into debt?" Macready rasped.

"I couldn't help it," said Phelps.

"Couldn't help it, sir! No-no-man has a right to live beyound his income. A speculator may incur liabilities, but no man with a fixed income is ever justified in a-a-a-living beyond it."

"Sir," said Phelps, turning away, "I came to see if you were disposed to help me. Since you are not, I suppose I must go to gaol."

"Don't talk stuff and a-a-a-nonsense!" said Macready. "How much do you owe?"

"I don't know sir."

"A pretty fellow you are to come and talk about money without-a-a-studying figures. Away you go! Come to me at twelve tomorrow morning with a full, true, and particular account of every debt you owe in the world. Don't leave out a-a-a-single shilling. Let me know the worst and we'll see what's to be done."

He shook Phelps's hand. The actor found himself outside. That sleepless night his table of debts reached four hundred pounds. Next day Macready took the paper, read it, glowered, drummed on his desk, strode about the room, and then, unlocking his cashbox, wrote a cheque for £450 and thrust it into Phelps's hands. "You remember how grim and grizzled he looked?" said Phelps, telling Coleman of the scene years later. "At that moment his face lit up with a rare and beautiful smile. It was a smile that could dignify (and sometimes almost deify) him." Phelps had just saved himself. As he hurried from the theater by the stage-door, a bailiff arrested him for thirty-six pounds. "Come round to the bank," he said. The bailiff was obliging, and the matter ended, thanks to a Macready that Bunn and his tribe would never understand.[19]

None of the vices except drinking seem to have tempted Macready greatly. He had one of the most dangerous habits an actor can have—that of fortifying himself for his work with alcohol, and though this did not lead in his case to the results that have sometimes followed, one does find, in that remorselessly honest diary, such entries as "I felt I had taken too much wine and could not trust myself" and "Drank beyond reason and went to chambers at a very late hour." Once at least he acknowledges that what he had drunk made him rude and profane. Once he speaks of having broken in upon "my teetotal experiment," and once he feels exceptionally well because of "the temperance of my life for the last week," but these terms are not defined. When the Pollock child was ill, he prescribed good English ale, or, failing that, "superior" stout. When he was in America in 1843–44, he was much taken with American cocktails and especially it seems with mint juleps. There are fewer references to smoking, but in 1866 he writes Bulwer that though he has tried several remedies for his asthma, he has found nothing better than the "pure Havana cigar."

His complete sexual decency was not due to any indifference to women, for he first fell in love when he was nine. He knew that "an actor has more temptation than other men"; sometimes it even seemed to him that *virtue is impossible in a theater*," but he must have known that it was difficult anywhere, for he was still very young when an acquaintance tried to unload upon him the pretty young mistress who had been passing for his wife. Yet it does not appear that Macready ever thought about women

[19] Quoted by permission of the publisher, George G. Harrap, London.

84

except in their relationship to men; he had no interest in "women's rights," and even his admiration for Portia was modified by her stepping over "the boundary of feminine reserve." He has a few vulgar references to women—"a nice piece of flesh enough, *rien autre*"—and he thought one girl who came to him in search of an engagement better qualified to be a "Cyprian," though he adds carefully that he did not tell her so. Once he ungallantly wonders whether all women are not alike, though he hopes not. Yet, for all his propriety, he was impatient with actresses who had scruples about showing their legs when his productions happened to require it, and he altered Helena Faucit's Imogen costume without her consent, though he also wished to put fleeced stockings on her because he thought her legs too thin.

A number of old flames bob up from time to time in the *Diaries*, one at least as an object of charity. In 1846 he read of the death of "Lettice, wife of the Rev. R. Green Jeston, aged 34," and was "shocked and grieved" by the recollections awakened of "the being whom I remembered in her first blush of beauty, whom I had loved, and who had loved me; who, I believe, through her life retained a deep feeling of attachment to me— whom I would have married, had our stars, adverse as they were, permitted." A reasonable number of women managed to fall in love with him in the days of his fame, but he was always wary. The Hon. Mrs. Norton was obviously not averse to making his acquaintance when he met her in 1835, and since we find her writing to Mrs. Macready at a later date, she must in a measure have succeeded, but though he thought her very beautiful, he did not, at the outset, trust her or want anything to do with her. In 1841 he decisively rejected the advances of an adventuress known as Mrs. St. Aubyn, who evidently tried to seduce him. He was not incapable of being "attracted and distracted . . . by a very pretty *demoiselle*" in a coach, and it is clear that he enjoyed the distraction, though he adds primly that "it would be much better that I should endeavor to turn my time to my mind's profit . . . instead of trifling it away in idle and not altogether harmless frivolity." But you had to be *very* pretty to bring that off, and he is more in character when he receives with "complacent indifference" the "violent advances" which one woman makes to him in a coach, and the same month goes to sleep to avoid conversing with another.

More interesting was the unknown girl who, in 1839, fell madly in love with him—or, rather, with his Claude Melnotte—across the footlights, and who wrote, threatening to destroy herself. He did not consider gratifying her, but he did arrange a meeting, at which he found her "a fine-looking young women, of modest deportment" and gave her fatherly advice. Perhaps it secretly flattered his pride to have an attractive girl lose her head over him, but he seems sincerely to have respected her. There is no doubt that her suffering was real, however foolish, and that his sympathy for her was quite genuine. Whether she found him less fascinating *in propria persona* than as Claude Melnotte I have no idea, but she seems wisely to have decided to go on living.

Within the theater, Macready was careful but not disgustingly prudish. On special occasions he was not averse to giving an actress a kiss of greeting, but he realized all the dangers involved in making a woman "acquainted with her own passions," and he refused at least one woman who wished to study with him because he feared being thrown into intimate contact with her. Sometimes he made a friend of an actress like Marie Huddart, with whom there seems at one time to have been some harmless kind of affectionate attachment followed by an estrangement, but he still considered such things "dangerous and ill-advised. A woman's company is always soothing, but it is a perilous indulgence." Only two women of the theater seem to require further consideration along this line. One was his principal leading lady, Helena Faucit, and the other was one of the great nineteenth-century divas, Maria Malibran.

I do not know when Macready first met Malibran, but he

refers to her in the very first year of his diaries—1833. When they met again in 1835, she saluted him

> most affectionately, and perhaps, I was to her what she was to me—a memorial of years of careless, joyous hope and excitement; she said I was not altered; I could not say what I did not think of her. I could have loved—once almost did love her, and I believe she was not indifferent to me. It often occurs to me on such recollections: how would my destiny have been altered! I should possibly have been an *ambitieux*—should I have been happier?— should I have had my Nina, my Willie and little Catherine? Left Malibran in very great depression of spirits.

This sounds as if he had known her before his marriage, but that was in 1823 when she was only fifteen, and she did not make her London debut until 1825. When she died, at twenty-eight, in 1836, as the result of a fall from a horse,

> the loudest clap of thunder in the calmest sunshine could not have given me a greater start. I felt as if my mind was stunned; it was a shock that left me no power to think for some little time. . . . I once could have loved her, and she has since said that she loved—"was in love with"—me. Had I known it for certain, I might have been more miserable than I am. Latterly she had decreased in my regards, and in my esteem she had no place.[20] The world is a sad loss to her, and she to it. Poor Malibran!

Vague as they are, these tantalizing references are interesting as establishing a connection between Macready and one of the most fascinating and unfortunate singers of the century.

As for Helena Faucit, it seems clear that she was seriously in love with him at the beginning of the forties and that she got herself gossiped about malignantly by the other women of the

---

[20] Probably because of her irregular connection with Charles de Bériot, to whom she bore a child out of wedlock, and whom she married in the year of her death. She had been married at seventeen to a much older man. In 1827 she left him, but the legal obstacles to her union with the man she loved were not cleared away until just before the end.

company.[21] Macready handled the situation both highmindedly and humanely, though he may not have been wise in discussing it with her at such length as he did. Sometimes her affection touched him, and sometimes it annoyed him, but he was still more annoyed when he saw her moving in to share his stellar glory. It has been conjectured that if Macready had been free, he might have married Helena Faucit, and that if he had been less high principled, he might have attempted to seduce her. Perhaps so, but the second alternative assumes that they were not themselves but a couple of other people, and is therefore hardly worth discussing.

Macready was a devoted husband and father, but in both aspects he was the same Macready we know elsewhere. He met Catherine Atkins on the stage when she was nine years old and characteristically began his association with her by scolding her because she did not know her lines. Later, after she had been bereaved, he tried to look after her; he himself says that " 'love approached me under friendship's name.' " Perhaps it would have been more accurate to say that love approached under the disguise of pedagogy, and he makes the blood run cold when he solemnly records that Catherine "never entirely relinquished the character of pupil, in wearing that which she so gracefully did, of 'wife and friend' . . . ." We are all familiar enough with mother-in-law trouble. Mrs. Macready had no mother-in-law, but, since she did have her husband's sister Letitia, she didn't miss her. There is no more horrifying tragi-comedy in literature than Macready's own account of the first meeting of Catherine and Letitia, of the "unmistakable disappointment, indeed repulsion," which Letitia registered, of how he himself rode in the carriage between two silent women, of how Letitia "retired to her room and lay till late in the afternoon on her bed, drowned in tears. Her

21 Miss Faucit was only twenty-three at the time, and her later impressive character may as yet have been partly unformed. She herself bears witness to Macready's kindness to her when she was ill, though it must not be forgotten that he needed her at the theater. See his letters to her in Sir Theodore Martin's *Helena Faucit (Lady Martin)* (Blackwood, 1900).

basic objection was that Catherine was a child, unqualified to be her brother's wife; therefore the marriage must be postponed while she continued her studies. "Catherine herself, she was confident, with the improvement she would make in the interim, would be happier in becoming my wife at a period more distant." Oddly enough, the girl accepted this arrangement, and when the probationary period was over, Letitia graciously wrote her a letter in which she affirmed that she could now honestly say that she loved her. So far as we know, the reconciliation was complete, and Mrs. Macready had her sister-in-law in her household (if it ever was hers) through the whole of her married life. But it may be that with those ten children she needed her.

Yet Macready loved Catherine deeply, sincerely, passionately, and the *Diaries* are full of his love. "Birthday of my beloved, my adored Catherine; God for ever and for ever bless her! Amen." "What would life be to me under the load of regrets that I should bear to my grave if I were to lose that dear woman?" "On this day ten years ago I was married to my beloved Catherine, whose affection, mildness, and sweet disposition have made the greater part of my life since that far event most truly happy." It is clear, too, that, for all her tractableness at the outset, Catherine was no vegetable. On May 4, 1833, while playing in Dublin, Macready received a letter from her. "I cannot call it unkind, because it was not intended to be so, but since she has been my wife I do not remember any pain or distress of heart to compare with the *dead pressure of misery* that she has laid upon my heart. . . ." Once, too, she upset him greatly by coming into his study, just as he was getting ready for bed, to tell him that the speech he had prepared to deliver at the Garrick Club was untactful and would only make him enemies. Though he found the objection "ill-timed, at least," he altered the speech before retiring.

If Macready was a pedagogue toward his wife, he naturally was unable to escape this role with his passionately loved children. "Dear Nina fell asleep in my arms in the dining-room and kept me some time from my employment. These blessed children, even when I am most busy, allure me from my resolves of diligence for a time; I cannot speak of the overflowing love with which I look at them." When they were sick—and when they died—his agony was terrible. But there were flashes of temper when Nina did not know her lessons, and when she did wrong, she had to be punished, two days handrunning if necessary, for, "thank God, my doting affection for these dear children does not, nor ever shall, make me guilty of such injustice as to spare my own feelings at the expense of their future, perhaps their eternal welfare." Lady Pollock suggests that his relations with the girls were smoother than with the boys because female instruction was more largely left to Catherine and Letitia.

The very first entry in Macready's diary (January 1, 1833) was a prayer:

> With God's merciful help I trust to make my conduct and use of my time during this year more acceptable in His sight than that of my previous life has been; and I enter upon it with prayers for His blessings on my wife, friends and myself. Amen!

This applied to his artistic life, his domestic life, and his life in every other aspect, for he certainly considered himself a Christian, though he insists on defining the term in his own way. One passage in his reminiscences shows him deriving considerable comfort from the sacrament, but ritual in general meant little to him, and sermons, it seems, even less, for he was almost as anti-clerical as anti-monarchist, and he despised clergymen as "these things"—tradesmen, "hypocrites," "villains," "liars to God," and "cheats to human nature," practicing "a base and bloody trade, extorting money by artifice and violence, and caring little or nothing for the immortal objects which ought to be . . . [their] care."

He believed in immortality and derived comfort from the belief, especially when it brought him the assurance that he had not lost his beloved children forever. He was not averse to metaphysical speculation, and Lady Pollock says he believed in a plurality of worlds, "a state of progression through other in-habited planets." At one time he dabbled in spiritualism, being, like most sensitive men who have investigated psychic phenom-ena, unable to explain the manifestations on any naturalistic basis, yet disappointed by their inconclusiveness and disgusted by their puerility. He opposed any purely secular, non-religious education because "I never was better in the hour of temptation for what is called knowledge, but I have been saved from some sins by the childlike habit of prayer." The new Biblical criticism held no terrors for him, for the brutality of the Old Testament sickened him, and he thought it blasphemous to refuse to apply human brains to Biblical and other religious problems.[22] Indeed, theology in general seems to have meant little to him; he doubted that Christ was a Christian in the theological sense,[23] and he even senses the possibility of moral corruption in the doctrine of the Atonement.[24]

All in all, filled as Macready's diaries are with conventional piety, I feel little indication in them of any sense of the abiding presence of God. He undoubtedly *believed* in God and acknowl-edged his allegiance to Him, but his real preoccupation was the work he had to do in this world, and, for the strength he needed to do it, he seems to me to have relied upon his family rather than upon God.[25] He understood himself when he wrote that "the

[22] In one curious passage, *Diaries*, I, 103–104 (February 9, 1834), Macready speculates on the possibility of Christians being bound by the laws in Leviticus. His primary concern here is to attack the arbitrariness of the Church in holding Christians to some part of the Jewish law but not all. But the larger question seems also to be in his mind.

[23] *Diaries*, II, 83 (September 22, 1840).

[24] *Reminiscences, etc.*, I, 475 (December 22, 1835): "The bulk of mankind, I incline to think, flies to a mediating and redeeming benevolence to silence the scruples of conscience and quiet the fears of an hereafter, where the awful ques-tions of their deservings may be made. They avoid atonement in their proper selves, and repose upon the sacrifice which Christ made." But of course it is the very point of Christian doctrine that atonement for sin *cannot* be made by a merely human being. After all his bitter struggles to correct his own faults, it seems odd that Macready should not have perceived this.

[25] See, e.g., *Diaries*, I, 315 (May 13, 1836): "Went to chambers in a wretched, wretched state of mind; thought of the villain who had in so cowardly and in-

more I hear or see of sects, *i.e.* the endeavor of individuals to flatter their own opinions by gaining assent to them among men, instead of attempting to reconcile them to God—the more I see the prudence of placing morality before religion." Only, it is more than sects that he is rejecting here. The element in religion that really attracted him was morality; perhaps he was even too moral—or moralistic—to be in the deepest sense religious.

Though William Charles Macready was an impressive and respectworthy figure, both as an artist and as a man, it is clear that he was not for all markets. In the ordinary sense of the term, he led a "blameless" life, yet he had faults which many persons found it quite as hard to forgive as the raffishness which he justly excoriated in many of his colleagues. It is clear that he lacked many attractive qualities, but it is also clear that he strove to encompass these, and if he strove in vain, this was not his fault alone. Human beings do not put themselves together, and libertines have no monopoly on the right to be judged charitably by their fellowmen. Most of the sharp things Macready said were evidently spoken; nothing could be more sweetly reasonable than such letters of his as I have been able to read. There is not much spontaneity, however, even about his reasonableness; he was almost as much the slave of duty as the young man in *The Pirates of Penzance*. Helena Faucit and his first wife agreed that he ought to have been a schoolmaster. Nobody was in a better position to know.

---

famous a manner attacked me in the *Times*. Felt that life was not worth holding on such terms, and, but for those dear ones who make it a duty to me, think I should either lay it down or put it to the hazard in punishing the scoundrels who are thus torturing me. These are neither religious nor philosophic thoughts, but I feel myself merely a weak, frail, creature, the sport of passion, and *in consequence* a very wretched being."

4

Edwin Forrest
(1806–1872)

T HE GREAT PROBLEM in Forrest's case is how to reconcile the legend of ruffianism that has accumulated around him not only with his aesthetic grandeur but, even more, with the devotion to high ideals which he always proclaimed and undeniably sometimes practiced. He could be arrogant, overbearing, even brutal, and though there is no evidence to show that he engineered it or desired it, his capacity as a good hater was certainly one of the elements that led to the worst riot in theatrical history, at the Astor Place Opera House in New York, May 10, 1849. His divorce scandal was one of the most shocking of the century, and even if Mrs. Forrest was as guilty as he said she was, his conduct was still disgraceful. Yet this man was not only the greatest actor of his time: he embodied in his own person the whole crescent spirit of nineteenth-century America. Forrest's enthusiastic biographer Alger is not merely partisan when he writes:

> He had an enthusiastic admiration of great men, and a ruling desire for the prizes of honor and fame. His soul thrilled at the recital of glorious deeds, and his tears started at a great thought or a sublime image or a tender sentiment. Friendship for man, love for woman, a kindling patriotism, a profound feeling of the domes-

tic ties, a burning passion for liberty, and an unaffected reverence for God, were dominant chords in his nature.

Even as a boy, he spontaneously attracted the interest and patronage of great men; later they accepted him as a friend and rejoiced to bear witness to their sense of his worth by offering him testimonial dinners on the slightest provocation. The state of California once sent him an official invitation to act there. Reared in poverty and self-educated, he collected a large library and made himself the unquestioned master of its contents.[1] He loved his country, cherished her welfare, and labored incessantly for aesthetic achievement even after disease had so crippled his powerful body that every step he took was pain. When he died, he left his fortune to provide a home for indigent actors, where they might spend their last days in a luxury to which few of them can ever have hoped to become accustomed.

Edwin Forrest was born in Philadelphia on March 9, 1806, the son of a Scottish father and a German-American mother. Always a loyal and loving son and brother, he worked at various jobs after the early death of his father, to help support the family and himself, and his mother hoped that the eloquence and presence which he early manifested would lead him to the pulpit. They led instead to the stage, in which he showed keen interest even in childhood, and when he was eleven years old, the anything but effeminate boy substituted for a sick actress at the South Street Theater, as Rosalia, a Turkish captive, in something called *Rudolph; or, The Robber of Calabria.* The apprenticeship of the future great tragedian embraced every conceivable kind of theatrical fare. He danced; he sang comic songs; he blacked his face; he even turned flip-flops at the circus. But his real debut was at the Walnut Street Theater, on November 27, 1820, as Young Norval, in Home's *Douglas.* Next he accepted an eight-dollar-a-week engagement with Collins and Jones, for whom he played in Pittsburgh, Louisville, Cincinnati, and elsewhere, and after the company had disbanded, he and some companions set out

[1] See Joseph Sabin, *Catalogue of the Library of Edwin Forrest* (Collins, 1863).

on a barnstorming tour of the back country, traveling by flat-boat, market-wagon, and on foot, and suffering great hardship. On February 4, 1823, he played Jaffier in Otway's *Venice Preserved* in New Orleans, where he also acted in John Howard Payne's *Brutus* and played Iago to the Othello of William Augustus Conway. In Albany, in 1825–26, he undertook Iago, the Duke of Richmond, and other roles with Edmund Kean, who encouraged him and influenced his style.

He made his first New York appearance at the Park Theater, June 23, 1826, as Othello, at a benefit for Jacob Woodhull, from which he passed, in the fall, to the new Bowery Theater, where he acted Othello, Damon, William Tell, and other heroic roles. His beginning salary was $25.00 a week, which was immediately raised to $40.00 for three performances, but Charles Gilfert sometimes "farmed him out" to other managers at $200 a night, which went into his own pocket. Though he had no contract, Forrest refused to leave Gilfert, for he considered his word as good as his bond, but when the time came to make arrangements for the following season, he told the manager that his price was just what he himself had established as his worth and received it. He was then just twenty-one years old.

In 1829 he returned to the Park, where he stayed for seven years. The year before had launched the first of his prize contests for American playwrights (William Cullen Bryant headed the committee), offering $500 and half the third night's receipts. The winner was the actor John Augustus Stone, the play the Indian drama *Metamora*, first acted on December 15, 1829, which remained permanently in Forrest's repertoire as his lifesaver of lifesavers. Two Robert Montgomery Bird prizewinners also remained fixtures: *The Gladiator* (1831)—by 1853 he had acted it five thousand times—and *The Broker of Bogota* (1834). In 1841, Robert T. Conrad gave him *Jack Cade*.

In 1834 he began an extensive sightseeing tour in Europe. In Paris he greatly admired Mlle Georges and Mlle Mars, but showed his real theatrical perspicacity by pointing out an unregarded "Jewish-looking girl," a "little bag of bones, with the marble face and flaming eyes—there is demoniac power. If she lives, and does not burn out too soon, she will become something wonderful." Her name was Élisa Félix, and she is famous in theatrical history as Rachel.

On October 17, 1836, Forrest began an engagement at Drury Lane in London, opening in *The Gladiator*, and this was followed by a tour of the provinces. On June 23, 1837, in London, he was married to Catherine Norton Sinclair. He was thirty. She was eighteen. He returned to America to play at the Chestnut Street, the Park, and the Arch Street theaters, and to make long tours to enormous receipts, and in 1845 he made his second professional visit to England, during which the foundations of his bitter theatrical rivalry with Macready were laid down. At the Princess' Theater, London, his *Macbeth* was hissed, and Forrest believed that Macready had headed a cabal against him. Shortly afterwards, he himself had the bad judgment to hiss Macready openly during a performance of *Hamlet* in Edinburgh.

Though Forrest's American public stood by him loyally, giving him tremendous demonstrations of confidence not only at the time of the Astor Place Riot but also after his separation from his wife,[2] when banners were unfurled in the theater proclaiming "The People's Verdict" as opposed to that of the court, which Mrs. Forrest had won, the strain told, and in 1857 his health broke. His last years were plagued by gout, rheumatism, and sciatica, which not only caused him great pain but robbed him of much of his famous grace and agility upon the stage. He talked of retirement and sometimes achieved it temporarily, but never for good.[3] When his style began to be regarded as old-

[2] They were legally separated in 1849 and divorced in 1852.

[3] When A. C. Wheeler met Forrest in Boston in 1872 after having had the misfortune to offend him by something he had written about him, he was greeted by a man who manifested of all signs of being about to have an epileptic fit. "You damned whippersnapper, have you come here to bark at my heels or to lick my boots?" Later he explained his position; "Who are you, sir, to order me off the stage? Have you set the limits to my career and fixed the boundaries of it? I can't leave the stage. Damn it, sir, it is leaving me. When you understand me you will

fashioned in the cities, he took to the road again and found that
he was still a thriller. In 1866, at Crosby's Opera House in Chicago, he averaged over $1,800 a night for the first ten nights, and
early in 1869, Woonsocket, Rhode Island (population 1,100)
shelled out $600 to see the dying lion as Jack Cade. At the very
end of his life, San Francisco sold seats for him at auction, the
first bringing $500. During his last season on the road, 1871–72,
he traveled seven thousand miles and played in fifty-two cities.
In the spring he collapsed in Boston, his final appearance on the
stage being as Richelieu at the Globe Theater, April 2, 1872.
Though he did not yet know that he was finished, something
impelled him to add a tag line of his own: "And so it ends." In
the fall he could only give readings, and it was Boston again
which heard the last of these, *Othello*, at Tremont Temple, on
Saturday afternoon, December 7. On December 12 he was found
dead, lying almost fully dressed upon his bed, with his dumb-
bells beside him. As a delicate boy, many, many years ago, he
had set out to "make" his body as Theodore Roosevelt was later
to "make" his, and he was still at it when death overtook him.

II

Forrest's two most obvious assets as an actor were a magnificent body and a magnificent voice. The body, however, was not
built quite according to the most highly favored stipulations of
today, for he was only five foot, ten, and decidedly stocky, ultimately carrying more than two hundred pounds.[4] He was also,
as we have seen, a physical culture fanatic, with a devotion to

respect me. Until you do, leave me." Still later he apologized: "Harkee, I may
have done you some injustice unwittingly, but you can understand that a bruised
man forgets the damned amenities at times." *Criterion*, September 23, 1899,
pp. 9–10.

[4] It is probably this fact, plus his persistence in wearing his own moustache and
goatee in most of his roles, that makes Forrest's photographs in costume less impressive than those of many of his contemporaries. Some of his early pictures have
a Byronic splendor, and one or two of the private photographs of later years an
impressive force and dignity, but many of the portraits in character suggest a
solemn Germanic "Pa-man," tagged out for a fancy-dress ball.

Turkish baths and everything else that the nineteenth century considered conducive to physical well-being, and he achieved a vast development of calves and biceps,[5] which he loved to display as fully as the mores of the day would permit in his Roman and Indian roles.[6] John Coleman speaks for all his admirers on this point:

> Imagine, if you can, some marble majesty of the elder world stepping down from its pedestal, instinct with life and motion. The head and shoulders are those of a demi-god. He is dark-eyed, dark-haired, olive-complexioned, with limbs of matchless symmetry—limbs of which every muscle can be clearly discerned through the transparent silken fleshings in which the majestic image is clad from head to foot. A simple flowing garment . . . falls from the left shoulder down to the waist on the opposite side, leaving the ample chest and the massive right arm quite bare.
>
> Try to conceive this gorgeous creature, making the stage alive with classic grace and dignity, and then you may form some faint idea of what this great actor was like in those days.

But not all his audiences felt thus, and though it was rarely denied that he handled his compact bulk with "ponderous grace," there were endless jokes about "the muscular school; the brawny art; the biceps aesthetic; the tragic calves; the bovine drama; rant, roar, and rigamarole."[7] James Henry Hackett thought his "pleasing black eyes" not very effective on the stage,

---

[5] There are stories about women fainting when he stepped on the stage. It is amusing that the intellectual Fanny Kemble should have exclaimed, "What a mountain of a man!" while the more "physical" Fanny Ellsler should have chosen instead to enlarge upon his "wonderful vocal organ" and "rarity of tone." "It was to his splendid acting that I paid tearful homage, and never in my life did artist inspire me with deeper admiration." Men were equally impressed, and Edmond S. Connor, an actor who was not on good terms with Forrest personally, exclaims, "And oh, the majesty of the man!" When Charles Kean saw him as Richelieu, he turned to his wife, Ellen Tree, and exclaimed, "Ellen, this is the greatest acting we have ever seen or shall ever see."

[6] Forrest took up a Greek attitude toward the beauty of the body; he would probably have much sympathy with the tendencies toward nakedness now in vogue; he might even adhere to the nudist movement.

[7] "Editor's Easy Chair," *Harper's Magazine*, Vol. XXVIII (1863), 131–33.

possibly because his inflexible brows, which arch low and near the bridge of the nose, impart when pursed together a grim severity to his countenance, thus seemingly rendering it incapable of much variety, or of sudden alternations, or of lightness of expression; his person generally, with his ample chest, long body, short and Herculean-proportioned arms and legs, does not conform to the ideal of an Apollo; nor is his ease, or grace of action, or carriage of body, remarkable or conventionally well-adapted to represent "the glass of fashion and the mould of form."

Hackett was no great admirer of Forrest, but perhaps it is George Wikoff who hands him the most unkindest cut of all when, out of his fencing experience with him, he declares Forrest to have been weak in the wrist!

The voice was more important. Forrest lived in the great age of American oratory, and had he chosen to enter the political arena, he could have met the greatest on their own ground; indeed he did just that when, in 1838, he addressed a great Democratic rally at Broadway Tabernacle and forthwith touched off a Congressional boom for himself! What is more important is that his own art shows the oratorical influence, even as Whitman's poetry does. His acting was basically elocutionary; almost indifferent to stagecraft, he scornfully dismissed the *mise-en-scène* that was coming into vogue in Shakespearean and other productions during his later years as "scene-painter's drama."

Winter says that "in moments of simple passion he affected the senses like the blare of trumpets and the clash of cymbals, or like the ponderous, slow-moving, crashing and thundering surges of the sea." It has been recorded metaphorically that Lear's curse upon Goneril "reverberated like a thunderstorm" and that when Richelieu threw the power of the church around Julie, "Forrest's bellow made the theatre walls tremble." Once when he cursed his dresser in the wings, waiting to make his entrance, the audience heard every word and applauded, thinking that his first line had been spoken off stage! Writes James E. Murdoch:

There are lines in *Othello* which seem to demand such a voice as his more than any other gift. One of them is—

Keep up your bright swords, for the dew will rust them,

in which, though he left the delicate irony unexpressed, the calm, deep sound seemed to suspend the clashing weapons by some inherent irresistible sway. Another is—

> *Silence that dreadful bell, it frights the isle*
> *From her propriety,*

of which the utterance was itself bell-like, but without harshness or clangor.

Nor was it only in Shakespeare that he could create such effects.

> I never heard anything on the stage [writes George Vandenhoff], so tremendous in its sustained *crescendo* swell and crashing force of utterance as his defiance of the Council in . . . [*Metamora*]. His voice surged and roared like the angry sea, lashed into fury by a storm; till it reached its boiling, seething climax, in which the serpent hiss of hate was heard, at intervals, amidst its louder, deeper, hoarser tones, it was like the Falls of Niagara, in its tremendous down-sweeping cadence; it was a whirlwind, a tornado, a cataract of illimitable rage!

And Alger says that when he went off in *Virginius* after denouncing Appius, his exit would "excite the wildest huzzas, the men in the pit standing with their hats in their uplifted hands, and the women in the boxes waving their handkerchiefs." Moreover, it must be understood that Forrest was not limited to *fortissimo* effects. He had a tremendous range; "he could sigh like a zephyr or roar like a hurricane"; he could command tears as easily as terror. Apparently inexhaustible, he was as fresh and sweet and strong at the end of a performance as he had been at the beginning.

This was heroic acting in the grand manner; we and our contemporaries meet its like only in the Wagnerian opera, but Forrest's elocution was never of the formal, old-fashioned variety, and James A. Herne, than whom there could be no more trust-worthy witness on this point, denying that Forrest was noisy, calls him "the most colloquial tragedian I ever heard." To be sure, he was often attacked for his naturalism also, and Winter speaks of the "snorts and grunts, the brays and belches, the gaspings and gurglings, the protracted pauses, the lolling tongue and the stentorian roar" which he affected in his death scenes.[8] In the early days he used a spurting red fluid in the knife with which he killed Virginia, but his maturer taste discarded this. For his *Lear*, which he considered his greatest achievement,[9] he studied insanity in lunatic asylums and elsewhere across the world, and made himself, or so he considered, an authority on the subject.

The accusation that Forrest was materially minded in his attitude toward his art is justified to the extent that he believed "that the purpose of acting was to show the exact truth of nature." He did not, like Joe Jefferson, try to extract the essence of experience and present it in a rarefied or poetic form. Horace Holley urged this ideal upon him early in his career, but he rejected it. It is difficult to be dogmatic concerning material which is no longer available for examination, but I have an idea that the very intensity of Forrest's acting may have done him a disservice by misleading his auditors. Robustious acting is not inferior *per se* to acting in a more quiet style; this is merely a matter of taste. What counts essentially is how profoundly the actor understands his character and whether he possesses the

[8] On the other hand, Winter testifies to Forrest's good taste in the last act of *Othello*: "The killing was done quickly and with judicious, artistic avoidance of coarse and horrible literalism. . . . The subsequent action, on the revelation of Iago's treachery, was nobly tragic. . . . The suicide was accomplished with one blow of a dagger, and the death was immediate." *Shakespeare on the Stage*, First Series (Moffat, Yard, 1911), 266.

[9] One of the best of all theater anecdotes concerns Forrest's reply to a gentleman who congratulated him on how well he had "played" Lear that night. "*Play* Lear! what do you mean, sir? I do not *play* Lear! I *play* Hamlet, Richard, Shylock, Virginius, if you please; but, by God, sir! I *am* Lear!" But this was in his later years when he considered that the world had used him hardly and had almost identified himself with the wronged king.

technical resources required to communicate his vision to the mind of his audience.

If he did fail in penetration, it was certainly not for want of trying. He studied both text and commentary unceasingly, always probing for deeper and deeper meanings, and when he had an author of distinction to deal with, he demanded an absolute textual fidelity from both himself and those who acted with him. Even in his last years he would not appear as Lear without having spent the day alone with the text. He did not prize originality of interpretation as such, for he believed that "there is generally but one mode positively correct, and that has not been left for us to discover." Though he knew the value of his voice, he never took even it for granted, nor trusted to it to help him bluff his way through a performance or a character. Instead, "he experimented with vocal colorings and pauses until he found voice patterns that conformed to the text and magnified and enriched the author's meaning."[10] It may seem odd that so vigorous an actor should have made so much of the pause; this, too, became the subject of endless jesting, and we hear of his taking up his everlasting rest on a period, going to sleep over a semi-colon, and spending an evening with a comma. But we must remember that some thought Forrest to lack fire in spite of all the noise he made, and that Hackett found his pathos "whining" and seeming "to spring more from a cool head than a warm heart," and complained that he recited the text of *Lear* as if it were prose. His *Macbeth* was often called too tame; he whispered his lines following the murder of Duncan. Even James Rees says that he habitually held his forces in reserve at the beginning of a play, except in *Lear*, where it would have been impossible to do so, since the climax of the Lear story (as distinct from the Gloucester story) occurs in the first scene.

Undoubtedly Forrest considered himself a great actor, but though he went on playing some of his roles for forty years, he never regarded one of them as a finished thing, and he could

[10] Richard Moody, *Edwin Forrest, First Star of the American Stage.*

recall only one night in his life when he had left the theater completely satisfied with his own performance.

> Satisfied! I shall never be satisfied in this world. The praise of men and gods combined could not elevate me an inch above the plane where my own consciousness has lifted me. Satisfied! Why, I go before the footlights sometimes with an aching sense of inefficiency, when only entire absorption in the character I have to sustain lifts me out of my own scorn. Satisfied! I should quit the stage at once if I was satisfied.

Gabriel Harrison says that Forrest often asked friends for suggestions to improve his performances and often adopted them. He admired Kean's Othello so much that when a friend told him his Iago was the better characterization, he never spoke to him again. His dominating nature and the blunt fact that he did not have a very good disposition contributed importantly to his celebrated "bearishness" in rehearsal, but part of the difficulty was the intense strain which his ceaseless quest for perfection imposed upon him. Socially he could relax and amuse his friends with imitations and recitations, but in rehearsal everything was grim and tense, with no toleration for slackness.

Neither did he think himself equally effective in all roles. Early in his career he refused to play Hamlet and Romeo because he did not consider himself ready; with Romeo the readiness never came. He did not like his Shylock nor his Sir Giles Overreach,[11] and he abandoned both. Obviously he had no natural gift for Hamlet, and his appearance in that role must have been almost ludicrous, yet he understood the character thoroughly.[12] His Othello was celebrated,[13] and his Coriolanus seems to have been very fine, but both he and his vigorously democratic audiences

[11] Which in Forrest's time was still almost as inevitable a touchstone for the serious actor as Shakespeare himself. See Robert Hamilton Ball, *The Amazing Career of Sir Giles Overreach* (Princeton University Press, 1939).

[12] Moody, *Edwin Forrest*, 402, seems to make this quite clear.

[13] See Barbara Alden, "Edwin Forrest's Othello," *Theatre Annual*, Vol. XIV (1956), 7–18; Marvin Rosenberg, "Othello to the Life," *Theatre Arts*, Vol. XLII, June, 1958, 58–61.

disliked the play, and he did not do it often. It is harder to understand why he should have been comparatively ineffective as Macbeth or Richard III or, for that matter, Shylock, for I should have thought that his style and temperament fitted him for all three. Winter says he failed to grasp the poetic or imaginative side of Macbeth. Perhaps the difficulty with the others was that he always disliked playing base or ignoble characters; he refused to portray Richard as the conventional, melodramatic villain and even toned down his physical deformity. Lear was probably his greatest role, especially in his later years, when it had been spiritualized through his own suffering, and there have even been those who have called him the greatest of all Lears. Winter, who disliked Forrest in general, admired his Lear, and so did Longfellow, who did not care much for his tempestuous Romans and Indians. But even here, so sympathetic a colleague as Lawrence Barrett found his work uneven:

> He passed over quiet scenes with little elaboration, and dwelt strongly upon the grand features of the characters he represented. His Lear, in the great scenes, rose to a majestic height, but fell in places almost to mediocrity. His art was unequal to his natural gifts.

Alger, too, was conscious of the limitations of Forrest's art. "He remained far from the complete mastership of his art in its whole compass." He lacked "physical and spiritual mobility," and was deficient "in bright, alert, expectant, rich freedom of play in nerves and faculties." "There was too much volition in his play." Once when he was asked, "Why do you enact that part in Macbeth as you do?" Forrest replied, "Because that is the way I should have done it if I had been Macbeth." Obviously there is a limitation in imagination here. That Forrest was a part of his own audience I should infer from the fact that he liked to read aloud, even when he was alone. Gabriel Harrison says, "Forrest always performed those characters well which agreed with his own emotions." I might add that nothing in any letter or journal entry of his that I have seen reflects anything other than a thoroughly conventional mind.

Whether this is true or not, it is still clear that much of the appeal of Forrest's acting was extra-aesthetic. Probably this is the case with the work of nearly all stage artists who achieve a celebrity at all comparable to his; however accomplished they may be in a strictly aesthetic sense, their special vogue is due to their ability somehow to incarnate some aspect of the time-spirit, in their persons as well as their art. In the case of this son of an alien father and a mother who was the daughter of immigrant parents, it was spread-eagle Americanism that was incarnated. It reached its evil apotheosis in the Astor Place Riot, when the Bowery Boys and all others who were silly enough to connect robust Americanism with rough manners set him up as the exemplification of American manhood and achievement as against the effete anti-Americanism of Macready and his kid-gloved champions at the "aristocratic opera house," and it was no accident that the rowdy Ned Buntline (Edward Zane Carroll Judson), best known as the author of the "Buffalo Bill" dime novels, who was primarily responsible for the riot if anybody was, should also have been one of the leaders of the Know-Nothing party.

Of course this does not mean that Forrest himself should be held responsible for the antics of such criminal lunatics or even that he was extremist in his political views. One commentator has compared his success story with that of Benjamin Franklin in his *Autobiography*, and the comparison has point. One side of the Franklin outlook developed into what we now call an "Alger story," and it seems quite suitable that Forrest should have employed a man named Alger to write his life. His audiences were the people, not the *cognoscenti*, and the people knew him as well as they know any film star today. Some of the lines in his plays became popular catchwords, and little boys went about saying to each other, "Metamora cannot lie," and "You sent for me, and I have come." Forrest was a Jacksonian Democrat, and plays like *Metamora* appealed to him, though he recognized their aesthetic limitations, because they expressed what he regarded as the American passion for freedom and the already old-fashioned Rousseauistic enthusiasm for the natural man. What he would call himself in these days of welfare states and global crusades, now that the Democratic party has been kidnapped by two wicked uncles named Woodrow Wilson and Franklin D. Roosevelt, is anybody's guess. In 1860 he supported Douglas, and though he lent no ear to the prophets of disunion, he never mustered much enthusiasm for Lincoln. He regarded Harriet Beecher Stowe as having traduced "the fame of her country" with *Uncle Tom's Cabin*,[14] but he was surprisingly free of blood lust at a time when it claimed far more moderate men than he was, and he himself seems to have told the story that when Lincoln came to see him in *Richelieu* he pointedly directed his reading of Bulwer's famous pacifist preachment straight at the Presidential box:

> *Beneath the rule of men entirely great*
> *The pen is mightier than the sword.*
> *Take away the sword.*
> *States can be saved without it.*

His dislike for what he regarded as degenerate aristocratic customs amounted to a passion; even when he was most in love with Catherine Sinclair, he indignantly refused her father's demand for a financial settlement as insulting both to her and to him, and he would probably have lost her rather than yield if she herself had not sided with him rather than let him go.

It is worth observing too that, even in the days of Cornelius Mathews, Forrest knew that it is not only American subjects which can be treated from an American point of view. The excoriation of Spanish tyranny in *The Spaniards in Peru* excoriated all tyranny by implication, and *Jack Cade* glorified the same champion of the people whom Shakespeare had ridiculed in

[14] Alice Kingsbury-Cooley, "Forrest, McCullough,—and Myself," *Overland Monthly*, Second Series, Vol. XXIX (1897), 604–19.

Henry Sixth, Part II. Bird's play about Spartacus, *The Gladiator*, was as clearly slanted (though under the inspiration of a very different ideology), and as clearly opposed to imperialistic oppression, as Howard Fast's novel on the same theme which in 1961 was made into a spectacular film, whose success proved that Forrestian interests and appeals are not yet quite extinct in the modern theater. When Forrest was in Sheffield, he paid his public tribute to the peasant poet who became the national bard of Scotland. And perhaps no other city in the British Isles welcomed him quite so passionately as Dublin, where he openly avowed his sympathy with the Irish nationalists and pointedly ignored England's Lord Lieutenant when he visited the theater in state.

III

Yet, however great an artist Forrest may have been, there is no denying that the contemplation of his life and career leaves a sour taste in the mouth. One may admire him and gladly acknowledge his greatness; one cannot but own that he came to the end of his life a bitter, disappointed man, with nothing but his own iron will to pull him through. And if this was not wholly due to the blows his prestige suffered in Astor Place and the divorce court, both these calamities still contributed importantly.

The immediate purpose of the Astor Place Riot was to prevent Macready from playing *Macbeth* at the Astor Place Opera House against Forrest at the Broadway, but actually the whole disgraceful affair was an expression of American rowdyism against everything British and genteel. To what extent was Forrest responsible for it? Only to the extent that any person who participates in a campaign of hatred or vilification against any other person may be called responsible for the undesired and unforeseen circumstances which may result from it. It should be stated emphatically that there is no question whatever to be raised as to the possibility of Forrest's having inspired or supported the rioters. He was a fair and open fighter, and there is no known instance of his having ever intrigued against anybody. It is true that he made no attempt to prevent the riot either, but at that stage of the quarrel, this would not have been possible for him. He had always had a gift for reading topical references into his plays, and just now his favorite lines in *Macbeth* were

> *What rhubarb, senna, or what purgative drug*
> *Will scour these English hence?*

Forrest undoubtedly hated Macready and was jealous of him; their rivalry ran clear back to his first visit to England, when they were both still saying the loveliest things to and about each other. Forrest never cared to have rivals approach his throne. In later days he even turned against his namesake, Edwin Booth, and he refused on any terms to open Booth's Theater, playing Othello to Booth's Iago, so that poor Booth opened instead as Romeo, giving, as he once told E. A. Sothern, the worst performance any actor ever offered in any play! When John McCullough burst in upon Forrest in April 1865 to tell him that John Wilkes Booth had killed Lincoln, and added that he could not believe it, Forrest replied, "Well, I do. All those God-damned Booths are crazy." There is an unpleasant suggestion here that if Lincoln had to be shot, Forrest would rather have had him shot by a Booth than by somebody else whom he did not know or have the pleasure of hating, and though I certainly do not believe that he *desired* what happened in Astor Place, I am aware of no oversensitive cries of *"Mea culpa"* emanating from him afterwards. On the other hand, I must immediately add that I do not believe Macready shows up in any more admirable light than Forrest. You may say if you like that his manners were better, but even that could be expressed by saying that he was considerably less frank and brash. There is no more evidence that Macready conspired against Forrest (as Forrest certainly believed) than there is that Forrest conspired against him,[15] but his own diary

[15] The strongest statement of the case against Macready is in Richard Moody, *The Astor Place Riot,* 46ff.

proves conclusively that his rival was a continual thorn in his flesh, that he kept him perpetually upon his mind, and that every decent word he gave him came from his conscience and not from his heart.

My interpretation of Macready's character is given elsewhere in this volume; with the other person involved in Forrest's divorce suit, I am concerned only as she affected him. On any assumption, his treatment of her was outrageous. If it was bad enough to describe her to James Oakes as "vain, trifling, lying, a drunkard, and by consequence a whore," and again as "a drunken female whose prostitutions and shameless acts have circled the world," it was considerably worse to air "the dishonor of my house" in curtain speeches and appeal from the verdict of the court to that of his audiences. Mrs. Forrest's admirable dignity and reserve, all the more impressive as opposed to her husband's violence, cracked after the trial only when she made a stage career out of her wrongs, appearing first, of all pieces, in *The School for Scandal*, and herself almost precipitating another riot on her first night.[16] Yet absurdly exaggerated as Forrest's charges

[16] It is only fair to add that the play was chosen not by "Mrs. C. N. Sinclair (late MRS. FORREST)," as she billed herself, but by George Vandenhoff, to whom she turned for coaching. See his *Dramatic Reminiscences . . .*, ed. by Henry Seymour Carleton (Thomas W. Cooper, John Camden Hotten, 1860). She went on to *The Lady of Lyons*, *Love's Sacrifice*, *Much Ado About Nothing*, and *The Patrician's Daughter*, and for some years functioned as actress-manager in California. She also appeared in London and in Australia. The consensus of critical opinion seems to have been that though her achievement was not by absolute standards first rate, it was remarkable under the circumstances. She attended Forrest's funeral and outlived him by nineteen years.

Few human situations own no touch of comedy. When the Forrests parted, he gave her, at her request, a Shakespeare, coldly inscribed "Mrs. Edwin Forrest, from Edwin Forrest" (previous inscriptions had read "From her lover and husband, Edwin Forrest"), also a large portrait of himself, and it was with these articles in the cab that he genteelly escorted her to the home of the Parke Godwins, where she was to take refuge. He later said that he proceeded to divorce because being "unwilling to submit to calumnies industriously circulated by my enemies that I had unmanfully wronged an innocent woman, the only choice open to me was either to assert my rectitude before the tribunals of my country or endure throughout life a weight of reproach which I trust my entire life proves undeserved." He fought his alimony assessment through court after court for eighteen years. In 1868 he was forced to pay Mrs. Forrest $64,000, of which her lawyers got $59,000.

against her finally became, I cannot believe that she was as blameless as the complete vindication which she enjoyed at the hands of a gallant jury would indicate. At the very least, we must admit in her a taste for somewhat rackety standards of living (probably shared with her family), plus a tendency toward libertarian views.[17]

All that we know of her relations with Forrest before the break would indicate that she was as affectionate toward him as he was toward her. Since she was English, and friendly with Macready, it has been suggested that she sympathized with the wrong party in the quarrel between the two actors, and that this turned Forrest against her, but there are letters in which she seems quite unwisely to have egged her husband on, instead of urging upon him the restraint which he so sorely needed. There can be no doubt that she was terribly in love with him at the beginning: "this is the handsomest man on whom my eyes have fallen." It can be argued that her failure to give him a living child (four babies were born dead or died shortly after birth) weakened his love for her, but there is no evidence for this. It is more likely that he never ceased to love her, and that this was the reason he hated her so bitterly, once her image had turned "black and hideous" in his eyes. "This state of things has distorted my peace of mind," he cried, "and is wearing out my life," and he never spoke a truer word.

Unquestionably he believed her guilty, for he was incapable of deliberate falsehood, and he was not such a fool as to bring his house down about his ears for nothing. But precisely because of his honesty and directness, he was the last man on earth to be able to deal wisely with the crisis which confronted him. Always fiercely loyal to those who were loyal to him, he had very little capacity for forgiveness under any circumstances, and what he suspected Mrs. Forrest of having done was the very last thing

---

[17] For the legal aspects, see Henry Lauren Clinton, *Extraordinary Cases* (Harpers, 1896), 71–73. Mary Clemmer Ames, *Outlines of Men, Women, and Things* (Hurd and Houghton, 1873) reflects contemporary opinion unfriendly to Forrest.

he could forgive. He himself would have said that no man could forgive such a wrong and retain a vestige of manhood afterwards. I suppose it says a good deal for him—and perhaps testifies importantly to his love for her—that he did not attempt to deal with the matter in Othello's fashion. He had tried to slug his way out of a good many difficulties, but even he knew that it was a little too late in the day for

It is the cause, it is the cause, my soul.

Indeed, he was not at all, in this crisis, the man of action he might have been expected to be. He brooded over his difficulties for a long time before he did anything, and he satisfied himself temporarily with a legal separation before he proceeded to a divorce. Once he even prepared a statement affirming his wife's innocence and required her to sign it. Nothing could have shown more clearly than such futilities how terribly he had been shaken.

The whole matter of Forrest's moral and spiritual outlook is involved here, and nothing about him is more interesting or, according to modern standards, more badly confused.

Forrest was not a pious man, but he was definitely a theist. For him God was "the Universal Cause" and "the Great Architect of the Universe," and he was much given to finding Him in nature in the standard, nineteenth-century pantheistic form, not only in great natural wonders like Niagara and the California redwoods, but even in a storm on Lake Erie: "If there are any infidels in Cleveland, let them come here, and look upon this magnificent element of creation, and let them go home and pray." There is one apostrophe to the cruelty of the sea, in which he takes up much the same attitude as Oliver Wendell Holmes, comparing the sea and the mountains in a famous passage of *The Autocrat of the Breakfast Table*. The most unusual idea that ever crossed his mind religiously speaking seems to have been his notion that this "Botany Bay of a world" was hell, whose inhabitants were being punished for offenses they had committed elsewhere.

Though Forrest was not a church member, Christ was "Our

Saviour" to him, and he loved the Lord's Prayer and ecclesiastical music, especially that of the Catholic church. Immortality he passionately desired, and sometimes he believed in it, but at other times he was assailed by doubts.[18] He sometimes found it hard to believe in the liveableness of life also, and though Henry Wikoff speaks of his "geniality, warm heart, and bounding spirits," there was a tendency toward moroseness in his make-up too, so that he would sometimes cry that life is "a wretched failure, and the sooner annihilation comes to it the better." This, of course, was in his later disappointed, embittered years, though it seems odd that the only time in life he was apparently in real danger of suicide was at the age of twenty, when he actually went so far as to buy arsenic with which he planned to poison himself. He did not even pretend to accept Christ's teachings about forgiveness. "I love my friends and hate my enemies, and no man who knows me will doubt my sincerity in this—and no man on earth will believe the hypocrite who says he loves his enemies." When the actor George W. Jamieson, in whose connection he had first doubted his wife, was killed by a train, like Dickens' Mr. Carker in *Dombey and Son*, even Forrest's God took on the lineaments of hate. "God is great," he wrote, "and Justice, though slow, is sure—another scoundrel has gone to Hell, I trust forever."

This is Forrest at his worst, and he could be almost as trying in his self-righteousness. Theoretically, to be sure, he knew that he was a very imperfect creature. "My faults are many," he told Alger, disclaiming all desire for a "whitewashing" type of biography, "and I deserve much blame." But hear how he goes on: "Yet after every confession and every regret, I feel before God that I have been a man more sinned against than sinning [it was

[18] Perhaps his strongest statement of faith is that quoted in "Reminiscences of Edwin Forrest," *Potter's American Monthly*, Vol. XII (1879), 369–73: "I suppose people say that Ned Forrest has no settled religious convictions, but they are mistaken. I see the faults and errors of my career, and God knows I have found little rest in life. Now that I am drawing near the end of my journey, I find great pleasure in thinking that there is another and a better state of existence, and thank God for it. God has been very good to me. . . ."

not for nothing that he cried, "I *am* Lear!"]; and, if the whole truth be told, I am perfectly willing to bear all the censure, all the condemnation that justly belongs to me." Again, he says, "I am not unwilling that my whole course of life should be scrutinized with justice and impartiality. When it shall be so all weighed together I have no fear of the result." He goes further yet: "I wish the great Day of Doom were not a chimera. What a solace it would be to all those whom man has so deeply wronged." And it is easy to tell what wronged man is in his mind.

Generally speaking, Forrest was anything but a dissipated man. Though he was no Puritan, he had seen too many careers wrecked by alcohol, gambling, and debauchery to run any chance of his own going the same way. He grew up in an atmosphere of poverty, dignity, and propriety, and when he established a home of his own, he sought to change only the first of these nouns. Furthermore, he dissociated himself completely from the raffish elements in his profession, and he had no patience with irregularities in any of the persons with whom he played.

He was no teetotaler, but he came close enough so that, at the end, when he could hardly stand on the stage, he refused the stimulant which James Oakes sought to give him, insisting that when he died nobody was going to smell alcohol on him. He was fortunate in that his natural tastes ran in the direction of simple, wholesome food: cold corn-meal mush in a bowl of milk was a carouse in his eyes. In early life he used tobacco, but when he became convinced that it was bad for his voice, he gave it up.

In New Orleans days, Forrest was a familiar figure in the picturesque underworld of that city, making special friends of the murderous James Bowie, inventor of the knife which bears his name, a river boatman known as Captain Graham, and a Choctaw Indian chief, Pushmataha. I do not pretend that Forrest moved among such people for any such motives as those absurdly alleged by Prince Hal in *Henry IV, Part I*, but I am sure that he was "seeing life" and cannily storing up experiences for future use, and I can well believe the story that one night, when he had been urged to gamble by his fellow-players in Cincinnati, he won everything they had, then threw the money on the floor, burned the implements of play, and never turned a card again.

In New Orleans, also, Forrest loved Jane Placide, a beautiful young actress, favorably known in the Southwest, over whom he challenged his employer, James H. Caldwell—or said he did—and when Caldwell laughed at him, he "posted" him as a coward in the first of his notorious "cards," later so disastrously directed, with other accusations, against Macready. Just what his relations with her were, we do not know, but from what we wrote of her when she died young in 1835,[19] they were almost certainly innocent, for Forrest was incapable of idealizing a woman who had outraged his ideal of womanhood. In the divorce trial testimony, he was accused of having committed adultery with the late Josephine Clifton, a distinguished actress with whom he had toured, but though there are various suspicious circumstances, nothing was really established. After his divorce, marriage became "legalized prostitution" in his eyes, though he was apparently still capable of interest in women, and we hear especially of two ladies, both, like his great friend James Oakes,[20] Bostonians. One is known to us only as "Nahmeokee," which was the name of Metamora's wife in the play. The other was cursed with the horrible name of Lillie Swindlehurst. He renamed her "Miss Lillie," made her a member of his company and paid her a suspiciously high salary for an inexperienced actress. At one time, she seems to have half-expected him to marry her.

[19] "And so Jane Placide is dead. The theatrical people of New Orleans have lost much. She imparted a grace and a force and dignity to her role which few actresses have been able so admirably to combine. She excelled in a profession in the arduous sphere of which even to succeed requires uncommon gifts, both mental and physical. Her disposition was as lovely as her person. Heaven lodge and rest her fair soul!"

[20] Forrest's friendship with Oakes was probably the most satisfying relationship of his life, and he permitted himself to describe it in language which no man would dare to use nowadays. Persons who are tempted to assume that there was an unnatural relationship between them should be bluntly informed at this point that they reveal a good deal about themselves and the age they live in but nothing about Forrest and Oakes.

But the most significant thing is yet to be told. When Forrest went to Europe, he recorded in his diary not only his visits to galleries and historic sites but also to houses of assignation, including the sanitary precautions he employed.[21] This may seem utterly irreconcilable to the self-righteous respectability which he professed. Actually, when one remembers and tries to understand the now almost incomprehensible nineteenth-century attitude toward sex, it was nothing of the kind. One sees, I suppose, another phase of it in the Southern planter's ability to have intercourse with slave women whom he regarded as almost subhuman for all other purposes. Sex was something dirty, but it was something that a man needed and must have, and need forfeit no respect by claiming. But if a woman needed it for any other purpose than to wear herself out bearing and rearing his children until she died, after which he could replace her and start over again, she was a "whore," and a man was automatically freed from all the obligations he felt toward "good" women. Forrest was greatly disappointed that the Russian prostitutes were so ugly; apparently he enjoyed himself more when he could see "the hectic flush of expiring beauty on the cheek of shame" as a "palliating witness to plead for . . . [her] lost honor." Did he ever think about his own, I wonder? Did he blush for himself? Or did he enjoy himself all the more for blushing? And did it ever occur to him that he had quite as much reason to blush as the girl, and probably considerably more, their respective provocations and positions in society being what they were?

It is amusing that Forrest, who had a gift for picturesque profanity should have been careful always to avoid swearing "before ladies or clergymen, less it should shock or grieve them." If a woman was willing to remain on the pedestal where he had placed her, as his mother and sisters were, or the actress Sarah Wheatley, whom he so greatly admired, then he would worship

21 The Diary, which is in the Harvard Theatre Collection, has had some pages cut out of it; one wonders what they can possibly have contained! Some of the divorce trial testimony indicated that Forrest continued to frequent houses of assignation after his marriage, but this is under dispute.

her all his life, but if she tumbled off, or even if he suspected she
had, then all the king's horses and all the king's men couldn't
put Mrs. Humpty Dumpty together again. I think there can be
little question that this is what happened to poor Catherine Sinclair. It may perhaps be worth remembering that one of Forrest's
friends in New Orleans once tied a cable around a bankside
bawdyhouse where he had been offended and pulled it into the
Mississippi, drowning its inhabitants, and Forrest himself, as a
youngster in a Cincinnati boarding house, once made such a fuss
over a woman whose morals he suspected that he had to be
rebuked and forced to apologize by no less a person than William
Henry Harrison. I do not know whether Forrest was "faithful"—
or would have remained faithful—to Catherine Sinclair, if she
had never given him reason to doubt her (that depends somewhat upon whether the stories about Josephine Clifton and the
others are true or not), but I do know that he loved her as sincerely as a man with such an orientation as his is capable of
loving, and that he was a good husband according to his lights.
If she had not soiled the image he had of her, he would certainly
have stayed with her to the end. I repeat that if we are to be fair
to Forrest we must remember how difficult changing conditions
have made it for us to judge his sexual mystique, and if we see the
nineteenth-century male as monstrously selfish and egotistical in
his relations with women, he might very well reply to us that in
thinking of sexual delinquency as natural to men but unnatural
for them, he was paying them a far higher compliment than
we do ourselves.

IV

But it would be brutal to leave Forrest on this note. If he was
an heroic actor, there were heroic elements in his personality
too. He has often been called a greedy man, and he certainly
bargained skillfully and remorselessly for his fees; the amounts
that he earned were very remarkable for his time. He made no
pretense of indifference to money, and when he was asked why

he had refused the Congressional bid, he replied bluntly that he could not afford to give his time for $8.00 a day when he might make $200 in the theater.[22] But he was very generous with money too and, except possibly in one area, wholly honorable. James Rees says that he gave away more than $40,000; Alger puts it at a quarter of a million. Alger's figure comes from Forrest's letter of August 28, 1870,[23] in which he also says that he gave away so much money that when he was earning $8,000 a year, he had to seek advances to cover his own living expenses. Elsewhere he says that he had only borrowed $200 in his whole lifetime and that he had lent two thousand times that sum, very little of which was ever repaid. In a letter to Alger, October 9, 1870,[24] he speaks of "the 'smiling damned villains' who under the mask of friendship borrowed my money and repaid it only by detraction, aspersion and calumny." Even Oakes does not seem to have been bashful about incurring pecuniary obligations, and this was the only point at which relations between him and Forrest were ever strained.

After the war he sent $500 to a Southern relief fund, and another $500 went to Chicago after the Fire of 1871. When the pilots of the towboat *Ajax* were drowned going to the relief of the steamship *Edwin Forrest*, each widow received $1,000. It was almost as a matter of course that Forrest went to the aid of any person whom he knew to be in need or whom he believed to have been treated unjustly. His grocer had a standing order to supply any customer who was hungry but could not pay and to debit Forrest's account. One day he received a note informing him a man he knew was ill and in want; within an hour he had sent $100 in a blank envelope. Once he overheard a minor actor in his company lamenting that he had been offered a good part

[22] This was not his only motive, however. "The duties of legislation, I thought, could not be adequately discharged without more preparatory study and reflection than I had yet found time to bestow upon the subject. . . ."

[23] Harvard Theatre Collection.

[24] Harvard Theatre Collection. Quoted by permission of Harvard College Library.

117

but could not accept it for lack of train fare. Forrest came in and dropped a purse in his lap. "There it is; don't say where you got it." Once, in winter, he removed his overcoat, wrapped it about a poor, sick man he had encountered, and had him taken where he could be cared for, and once a woman who had tried to sell him a picture because she knew he was a collector, and it seemed the only one of her possessions that could possibly have any value for anybody, found herself and her family removed to comfortable quarters at his expense, with the picture hung on her own walls. Forrest loved children and animals and once set the broken leg of a little turkey and nursed and fed it in a basket until it was well. In his last years he was fond of standing on a street corner near a public school that he might have the pleasure of watching the children. There is even a record of his having once walked the floor all night with a sick baby in his arms so that the baby's mother might rest. There can be little doubt that the great tragedy of his life was his failure to become a father.

The great exception to his generosity is his dealings with dramatists. He encouraged the development of an American drama, but he did very little to help dramatists to live by it. He may not have been wholly at fault technically in his quarrel with Robert Montgomery Bird (which caused Bird to give up playwriting), for they were operating under the loose kind of verbal agreement which the nineteenth century seems to have loved, and which each party was free to interpret according to his own interest, but he certainly was not generous or farseeing. Forrest made a fortune out of *Metamora*, but its author, John Augustus Stone, drowned himself in poverty and despair in the Schuylkill River, and he probably did not get much satisfaction out of the handsome tombstone which was erected "In Memory of the Author of *Metamora* by his Friend E. Forrest." It is only fair to add, however, that, in this case, Forrest had often aided Stone during his lifetime, and also that the touting of his good deed which he achieved in the monument was quite exceptional. In most cases he almost literally obeyed the Scriptural injunction not to let his left hand know what his right hand was doing.

We have all heard enough and to spare of Forrest's violence at rehearsals, but James A. Herne, who saw him "under all sorts of conditions," never saw any of "the discourtesies, not to say brutalities, with which he has been charged. I know that his company idolized him." Mrs. John Drew thought him the fairest actor she ever played with and the one least disposed to cheat another member of the cast of his opportunity or his glory.[25] Once he undertook to play *Virginius* for Cooper's benefit, but when he learned that Cooper's daughter would feel easier playing Virginia to her father rather than to him, he gladly relinquished the role, contenting himself with the supporting part of Denatus. To be sure, I get the impression that he was something of an autocrat even in his kindness. One letter to Gabriel Harrison begins: "Dear Sir:—It is my desire that you visit me on Thanksgiving day, Thursday, 25th, and take thanks with me." Catherine Reignolds Winslow wrote a touching account[26] of how kind he was to her when, coming green to New York in search of a theater career, she had the nerve to go to his hotel and ask for him. He came out to her, listened patiently, trained her, and gave her a place in his company. But she adds: "It will always be a sincere regret to me that, while he lived, I could not express myself to my benefactor as my heart prompted. So reserved, so business-like, so impersonal in his teaching was he." And no doubt he had one attitude for fine artists like Mrs. John Drew and for promising newcomers and quite another toward the slack incompetents with whom his lot was all too often cast. One night a young actor blew up in his lines and rushed from the

[25] Incidentally Mrs. Drew loathed the gentlemanly Macready, "a dreadful man to act with; you had the unpleasant sensation of knowing that you were doing nothing that he wanted you to, though following strictly his instructions. He would press you down with his hand on your head, and tell you in an undertone to stand up!"

[26] *Yesterdays with Actors* (Cupples and Company, 1877).

stage in tears, feeling that he had ruined the play and his own career with it. Forrest followed him to his dressing room to comfort him, dried his tears, and assured him that the same thing could happen to the best actor in the world, and that he still had it in him to live it down and do fine work. And he could sometimes be very kind even to mediocrity. An actor late for rehearsal was met one day with a stern rebuke. He explained that his child had died during the night, and Forrest, instantly mollified, pressed $50.00 into his hand and sent him home. But he did not need great calamities to soften him. One day he had great difficulty getting an actor to speak a line the way he wanted it. Having demonstrated several times, he asked impatiently, "Can't you speak the line like that?" "No, sir," replied the actor, "if I could, I wouldn't be working for $5.00 a week." "Is that all you get?" asked Forrest. "That's all, sir." "In that case, you may speak the line any way you like." But he saw to it that more money was forthcoming.

These things do not cancel out Forrest's faults, but they deserve to be remembered alongside of them. It is significant that those who knew him best generally loved him most. William Winter goes much too far when he speaks of him as "diseased with arrogance, passion, and cruelty." There are passages in Winter's criticism which are quite as cruel as anything Forrest ever said or did. His "dram of eale" was his unconquerable self-will. He confronted life unflinchingly, bent on subduing it on his terms and forcing it to do his will, and when it resisted him, he would break his heart rather than yield to it. Cry "Forrest, be merciful unto me, a sinner!" and he was yours, but if you spoiled his ideal of you, it would be very hard for him to forgive you. Add to this the tendency toward melancholy brooding over his own wrongs, the fondness for overdramatizing, and the power of becoming imprisoned in his own concerns which was always characteristic of him, and you get—well, you get nothing short of the misery with which Edwin Forrest was plagued throughout his later years.

On the evening of November 22, 1872, William Winter was sitting in Steinway Hall listening to Forrest read *Othello*. Suddenly he felt sure that the great actor was nearing the end of his road and that he would never hear that voice again. When Forrest came to the great speech in Act III, scene 3, which ends with "Othello's occupation's gone," he "spoke it from his inmost soul,—pouring forth in those few words an agonizing sense of utter failure, forlorn wretchedness, and irremediable woe." Desiring that these should be the last words he would ever hear Forrest speak, Winter rose and left the hall. He waited just one day less than three weeks for his presentiment to be fulfilled.

If this was a case of what it is now fashionable to call extrasensory perception, it is not the only one in which Forrest has figured. Many years later, one of his guests in the Edwin Forrest Home at Springbrook, was sitting by her window one evening when she saw him approach the house. She rose to greet him, and he stopped on the walk below and lifted his hat. "Madame," he said, "I shall soon have the honor to welcome you to a sweeter home than this."

The next morning at breakfast she told Forrest's other guests of her experience, and before evening came again he had kept his word.

5

Edwin Booth
(1833–1893)

Edwin booth may or may not have been the greatest of America's classic actors, but there is no doubt that he has been the most dearly loved. His melancholy but irresistible charm reinforced the lure of his genius—his charm plus the fact that he and his whole family lived in so lurid a melodrama that even a Bowery audience must have hooted it off the stage as unconvincing. For Americans at least his is the name that comes first to mind when one thinks of Hamlet, yet there is division of opinion as to whether or not this was his greatest role, and he himself sometimes obviously preferred other characters. "Copey" of Harvard thought Richelieu, Bertuccio,[1] and Iago his finest characterizations, with Shylock, Richard III, and Hamlet "as a good second group," the reason being that he played the Prince of Denmark "on stilts," as it were, "taking the stage" and striking attitudes, keeping more of the manner of the "old school" than he had retained in his other roles. For all his admiration, young Otis Skinner thought Booth's Hamlet cold and mechanical at times, as if he were letting it play itself, and John Ranken Towse saw it as an assemblage of amazing "points" that failed to add up

---

[1] In Tom Taylor's play, *The Fool's Revenge*, which is the *Rigoletto* story.

to a complete or consistent characterization, "a mosaic of precious but ill-adjusted gems rather than a perfect jewel." Henry A. Clapp and William Winter[2] seem to place his Lear first, though both fully realized that Hamlet suited Booth's temperament like nothing else he played. "His eyes, after the fourth scene of the first act," writes Clapp, "never lost the awful light which had filled them as they looked upon his father's ghost; his voice never quite lost the tone which had vibrated in harmony with the utterances of that august spirit." When Mrs. D. P. Bowers, who afterwards acted with him, first saw his Hamlet, she was not sure that as a work of art, it was markedly superior to what she had seen before, "but as an embodiment of a noble yet complex soul

[2] *Life and Art of Edwin Booth*, 108. Elsewhere (page 153), Winter grants Booth supremacy "in all characters that evoked his essential spirit—in characters which rest on spiritualised intellect, or on sensibility to fragile loveliness, the joy that is unattainable, the glory that fades, the beauty that perishes. . . . Hamlet, Richelieu, Faust, Manfred, Jacques, Esmond, Sydney Carton, and Sir Edward Mortimer are all, in different ways, suggestive of the personality that Booth was fated to illustrate." Of these he played only the first two and the last (in Colman's *The Iron Chest*). Again, Winter says (page 223): "Taking Richelieu, Hamlet, Lear, Iago, and Bertuccio together, the observer had a complete exemplification of his style and method." See, also, *Shakespeare on the Stage*, 340. The hypercritical Alfred Ayres, "Edwin Booth," *Theatre*, Vol. II, May, 1902, 19, put Booth's Richelieu first but considered both his Iago and his Richard III superior to his Hamlet. There seems little doubt that his Iago was superior to his Othello; see A. C. Sprague's "Edwin Booth's Iago: A Study of a Great Shakespearean Actor," *Theatre Annual*, 1947, pp. 7–17. The case against his Hamlet was probably most effectively stated by an editorial writer in *The Nation*, Vol. II (1866), 395–96, obviously not unfriendly to him, upon his emergence from the retirement which followed Lincoln's assassination, who described the characterization as

> beautiful, elegant, graceful, exquisitely refined and delicate, but neither intellectually nor morally strong. It is a romantic and sentimental Hamlet, pensive but not deeply reflective; sad, with the low-spiritness of the morbid temperament increased by a tragic experience, not with the settled sorrow of a great soul steeped in thought and agony. He is vacillating and weak; he drifts before circumstances, instead of taking his stand on reason and conscience with a purpose to control fate. His action is that of a man of impulse; his gesticulation is feeble; his declamation smooth, easy, balanced as if no profound emotion was in him. He is distinguished from those about him by the finish of his artistic elaboration, rather than by the grandeur of the traits which he impersonates.

The writer conjectures, further, that Booth was divided between two different traditions of acting—the romantic and the natural, without himself ever having made a choice between them.

environed by a body of singular charm and comeliness . . . it was vastly superior."

Booth himself seems to have recognized all this, and it was recognized with equal clarity by those who were closest to him. In 1879 a madman took two shots at him while he was playing Richard II at McVicker's Theater in Chicago, and he behaved like a hero. But, he says, "my temporary self-control gave way after a day or two to a highly nervous excitement—a condition similar to that which I believe Shakespeare illustrated by Hamlet's frivolity after the ghost is gone, and the terrible tension of his brain is relaxed." His adored first wife, Mary Devlin, called him "My Hamlet," and when his daughter Edwina was a little child, she had difficulty distinguishing between her father and the character. The resemblance was so inevitable that it seems to have been understood even by the ill-starred younger brother, John Wilkes, the slayer of Lincoln, who never apparently understood anything else. "No, oh no!" he cried on one occasion, when his own Hamlet was praised. "There's but one Hamlet to my mind—that's my brother, Edwin. You see, between ourselves, he is Hamlet—melancholy and all."

Edwin Booth was born on his father's wilderness farm near Belair, Maryland, on the night of November 13, 1833 (he once told Edwina that his grandmother always insisted the fifteenth was the correct date). Mark Twain came into the world with Halley's Comet, which returned, seventy-five years later, to usher him out again. Booth's auspices were somewhat less spectacular, but he was born with a caul, under a remarkable shower of meteors, and when he came to die, at The Players Club, which he had founded, all the lights went off, and then on again, the moment before his passing, and during his funeral, the Ford's Theater building in Washington, where his brother had killed Lincoln, collapsed suddenly, killing more than twenty persons.

He was the seventh of the ten children of the English-American tragedian, Junius Brutus Booth, and Mary Ann Holmes, who had been a London flower-girl. One great-grandfather was a

Portuguese Jew. There was also some Welsh blood. The rest was English.

All the Booth children were technically illegitimate. When Junius fell in love with Mary Ann Holmes, he deserted wife, child, and career to take her to America. Though he afterwards visited his English family, they knew nothing about his American domestic arrangements until many years later, when the son, Richard, came to America to be with his father. Then Adelaide Delannoy Booth followed. Having failed to persuade her husband to return to her, she divorced him in 1851, and proceeded to drink herself to death. As soon as the divorce had been granted, Booth married his Mary Anne, who, since the day he first laid eyes on her, had been the only woman in the world for him.

The irregularity of her connection with Junius Brutus is the only blot on Mary Anne's escutcheon; she was the stable side of the family, and though she may (especially with John Wilkes) have been an overindulgent mother, she was a noble-hearted woman, devoted to her mate and her children without reservations, and facing up heroically to the terrible blows which life dealt her. Of the father it is impossible to give even a glimpse in his son's portrait; were this to be attempted, he would surely steal the show. One could easily fill a paper the length of this one with anecdotes illustrative of his eccentricity, unconventionality, and outrageousness. Junius Brutus Booth was a drunkard and, in his later years increasingly, a madman, but to describe him thus is to give the reader almost no idea of his character. An intelligent, high-souled man with strong mystical tendencies, he was so sensitive and tender-hearted that he not only refrained from eating meat, but even refused to permit insects and noxious reptiles to be killed. In a sense, he made a shipwreck of his life, but like many such persons, he had a far more precious and dangerous cargo to carry than many of those who come safely to harbor.

He never encouraged Edwin as an actor; when the boy went

on the road with him, it was as his guardian. This sometimes involved dogging his footsteps through the night or locking him in his hotel room. Edwin's first stage appearance really worth noting was as Tressil in his father's *Richard III*, at the Boston Museum, in 1849. He first appeared in New York as Wilford in *The Iron Chest*, at the National Theater, in 1850; the next year he enacted Richard III on the same boards, literally on the spur of the moment, when his father, in a freak of whimsy, refused to go on.

In 1852 they went to California together, and when the father started home, the son stayed behind. Junius Brutus died on the way, November 30, on a river steamer, just below Louisville, and Edwin blamed himself bitterly for not being there to look after him; this was the first of his many great sorrows. But by now he himself was in the midst of a California apprenticeship as variegated and, on occasion, as humble as Edwin Forrest's had been in the southeastern hinterlands. In San Francisco and in Sacramento, he played with and under the direction of Forrest's estranged wife, and when all else failed, he toured the mountains and the mining camps. Blackface was not unknown to him, and he was once billed with a girl whose only claim to fame was that she had run off from the Mormons.

In 1854 he went, with other players, to Hawaii, Australia, and the South Seas (Laura Keene was of the party, but this did not last long). He did not come back east until 1856, and the real beginning of his career as a leading actor of quality dates from his success as Sir Giles Overreach at the Boston Theater, on April 20, 1857. On May 14, he played Richard III at Burton's Metropolitan Theater in New York.

In 1858, in Richmond, he enacted Henry V in the first American production of the Shakespearean play, and it was during his engagement in this city that he met Mary Devlin, whom he married on July 7, 1860; their only child, Edwina, was born in London, December 9, 1861, where her father had opened at the Haymarket in September as Shylock, followed by Sir Giles and

Richelieu. Mrs. Booth died, suddenly and unexpectedly, at Dorchester, Massachusetts, February 21, 1863, while her husband was playing in New York.

Seven months later to the day, Edwin Booth began his management of the Winter Garden Theater, where, on November 25, at a benefit performance of *Julius Caesar*, he played Brutus to the Cassius of the younger Junius Brutus and the Mark Antony of John Wilkes. On March 26, 1865, he ended his famous one hundred nights run in *Hamlet*.

Edwin Booth was acting in Boston in April, 1865, when the terrible news came that his brother had killed Lincoln. For the time being, all Booths were proscribed, and nearly all actors; some fools even raised the cry of anti-Semitism. Booth supposed at the time that he had left the stage permanently, but his obligations were great, acting was the only thing he knew how to do, and it was soon made clear to him that no sane person could hold him guilty of his brother's crime. He reappeared as *Hamlet* at the Winter Garden on January 3, 1866, where despite the rabble-rousing hysterics of the New York *Herald*, he was received with such enthusiasm as few actors have ever awakened. It was one of the great nights of the American theater and a high water mark for American common sense and decency. Notable productions of *Richelieu* and *The Merchant of Venice* followed.

On the night of March 22–23, 1867, the Winter Garden burned down, and Booth proceeded to the construction of a million-dollar playhouse in Twenty-Third Street, at Sixth Avenue. The cornerstone of Booth's Theater was laid on April 8, 1868, and the curtain rose for the first time, on *Romeo and Juliet*, February 3, 1869, with Mary McVicker, stepdaughter of the Chicago theater magnate, whom Booth was to marry on June 7, as the Juliet. *Othello* and *Julius Caesar* followed; during the run of the latter, which began on Christmas night, 1871, Booth appeared, at different times, as Brutus, Cassius, and Antony. Dion Boucicault said Booth's was the only theater in the world he had ever seen properly managed, and Joseph Jefferson said it was run like a counting-house before the curtain and like a church behind it. The box office did not, as has often been said, fail to support it, but unfortunately Booth himself was far too guileless, dreamy, and inefficient to be a good businessman. Moreover the financing of the entire project had been insanely handled. In 1873 he gave up management, and in 1874 he declared bankruptcy. For the rest of his life he was a traveling star.

In the fall of 1875, Booth offered a distinct novelty for the time in the shape of a production of *Richard II*. In 1880–81 he made a second professional visit to England. This began badly at the Princess' but picked up steam notably in a series of joint appearances with Sir Henry Irving and Ellen Terry at the Lyceum, the two male stars alternating as Othello and Iago.

Booth's domestic situation could, at this time, hardly have been more miserable, for his second wife, always something of a domestic tyrant, had now become hopelessly insane.[3] Part of her malady was an intense hatred of both her husband and his daughter, and though James McVicker had notably assisted Booth when he lost his theater, both he and his wife seem incredibly to have believed everything Mary's sick mind dredged up. The whole party returned to America in the summer of 1881, and on November 13 poor Mary McVicker's sufferings came to an end. The Reverend Robert Collyer, who had known her from childhood, is said to have included in his funeral oration references decidedly derogatory to her husband.

Next spring, Booth again went to England, reappearing at the Princess' and touring the provinces, and in 1883 he met what was perhaps the overwhelming success of his life in a series of bilingual performances of Shakespearean tragedy in Berlin, Vienna, and other German cities.

Thereafter his life consisted of touring in America and (at the end of 1888) the founding of The Players, to whom he gave the house in Gramercy Park, where actors might have the privilege

[3] For Mary McVicker Booth, as an actress and a personality, see Winter, *Life and Art*, 52–55.

of association with other gentlemen, and an increasingly hope-less struggle against disabling illness. He acted with Madame Ristori in *Macbeth* in 1885 and with Tommaso Salvini in *Hamlet* and *Othello* in 1886. In 1887 he joined forces with Lawrence Barrett, who undertook the management of his tours. In 1889, Helena Modjeska was a member of the Booth-Barrett company. Barrett died, almost on the stage, on March 20, 1891, and Booth's final appearance was made as Hamlet, at the Brooklyn Academy of Music, at a matinee performance on April 4, 1891. On June 8, 1893, he died in his rooms at The Players, and was buried in the New England pantheon, Mount Auburn, in Cambridge, Massachusetts, where he sleeps beside Mary Devlin and the poor little child whom he fathered by Mary McVicker, in the shadow of a monument designed by the great and tragic Stanford White. The interment was at sunset, and Thomas Bailey Aldrich described it, in a letter to Winter, in words which have often been quoted for their beauty:

> There in the tender afterglow two or three hundred men and women stood silent, with bowed heads. A single bird, in a nest hidden somewhere near by, twittered from time to time. The soft June air, blowing across from the upland, brought with it the scent of syringa blossoms from the slope below. Overhead and among the trees the twilight was gathering. "Good-night, sweet Prince!" I said, under my breath. . . . Then I thought of the years and years that had been made rich with his presence, and of the years that were to come, . . . and if there had not been a crowd of people, I would have buried my face in the greensward and wept, as men may not do, and women may. And thus we left him.

II

Augustin Daly called Booth "the greatest tragic actor of his time, and beyond dispute, the noblest figure, as man and actor, our stage has known this century." "No actor of his time so completely filled the eye, the ear and the mind with an ideal of romantic tragedy," says Otis Skinner. "Extravagance never marred his work; he was a living illustration of Hamlet's advice to the players concerning the temperate smoothness to be begot in the torrent, tempest and whirlwind of passion." And E. H. Sothern adds that "Edwin Booth's genius shone like a good deed in a naughty world. His light was so steady and pure and his acting so free from exaggeration that he baffled imitation, although all the ambitious actors of my early days took him as their ideal."

He had a tremendous advantage, to begin with, in his appearance. His face was not handsome; it was beautiful, "the most noble face I ever looked upon," said Joseph Jefferson. He looked like a great actor (when he walked on the street, heads turned to gaze after him), which is to say that he looked the way a great actor is supposed to look, and as no actor dares to look nowadays. But it was a face which uplifted while it thrilled, for essentially its beauty was not of the body but of the spirit. "It was the most beautiful face I had ever seen," thought young Kitty Molony, "and the saddest." Nor was Ellen Terry less impressed: "I have never in any face, in any country, seen such beautiful eyes."

Winter says they

> were dark brown, and seemed to turn black in moments of excitement, and to emit light, as if they were suns, and they were capable of conveying, with electrical effect, the most diverse meanings,— the solemnity of lofty thought, the tenderness of affection, the piteousness of forlorn sorrow, the awful sense of spiritual surroundings, the woeful weariness of despair, the mocking glee of wicked sarcasm, the vindictive menace of sinister purpose, and the lightning glare of baleful wrath.

It goes without saying, then, that they were not always gentle; one reviewer speaks of them as sweeping the stage like basilisks. But whatever their mood or color, nobody ever doubted their vividness; people who were taken to see Booth in childhood have remembered them through a lifetime, and thought of the character he portrayed in terms of Booth's eyes. The voice, too, was splendid, though it lacked the power of Forrest's; David Belasco says that it kept him awake all night after first hearing it. "Its sweetness and strength spoke to the inner even more than to the outer ear," wrote Charles T. Copeland. "It stirred not only the blood but the spirit."[4]

He had other natural advantages. Like all sensitive people, he hated the notoriety which goes with a great theatrical career, but he soon learned how to take the "crickets" (critics) in his stride, and, not being a vain man, he enjoyed George L. Fox's burlesque of his Hamlet greatly. He was not naturally a good "study" (Edwin Milton Royle, who played with him, says he was "never very perfect in the lines of Lear"), and acting was a physical strain for him, but he never knew the meaning of stage fright. His father had always tried to keep all day in the character he was to play at night. Edwin never lost his grip on a character, and he could weave in and out of it with ease; consequently he never repeated himself mechanically but remained alert to all that was happening on the stage and ready to take advantage even of the blunders and accidents that occurred and build them into his performance. In 1876 he himself wrote that though he had played Hamlet hundreds of times, he was still learning many things about the character that until now had been hidden from him. He was famous for his listening on the stage, and the first time young Julia Marlowe saw him, she was most impressed not by the eloquence of his speech but by the eloquence of his silence. It is interesting that when he did sometimes permit his personal emotion to become involved in his playing, he was not at his best, and after he thought he had given the performance of his life in *The Fool's Revenge*, his daughter came back stage

---

[4] In 1890, in a hotel room in Chicago, Booth recorded "To be, or not to be" and Othello's speech to the Senate on wax cylinders which later came into the hands of Professor Frederick L. Packard, Jr., of Harvard. It proved impossible to re-record the *Hamlet* successfully, but the *Othello* was re-recorded, and part of it is included in Professor Packard's tape, "Styles in Shakespearean Acting, 1890–1950," published by Creative Associates, Inc., of Boston. The closest description of Booth's reading is in Henry A. Clapp, "Edwin Booth," *Atlantic Monthly*, Vol. LXXII (1893), 307–17.

to find out whether he had been ill, never having seen him give the character so badly![5]

Yet Booth was not universally admired. His extreme detractors claim that he had no basic or consistent underlying conception of the roles he played, or, more brutally, that he relied primarily on stage "business" and did not really understand what he was doing. In view of the notes he contributed to the "New Variorum" Shakespeare, the prompt-books of his acting editions, published under the editorship of William Winter, and his papers on his father and on Edmund Kean in the Matthews and Hutton *Actors and Actresses*, this seems too absurd to consider seriously. Booth's respect for the Shakespearean text was not up to modern standards, but it was considerable for its time. He does not, however, seem to have achieved any very elaborate theory of acting. He knew that his style was "quieter" than his father's, and that he was aiming at the imagination of the audience, but he never went much farther than that. When John E. Russell begged him not to elaborate upon or refine his characterizations further, he replied amusingly:

> I appreciate all you say, my dear boy, but if the great gods will have it so—how in hell can I help being refined? (The above is a specimen of it.)—I can't paint with big brushes—the fine touches come in spite of me and it's all folly to say "don't elaborate—don't refine it"—I can't help it. I make desperate attempts to "pitch in" but there's no pitch in me—I'm too damned genteel and exquisite, I s'pose, and some buster with a "big woice" and a broad axe gesticulation will oust me one of these fine days.

Nevertheless, Booth was far from being wholly "modern" in

[5] Booth's self-possession on the stage entailed also one other, perhaps less fortunate, consequence: it sometimes led him to "kid" his fellow players or whisper "asides" which made it difficult for them to keep a straight face. Once, disgusted by an apathetic *Richelieu* audience, he deliberately burlesqued the play from the curse of Rome scene to the end. Yet I think one must almost forgive one interpolation in *King Lear* in a mosquito-infested theater. "What is your study?" he asked his Edgar, and young Frederick Warde replied properly, "How to prevent the fiend, and to kill vermin," whereupon Booth queried further, "Skeeters an' sich?"

his technique. "By the time I saw him," writes Copeland, "although there was (and continued till the end to be) an ever-lessening degree of old-fashioned theatricality in his impersonations, he seldom, even in *Richard III*, played obviously for points." But it is clear that his performances were constantly interrupted by applause, and that he wanted it thus and was troubled when he failed to secure it. Skinner says that though he was "a small, even a frail man, I could swear that at times in *Othello* and in *Macbeth* he was seven feet tall." He used physical as well as spiritual means to create such an effect, and he knew every trick in the book; when he hurled the curse of Rome in *Richelieu*, he raised himself on tiptoe inside his long cardinal's robes and extended his arms as high as possible above his head while every other actor on the stage bowed before him.

One auditor objects that he lacked repose ("he was always gesticulating with his forearm or shaking his finger at somebody"), but this does not seem very penetrating. To begin with, there is a conflict of testimony here (Clapp actually says Booth was sparing in gesture), and insofar as he did gesticulate, he seems to have been trying to break away from the older style of formal declamation that he had known in his youth, as if he wished to load every rift with ore, making his long speeches a part of the performance and not so many interruptions of it. Copeland stresses too his sparing use of emphasis in his declamation: he relied rather "upon the subtler means of inflection and quality of tone." Yet it is clear from Otis Skinner's description that gesture and declamation often combined into more elaborate display pieces than contemporary actors favor:

> Shylock's line to Bassanio, "Would'st thou have a serpent sting thee twice?" was accompanied by a darting movement of the right hand—the finger-tips closed, resembling a serpent's head—forward and back on a flexible wrist. It was the striking of a snake. Macbeth's "The crow makes wing to the rooky wood" was pictured by a waving of hand and forearm as undulating as Ruth St. Denis in an oriental dance.

Booth was an uneven actor, and nobody has ever pretended that he was equally successful in all his roles, or that he was always at his best even in the roles which favored him; to have a full understanding of what he could do with a part, you had to see him in it again and again. His Othello had many beauties, but it was too subtle and intellectual to be the Moor that Shakespeare drew. He emphasized Macbeth's perverted mysticism to bring the role more within the range of his own capacities. He idealized and poetized his Richard II to the extent of giving him a Christ-like make-up, which if not a glaring misunderstanding of the character was perilously close to blasphemy. Booth never spoke a line on the stage whose meaning he had not pondered from every conceivable angle, but he disliked the drudgery of rehearsals and would go to any length to escape from them. Sometimes, especially during his later years, he was lethargic and mechanical, and Edwin Milton Royle frankly states that in the South the Booth-Barrett tour degenerated into "a money-grabbing device. Much of the time we played twice a day, like a travelling vaudeville show."[6] He must often have felt what he once remarked to Modjeska: "I wish I had all my strength and vigor to play this as I ought to play it." But he was always capable of walking through a play up to a certain point, when he would suddenly catch fire, and then, as Sarah Bernhardt would say, "God was there." He was a dreamer by temperament who got his best effects not by logic but by intuition, and the same spiritual quality which imparted a wonderful poetic charm to his interpretations could, when it failed to work, also conjure up an atmosphere of vagueness. As his great friend Adam Badeau put it, "he was uneven and fitful in everything, but in every part he played he did something that no other actor could rival."

Though much has been said here and elsewhere about the spiritual quality in Booth's acting, it should not be forgotten that he played his share of villains, both robustious and quietly

---

[6] On the financial aspect of Booth's career, see Sally MacDougall, "Edwin Booth Counted His Ducats," *Century*, Vol. CXVII (1928), 198–204.

malicious.[7] Perhaps it was merely his natural modesty which made him dislike playing lovers, but in view of what he himself tells us of the difficulty he had in expressing even his love for Mary Devlin, I doubt it. Badeau thought his Romeo satisfactory only in the duel scene: "there was a lack of tenderness in his eye, and of ardor in his tone; even the gestures were tame. He was not anxious or persuasive enough; he was too confident, or too indifferent." He seems to have been much better in the wooing scene in *Richard III*, which is particularly interesting in view of Winter's statement that Booth's comedy was never outstanding except when it included an element of bitterness or sardonicism. Listen to this critic, further, on some of Booth's evil roles. His Iago roused admiration "by a lithe, clear, rapier-like elasticity, both physical and mental, and by a cool, involuntary, cruel, veiled humor, which was made to play, like a lambent flame of hell, over the whole structure of the work." His expression "of the dissimulative part of Gloster's conduct was beautiful in its diabolic, glittering, serpent-like, specious craft." His Cassius was "comet-like, rushing, and terrible—not lacking in human emotion, but colored with something sinister." In *The Fool's Revenge* he "gave an embodiment of horrid yet pitiable deformity, mental as well as physical." As Pescara in *The Apostate* his "dangerous, jeering, menacing duplicity was so terrible that often it impelled the spectator quite over the line of terror, into the shuddering mood of hysterical laughter." These are not idiosyncratic judgments. John Ranken Towse thought the Iago "enveloped in an aura of evil." Kitty Molony says that "the audience was with him every moment" and "gurgled at his dia-

[7] In view of all that has been said about the quietness of Booth's style as compared to that of his predecessors, Mrs. D. P. Bowers, who played Julie to both Forrest's Richelieu and his, is very interesting. "Forrest's method . . . was to work up gradually to the climax, giving the words with all the strength of his marvelous voice, until it seemed as if a tidal wave were about to overwhelm everything. Booth reached his climax here with startling suddenness, and the words were shrieked out with an intensity that was awful. It came like an electric flash out of a clear sky, seeming to inspire a terror that was supernatural and a warning prophetic of annihilation." "Memories of Edwin Booth," *Californian*, Vol. V (1894), 471–78.

bolical triumphs"; she adds that the role tired him less than any other he played on the tour she shared. And though Ellen Terry felt that his Iago was much less effective than Irving's, the reason was that Booth was "always the snake in the grass; he showed the villain in all the scenes."

Booth's attitude toward acting differed widely from time to time. Sometimes he professed neither to enjoy it nor to respect it. "I've led a useless life." One can understand why he should have turned against it after Mary Devlin's death. "When I was happy my art was a source of infinite delight and pride to me, because she delighted in my success and encouraged me in all I did; I had then an incentive to work, to achieve something great. But my ambition is gone with her; it can give me no pleasure to paint a picture of my grief and hold it up as a show for applause again." But he spoke slightingly of his art at other times also, and he certainly does not show a very intelligent sense of human values in general when he declares that "very great writers may stand full length among the statesmen and warriors, but as a rule, they, with artists, especially actors, should be permitted only an occasional bust in some quiet corner." There were even times when he thought art enervating in itself ("my fancy world where I dream my life away"), obscuring the difference between dream and reality and hopelessly confusing the actor with the parts which he played. "I believe you understand how completely I 'ain't here' most of the time. It's an awful thing to be somebody else all the while." And one thinks of Keats: "A poet is the most unpoetical of anything in existence, because he has no identity; he is continually in for and filling some other body."

But this is far from being the whole truth, and I do not for a moment believe that Booth really disliked the theater. "Since the talent God has given me can be made available for no other purpose, I believe the object I devote it to to be worthy of self-sacrifice." His ambition appeared at the outset in the determined way in which he pursued his desire for a stage career despite the opposition of his father, and I think it shows even more clearly in 1860, in his advice to Lawrence Barrett: "Don't turn up your nose at the stock, Larry, a position can be made there to command respect and admiration for all true lovers of the highest of all arts." For Larry, but not, it seems, for Ted. For he goes on: "I'd rather there was no such thing as *starring*—I'd rather stay in one place and have a home, but of course I'd like to have A.1. in my trade." (Don't do as I do, Larry; do as I say.) When Booth was in England, he even grumbled because royalty had not been to see him, and nothing could be franker or more winning than his whole-hearted rejoicing in the reception he was accorded in Germany; "I have just accomplished the one great object of my professional aspiration. . . . This is the realization of my twenty years' dream. . . . I cannot tell you of my triumph tonight without a gush of egotism—and you know how difficult that is for me." And it seems to me more than a little suggestive that when Kitty Molony told him he took curtain calls as if he had been insulted, he replied that that was exactly how he felt, explaining that he considered himself an interpreter, not an entertainer, and that it seemed to him degrading to be obliged to accept the plaudits of those who did not actually know whether he had done his work well or ill. To be clapper-clawed with the palms of the vulgar seems to have given him little pleasure.

The thing for which Booth was most often criticized during his later years was the inadequacy of his support.

> I saw him in everything that he played from 1875 up to the date of his retirement [says John Ranken Towse], and—until he came under the management of Lawrence Barrett—I can not recall any occasion upon which he was surrounded with a decently adequate cast. The tacit assent which he gave to some of the worst features of the star system was deplorable. His own brilliant work helped to keep the literary drama upon the stage, but left it desolate when he departed.

Booth was not careless when he himself was *producing* plays, though even then he was quite capable of assigning roles to personal friends who were not capable of playing them effectively, and it is hard to believe that Mary McVicker can ever have been the Juliet he needed to open Booth's Theater. After his bankruptcy, however, he apparently had no strength or inclination to think about anything except his own roles. It must be clearly understood that he did not surround himself with boobies, as some actors have done, so that he himself might shine more brightly. Few great actors have co-starred with so many great contemporaries, and none has been more warmly spoken of by other players. "I never met one in my profession," says Mrs. Bowers, "so generous to his brother and sister artists in the matter of dramatic points as he." He was equally considerate of beginners in his company and of the underlings about the theater. "I have frequently seen him," says John Malone, "during a performance, while waiting for his cue, walk across to his dressing-room and bring out a chair for himself rather than ask anyone else to do it." He once dropped two plays from his repertoire to avoid the necessity of telling a young actress that she was inadequate in the roles that had been assigned her and would have to be replaced.[8]

It should be clearly understood, however, that Booth knew his own value, both in itself and in its relationship to that of others, and that he never had the slightest intention of being imposed upon.[9] His correspondence with his difficult colleague Lawrence Barrett shows this very clearly. Booth is forbearing far beyond most men, but when he needs to lay it on the line, nobody can do it more effectively. "I think it is definitely proved

[8] The famous story that he was once taken literally when he insisted on a Detroit manager's taking down "The World Renowned Young American Tragedian," etc. ("I wish to be billed as simple Edwin Booth") seems adequately vouched for by Barton Hill, "Personal Recollections of Edwin Booth," *New York Dramatic Mirror*, Christmas Number, 1896, pp. 2–9.

[9] Booth had his "views" about his contemporaries, and both Modjeska and Edwin Milton Royle testify that though he liked Henry Irving personally, he did not rate him highly as an actor. (He also seems to have felt that David Garrick had been overpraised.) He called Tennyson "a vain old man" and said that Browning "was always talking about himself, saying things it would have been in better taste to let others say."

that the 'draught' to this house lies in *my* name, and it follows that greater prominence should be given to the article that sells best." "I cannot afford to *star* those who have proved to be un-profitable to me. . . ." And when Barrett blows up and writes him a cruel "Dear Sir" letter, Booth endorses it, Edwin Forrest-wise, "Preserve this as a souvenir of the blackest ingratitude." As for minor actors, during his later years they might do as they liked on the stage insofar as they did not come into contact with him, but when they did, there was never any question that where Mac-Gregor sat was the head of the table. "Your costume is more a high-light than a background, but after my exit you may do what you please."

III

But what was Booth besides an actor? He loved nature, es-pecially trees (to which he was inclined to attribute conscious-ness), but music meant little to him and the plastic arts little more. Sports and games did not exist so far as he was concerned. He felt his lack of formal education keenly, but when Mrs. Richard Henry Stoddard priggishly advised him to "cultivate the intellectual," he replied that this was "impossible for him." "I have only just discovered that I know infinitely less than nothing," he wrote in 1876. At an early stage, Adam Badeau took him in hand, discussed his roles with him, hunted up books and pictures, and earnestly considered all possible avenues of im-provement, and Booth was very grateful for this. Brander Mat-thews says he was delighted with the success of his contributions to the *Actors and Actresses* series and anxious to know how they were being received. He collected a good library and, like most intelligent men who are much alone, he read a good deal. Some-times he mentions a title—Motley's history or Marie Bashkirtseff's journal—in his correspondence, but I do not feel that reading was actually a passion with him. Much of it seems to have been done in the books of those with whom he was personally acquainted.[10]

[10] J. A. Watrous, "Side Lights on Edwin Booth," Chicago *Daily Journal*, July

For politics he cared not at all, and he never voted until 1864, when he supported Lincoln "in pure admiration of his noble career and his Christian principles." Though he realized that army life would be impossible for one of his temperament,[11] he was a strong Union man, and once victory was assured, he waited impatiently for the spring of 1865 in pathetic ignorance of the grief and shame it was to bring him. His provincialism in London seems a little childish, as when he draped a Stars-and-Stripes canopy over Mary's bed so that Edwina might be born under the flag. In Europe again in 1883, he admired Germany and disliked France.

Booth seems to have thought little about—and cared little for—men in the mass. As for individuals, he himself said that he always "either loved or detested," but I should say he was often too indifferent for either. "I love those best who let me alone," he once said. He might have added, with Longfellow, that he had been "bored so often." "He had stage-fright everywhere but on the stage," says Edwin Milton Royle, and when the company at table stopped talking to hear what he was going to say, he forgot it himself and couldn't say it. "Saw Booth at the Goulds," wrote Louisa May Alcott in her journal, "a handsome, shy man, glooming in a corner." When they went into Boston society, both he and Mary Devlin very soon got enough of Mr. and Mrs. James T. Fields, and I doubt that they cared much more for Julia Ward

---

26, 1906, tells of Booth's being entertained by Covert Masonic Lodge in Omaha, on one of his visits there. Asked for his favorite poem, he replied that his favorite *hymn* was "Jesus, Lover of My Soul," and repeated it. He was glad to be asked, further, for his favorite piece of prose, which was the Lord's Prayer, "the most beautiful, impressive, ennobling, unforgettable piece of prose ever preserved in this world," and which he recited with bowed head.

11 "If it was not for the fear of doing my country more harm than good, I'd be a soldier, too; a coward always has an 'if' to slink behind, you know. Those cursed bullets are awkward things, and very uncivil at times, too; and as for a bayonet charge, I don't hesitate to avow my readiness to 'scoot' if there is a chance. I'd be cashiered or 'broke' in two after the first day's roll call. Bull Run would be nothing to the run I'd make of it." Eleanor Ruggles illuminatingly parallels this to Lincoln's own declaration: "I have moral courage enough, I think, but I am such a coward physically that if I were to shoulder a gun and go into action, I am dead sure that I should turn and run at the first fire—I know I should."

Howe, though she was very loyal to Booth at the time of Lincoln's death. Booth went to Mrs. Howe's parties, but once there he preferred sitting on the floor and playing with little Maud to talking with her guests. And he missed his chance of being E. H. Sothern's godfather because he was afraid he could not fulfill the obligations involved. Perhaps he did not think Edwin Forrest had been notably successful in his ghostly sponsorship of himself!

With friends like Thomas Bailey Aldrich, William Winter, or Adam Badeau it was different, and even with those with whom he was thrown into close contact on his long tours. Henry Holt never sought him out at the Century Club "because he appeared to me to be affected," as if he were playing Hamlet all the time. But when the introduction was finally made, he found Booth "as natural and genial as anybody else, and I well understood from that little talk why he was so deeply and widely beloved." His conversation seems to have been largely monologue, yet Modjeska listened to it enraptured. "He never says too much or too little, and that's what makes everything he says so interesting." Yet I wish I knew how she felt when, upon some idiot's having started a story that they were having an affair, he stated publicly that the charge was absurd because they were old enough to have grandchildren! In *Behind the Scenes with Edwin Booth*, Kitty Molony has preserved a priceless record of his frolics with a group of young actresses, all of whom were quite innocently in love with him. "Mr. Booth was eternally young," she says; "younger than we, when at play."

Above all else, his heart and his purse were ever open to human need. After he had shot at him in McVicker's Theater, the lunatic Mark Gray tried to borrow money from him. Gray must have been the only person he ever refused; he even sent theater tickets to the crazy Boston Corbett, who asked for them on the ground that "I am the man who shot your brother." There is a letter in his daughter's book in which he suggested that a subscription be organized to relieve a certain person in need; he "cannot alone render much assistance," but he enclosed a check for $500. In 1866 he sent $1,000 to a friend in Charleston.

> The earthquake horror reminds me that I have (or had) many dear friends in Charleston. I can't help all of 'em, but if the enclosed can relieve you and the dear ones—use it—would to God I could offer more. Bad as it is, it might be worse. The Almighty loves us, despite his chastisements. Be true to him. He will not desert you. My life has been a chapter of tragedies, as you know, but I have never despaired—never lost my "grip" of the "eternal truth." The worst is not so long as we can say, this is the worst.

Charles S. Abbe tells of two instances in which he sent checks for $2,500 each to two poor widows. "To my certain knowledge," said William Bispham, "he gave away in charity more than most men would consider a fortune." He even rebuilt the tobacco barn which was burned down when John Wilkes was captured in it. "I have seen him blush like a girl at the receipt of a letter of thanks," says Laurence Hutton, "and run away like a coward from the gratitude of those he had helped." Since he was a human being, I suppose he must at some time have been unkind to somebody, but apparently no record of this has been preserved. "I would rather a thousand times be hurt than hurt another," he says, and his whole life proves that this was no empty boast. He showed mercy even to the worthless woman who tried to blackmail him by pretending that he was the father of her child, for after she had been trapped by a theatrical trick based on another actor's resemblance to him, he refused to prosecute. "Get her confession in writing, give her some money, and send her back to San Francisco."[12] And since he was his father's son, it

[12] The only sour note is struck by his curious reply to David Anderson's compliment to him upon his generosity: "Well, life is uncertain and I've been successful. I don't want generations hereafter to say, 'He took care of his money and never thought of others.'" This is a little like the man with an invalid wife of whom Gamaliel Bradford tells: "When I stand by her grave, I do not wish to have anything to reproach myself with." But I am sure Booth does not do himself justice. What, however, shall we make of this as manifesting a strange streak of economy: "This hotel ink and paper are vexatious; if my business continues good I'll buy some better material"?

should not be necessary to add that his kindness embraced animals also. The most touching example is that of the pet lamb which repeatedly thrust itself upon him one day while he was studying a role out of doors; he pushed it away and finally slapped it gently with his book; the lamb would never thereafter come near him, and he could never forgive himself for having wounded it so. But the most extreme case is that of the flies he poisoned. At first he was amused by their antics after having tasted the stuff. "But suddenly I realized that as death was not instantaneous they must be *suffering*, and I have been grieved about it ever since."

If Booth had a gift for friendship, he had an even greater gift for love. First of all there was the family into which he was born. No man ever loved his family more than Booth did, and none ever paid a higher price for loving. His mother, indeed, never failed him. But his boyish guardianship of his mad,[13] drunken father robbed him of his youth, and his brother's murder of Lincoln would have broken his heart if Mary Devlin's death had not anticipated it. "All my life I have thought of dreadful things that might happen to me," he told Winter in later years, "and I believed there was no horror that I had not imagined, but I never dreamed of such a dreadful thing as *that*." It is not literally true that though he kept John Wilkes's picture in his bedroom as long as he lived, he never spoke of him, but the recorded occasions

[13] Edwin Forrest's blunt judgment, "All those God-damned Booths are crazy" has been quoted elsewhere in this volume. Junius Brutus Booth certainly had a crazy streak in him, and if John Wilkes was sane, he must have been one of the greatest fools in recorded history. Rosalie seems to have been somewhat simple, and it is difficult to believe that Asia Booth Clarke's treatment of Mary Devlin, who was an angel in human form if there has ever been such a creature, was that of a well-balanced woman. In *The Elder and the Younger Booth*, Asia praises Edwin as "the kindest and most tender of sons to an erratic father and to a widowed mother, in every other relation, as brother, husband, father, friend, worthy of affection and of all praise." His kindness and tenderness as a husband she disliked too much even to be able to mention it! In the next generation, Junius Brutus Booth III killed his wife and himself. Edwin's second wife, Mary McVicker, lost her mind, and even Edwina, before her successful marriage to Ignatius Grossmann, had to get herself engaged to a man who must break down, fortunately, this time, before the engagement had had time to ripen into marriage.

are very few.[14] I know of nothing more pathetic than his reply to Richard Harding Davis when the latter apologized to him after having inadvertently remarked that he possessed a playbill of Ford's Theater the night Lincoln was killed that he would like to give to the club. "Do not apologize. I really took satisfaction in your forgetting. It shows that at last there are some people in the world who do not associate me with Lincoln's death."[15] When his dead brother's theatrical costumes at last came into Edwin's hands, he burned them.[16]

Mary McVicker, Edwin married because he admired her and wanted a home for himself and his little girl.[17] Toward her he seems to have fulfilled all the obligations of a husband, and when her world crashed around her, he went not only the second mile but the third and the fourth and the fifth. But the woman he loved was Mary Devlin, and he was the kind of man who understands Ambrose Bierce's saying that he who thinks he has loved twice has not loved once. It is not conceivable that Booth can have failed in tenderness toward Mary McVicker, but it is pos-

[14] See Grossmann, *Edwin Booth*, 227–28; also Goodale, *Behind the Scenes*, 95. Actors very rarely commit crimes; it seems strange that the most famous crime in American history should have been committed by an actor; it seems stranger still that Edwin Booth, brother of the assassin, should personally have saved Robert Lincoln from falling under a train (see Lincoln's own account, correcting inaccuracies in other reports, *Century*, N.S., Vol. LV [1908–1909], 920), and that, upon her first voyage to America, an actress, Sarah Bernhardt, should have saved Lincoln's widow from a shipboard fall which might well have proved fatal. These are simply additional examples of the strange coincidences and melodramatic encounters which make the sober history of the Booths stranger than fiction.

[15] W. W. Ellsworth, *A Golden Age of Authors* (Houghton Mifflin, 1919), 19.

[16] See Skinner, *The Last Tragedian*, 143ff. Edwin Booth's first appeal to Secretary of War Stanton, that John Wilkes's body might be returned to his family for burial, got nowhere, which should surprise nobody. It is more disappointing that Grant should have ignored a similar appeal, especially since he had written Edwin, promising to serve him should it ever fall within his power, at the time of Robert Lincoln's near-fatal accident. See H. H. Kohlsaat, "Booth's Letter to Grant," *Saturday Evening Post*, Vol. CXCVI, February 9, 1924, pp. 20, 56. The final, successful appeal was made to one of the most underrated of American presidents, Andrew Johnson, who issued his order of release on February 15, 1869.

[17] He had previously been engaged to a Blanche Hamel, but John Wilkes's crime had taken care of that.

sible, and even likely, that she may have known that he could never love her with the passionate, possessive love she felt for him, and if she did, the knowledge can hardly have been helpful to a woman of her cast of mind. She had, moreover, been an ambitious, though not, apparently, a very talented young actress, and if it was at his insistence that she gave up her career, this too may have been bad for her.

Mary Devlin he adored. We have some of her letters, and she could not have been more worthy. But the frankest expressions of his feeling for her that have come down to us are in letters to others written after her death.

> I see her, I feel her, hear her, every minute of the day. I call her, look for her, every time the door opens; in every car that passes our little cottage door, where we anticipated so much joy, I expect to see the loved form of her who was my *world*. God only can relieve me: nothing on earth can fill the place of her who was to me at once wife, mother, sister, child, guide, and savior. All is dark; I know not where to turn, how to direct the deserted vessel now.

He sought assurance of her continued existence through spiritualism, but the attempt was inconclusive. When the storm raged, or a bird sought admittance at his window, he would be seized by the wild hope that Mary was trying to reach him. "Would I either did not believe at all or were convinced beyond all doubt! This half humanity is a hellish state to be in. This dangling between the fiend and God is worse agony than to be damned outright." "I'm black—black as hell within and I hate to look there." Too black, by far, to hope for communion with that bright spirit. If she had not left a hostage behind her in the shape of a daughter who had inherited much of her own nature, and with whom Booth was to enjoy as satisfying a father-daughter relationship as is anywhere on record, one shudders to think what might have become of him. In 1865 he wrote, "All my hopes and aspirations now are clustering like a halo about my baby's head; to rear a monument to the mother in her child is my life-study now."

He reproached himself bitterly for not having sufficiently expressed his love for Mary while she was alive:

> When I recall the many sad trials I have given her, and the little joy, save in her own devotion, she derived in her connection with me, I cannot but think that God removed her from a life of misery, perhaps; for although my love was deep-rooted in my soul yet I could never show it; I was ever cold, indifferent and even have made her weep most bitterly when like a statue I received her devotion.

But that was not the worst of it. For Booth had inherited his father's "devil," and it was not until after his wife's death that he completely conquered it. In his remorse he wrote, "Before I was eighteen I was a drunkard, at twenty a libertine."[18] The

[18] This is probably too harsh a self-judgment. Edwin's libertinism, at any age, has left no trace, and if it be replied that libertinism often does not, one should remember that that of John Wilkes left plenty. Certainly there is no suggestion of libertinism nor of anything even remotely related to it during any of the years we knew Booth well. His bowdlerizing of Shakespeare's text was considered extreme even in his own time.

The letter to Mrs. Stoddard from which the above quotation is taken has apparently been printed in full only in Dolores Marbourg Bacon's valuable article, "The Heart of Hamlet," New York *Herald*, Magazine Section, November 1, 1903, pp. 1 ff.

... I remembered how she wept when I laid my blackened heart bare to her. She covered it with her goodness and kissed away many dark stains from it which now, I fear, begin to show their damnable dyes again. You might think that I had been the author of most horrible crimes when I speak of my past, might you not? It is not so, however, but I have been full of sin, up to the top of all that dissipation, evil associations and sensuality could lead me to, except, of course, murder, robbing and such petty offences, although the perpetrators of such things have been my companions. I don't think I am to be blamed for what I may have done, for I was neglected in my childhood and thrown (really, it now seems almost purposely) into all sorts of temptations and evil society. Before I was eighteen I was a drunkard, at twenty a libertine. I knew no better. I was born good, I do believe, for there are sparks of goodness constantly flashing out from among the cinders.

"I never was at school more than a week at a time. I grew up in ignorance, allowed by an indulgent mother who knew nothing more than that she loved her child, and a father who although a good man, seemed to care very little what course I took. I was allowed to roam at large, and at an early age and

night his wife died in Dorchester, he was staggering on and off the stage in New York, too drunk to open and read the telegrams which the doctor was sending him. When finally he arrived home, he went into the room where her body lay and remained there for hours. By the time he came out, he had won his battle. But Mary had had to die to save him.[19]

A priori such an experience might seem ideally calculated to reinforce Booth's always strong religious feelings, but one would hardly expect whatever religion emerged from it to be strongly marked by health or joy. And in his case both these expectations are fulfilled.

Melancholy is often produced by the absence of a satisfying religious faith and a consequent loss of faith and satisfaction in life itself. Spenser understood this when he created the three

in a wild and almost barbarous country where boys become old men in vice very speedily; but after satiety remorse set in like a despair, and like the devil when he was taken ill I resolved to become a saint and throw off the hoofs and horns. I could not do it. Sin was in me and it consumed me while it was shut up so close, so I let it out and it seemed to rage and burn more fiercely than ever. All the accumulated vices I had acquired in the wilds of California and the still less refined society of Australia seemed to have full sway over me and I yielded to their bestializing voices. I added fuel to the fire until the angel quenched it and made me, if not a man, at least a little worthier than I was. There was one spark, however, left untouched. It was merely covered, and it occasionally would ignite; still the angel kept it under. I dread lest it get full headway again. Through all this vice I, of course, suffered tortures, at times bodily pain and mental agony. These in time left me sad mementoes which I must carry to the grave.

[19] It does not seem to have been literally true, as has sometimes been asserted, that Booth never raised a glass to his lips again. See Ruggles, *Edwin Booth*, 299, and cf. the references to German beer in Skinner, *The Last Tragedian*. Nevertheless the battle had been won, once and for all; there was no turning back, even when he was overwhelmed by his brother's crime. In England the water glass by his plate astonished his hosts, and on the tour Kitty Molony describes, he would not allow even beer to be brought into his private car. Of course the gossips never believed any of this, and in his last years, when he sometimes staggered on the stage under an attack of vertigo, he was often reported to have been drunk. In a way, this was less unjust than it seems, for while Booth was not drinking, he was slowly killing himself with the incessant, intemperate smoking which all reliable opinion seems to hold responsible for his early breakdown, and I do not know why it should be considered more moral to commit suicide with one poison than another. From time to time he talked about trying to cut down; on the other hand, he even tried to teach the girls in his company to smoke on one of his tours; see Goodale, *Behind the Scenes*, Chapter XVIII.

knights Sansfoy, Sansloy, and Sansjoy. Sometimes, however, it is associated with religion, as it was in Booth's case, and for all the influence belief exerts upon conduct, one may perhaps be permitted to doubt that it profoundly alters temperament.

Melancholy was certainly a matter of temperament in Booth's case, and heaven knows that he had suffered enough to make any amount of depression on his part seem reasonable. Perhaps, even, it was the family heritage of madness which came through to him in the milder form of melancholia, but if so, it never went to the length of really throwing him off balance. One of his favorite quotations was from *Richard II*:

> *Nor I nor any man that but man is*
> *With nothing shall be pleased till he be eased*
> *With being nothing.*

He was not, in the usual sense of the term, a "pessimist"; he entertained no convictions about the worthlessness of life; one does not gather that his melancholy was an ideational matter at all, or that he had any interest in ideas for their own sake. Neither did he "catch" it from the specific "Romantic" melancholy which was still in the air in his time; as Gamaliel Bradford observed, "so far as his recognition of them is concerned, Rousseau, René, Byron, Shelley, George Sand, Obermann, might never have existed."

Booth's hymn to death finds its most eloquent expression in the strangest letter of consolation ever written, sent to Winter after the death of a son:

> I cannot grieve at death. It seems to me the greatest boon the Almighty has granted us. Consequently I cannot appreciate the grief of those who mourn the loss of loved ones, particularly if they go early from this hell of misery to which we have been doomed.

And again:

> Why do you not look at this miserable little life, with all its ups

and downs, as I do? At the very worst, 'tis but a scratch, a temporary ill, to be soon cured, by that dear old doctor, Death—who gives us a life more healthful and enduring than all the physicians, temporary and spiritual, can give.

Thus expressed, the praise of death almost approximates an affirmation of life—or at least of beauty, which is an aspect of life. I have no doubt that Booth knew the dark night of the soul, especially during the hours when "vulture thoughts" o'ercame while he struggled for sleep, sometimes until dawn. He had, too, what Henry James called "the imagination of disaster"—"the feeling that evil is hanging over me, and that I can't come to good." Yet I cannot but feel that when he says he "never knew a really happy day," he is blowing out the gas to see how dark it is, though always quite without the bitterness that went along with Mark Twain's performance of a similar act. Booth had one of the "corniest" senses of humor of any great man I know; as he himself says, "I'd have my joke, though I were beaten dead for't." ("You are dealing with a *Wampire!* I axes more nor what I gives, as you will surely find to your cost some day.") This humor informs every page of his letters, and it was equally prominent in his face-to-face intercourse with his friends, in early life in the form of "guying" and practical jokes, later in gentler though not more subtle ways. Some of this may be what the Germans call *Galgenhumor,* as when he had the bullet which had been fired at him mounted into a watch-charm, inscribed "From Mark Gray to Edwin Booth." But much of it is too genial for that. Booth always disliked stiffness and wanted "jolly" people around him, and when he was badly injured in a carriage accident in 1875, the upset struck him as so ludicrous that those who ran to his aid found him laughing. Otis Skinner says he never heard Booth laugh aloud, but Edwina suggests that he restrained hearty laughter because it affected his asthma; the impulse was there. Mary Devlin thought him, like Shelley, " 'a phantom among men'—'companionless as the last fading storm,' and yet my spirit ever seems lighter and more joyous when with you." Above all, Booth always had good advice for others who were in danger of being engulfed by what possessed him: "You mustn't be so in love with melancholy as to flop over into the dumps at every little adverse puff. I really believe if some of your well-wishers would get square mad with you and give you a sound scolding it would do you more good than expressions of sympathy." None of this means that his own sadness was feigned or insincere, but it did partake of unreality to the extent that it shared the curious dream quality which somehow infused his whole life—the good and the bad together, his sorrows as well as his triumphs and successes. In this sense, Mary was a dream too, and John Wilkes was a dream, and Lincoln and God, and the whole wide universe together. Like Jacques in *As You Like It*, he subsumed it all into "a melancholy of mine own, compounded of many simples, extracted from many objects," and if there was pain in it there was also beauty, and sometimes one could hardly tell the two apart.

About his own religious faith, however, there was no question whatever. "Adieu," he concludes one letter to Horace Howard Furness; "and may Christ be before thee, behind thee, and round about thee!" He would not act on Good Friday and thought even the Oberammergau Passion Play irreverent. Very nearly the sternest words he ever wrote were addressed to a clergyman who had written to inquire whether there were not some way for him to attend a performance at Booth's Theater without running the risk of being seen by a member of his congregation: "There is no door in my theater through which God cannot see." And certainly the most beautiful words he ever wrote were sent to his friend Adam Badeau and to Mrs. Richard Cary, the widow of another dear friend, who was killed in the Civil War:

> Believe in one great truth, Ad.—God is. And as surely as you and I are flesh and bones and blood, so are we also spirits eternal.

And again:

> Life is a great big spelling-book, and on every page we turn the

words grow harder to understand the meaning of. But there *is* a meaning, and when the last leaf flops over, we'll know the whole lesson by heart.

Though Booth is said to have done considerable religious reading during the last years of his life, I would guess that it must have been purely devotional in character; there was nothing intellectual about his faith, and its expression achieves everywhere the winning simplicity of a child. Unlike Edwin Forrest, who made a point of never forgiving an injury, Booth forgave everybody. On the lowest level of his belief, he was as enslaved to superstition as even Sarah Bernhardt, regarded his caul as a talisman to protect him from danger, would not allow peacock feathers to be brought into the theater, and regarded a broken mirror as sure to inaugurate a streak of bad luck. He experienced premonitions; if he had not, for no reason at all, shifted his position on the stage, Mark Gray's bullet would surely have got him, and he once shifted, with similar aimlessness, under a coconut tree, just before the coconut fell where his head had been. On a higher level, he believed, though sometimes tortured by doubt, in the interest in human affairs and human welfare maintained by just spirits made perfect.

> May not those who yearn to see me carry out the ideas we love to think worthy of a life's hard labor, rejoice now to see a step made toward the fulfilment of what is true and beautiful in art? I think they do; and in this belief I begin to realize the usefulness of my labor, and to appreciate what I once deemed worthless.

He had—or thought he had—psychic experiences at the time of Mary's death, and when Keller the magician demonstrated that he could do everything the spiritualists did by material means, his faith was unaffected:

> Keller, . . . so far as physical manifestations go,—has settled the question, unless he, as spiritualists declare, is a medium, and calls his "wonders" tricks for mere money-making. I don't believe it; I think he is honest, and yet I've had such strange experiences in

that direction that I'm inclined to accept almost everything that savors of mystery as supernatural.

Two years after Mary's death, his faith was firmly founded, long enough at least for him to write Mrs. Cary:

> But, my dear friend, a light from heaven has settled fully and firmly in my soul, and I regard death as God has intended we should understand it—as the breaking of eternal daylight, and a birthday of the soul. I feel that all my actions have been and are influenced by her whose love is to me the strength and the wisdom of my spirit. Whatever I may do of serious import, I regard it as a performance of a sacred duty to all that is pure and honest in my nature—a duty to the very religion of my heart. Since Mary went to join our dear Richard in Christ's dear love, I've grown clearer in mind and heart, faithful and wise in soul, and fearless as to the gloomy passage they have taken.

They have all gone into a great world of light,

and we have found them, then, in losing them, as the excellent becomes the permanent. A certain temperament will inevitably ask at this point how such faith could coexist with Booth's sadness. I find no indication that Booth ever read Melville, but he might very well have agreed with him that "the truest of all men was the Man of Sorrows," and that "Great Love is sad; and heaven is Love. Sadness makes the silence throughout the realms of space; sadness is universal and eternal." For him, at least, grief held theophanic qualities: "Oh, I feel such an intense love for God when sorrow touches me that I could almost wish my heart would always ache—I feel so near to him, I realize his love so thoroughly, so intensely, at such times." Some readers will turn in disgust from what they consider the self-indulgent morbidness of such an utterance; personally I am more inclined to squirm when he writes of Mary Devlin's death that "nothing but the blow which fell could have awakened me. I learned to feel it was in kindness, not anger, that God spoke thus to me." If I were a drunkard, I think I should feel that my wife's death was too high a price to pay for my salvation, but perhaps the arbitrary conception of God presented in the Old Testament had conditioned Booth to accept such a sacrifice, and it might even be argued that a Christian cannot reject it either without also rejecting the sacrifice of Christ.

Life, Samuel Butler used to say, is a pragmatic habit, and therefore the question "Is life worth living?" is a question for an embryo, not for a man. Great tragedy raises our spirits even while it depresses them because it lends dignity and stature to human beings. If the world destroys a Tess of the D'Urbervilles, that same world has had the power to produce her, and a world which can produce such goodness is not all bad. Without the omniscience of God, it is perilous to dismiss as worthless even lives which seem to the observer to have been wasted or cast away. "Apparent Failure" reflects Browning's conviction of this as to the suicides in the Paris morgue, and Booth's devoted friend Aldrich wrestled with the same problem in "Broken Music," the fine poem he wrote in memory of Amy Levy, a minor but genuine young English poet who killed herself. Whatever his faults, sorrows, and limitations may have been, Edwin Booth sweetened and uplifted life for a whole generation of playgoers, and, as Gamaliel Bradford says, much of the charm remains even for us "who read of him in old and dusty books." If there was toil and anguish for him where his audience knew only exhilaration and enjoyment, he cannot have been wholly unmindful that his too was the victory.

6

Sir Henry Irving
(1838–1905)

W<small>HEN AN AMERICAN REPORTER</small> asked Irving the not un-
typical reporter's question, "To what do you attribute your success, Sir Henry?" the great man replied simply, "To my acting."
It is perhaps the finest response to reportorial probing on record.
But coming from him it has a special force.

When Irving chose the theater, everything was against his
choice, even his mother's conviction that actors belonged to the
devil. But the shades of his Methodist forebears may be seen
peering over his shoulder in his consistent references not to his
"profession" but to his "calling." But in *Who's Who* he also
called it his "recreation," and when he was asked what he did
for exercise, he said, "I act." "If I have in any way deserved
commendation," he declared, "I am proud that it is as an actor
that I have won it," and when, late in life, a friend asked him
what he would do if he were told he would live ten years if he
would rest and only two if he continued to act, he replied instantly, "I should act." During the same period he remarked
plaintively to Gerald Lawrence, "It is a sad thing, just as one is
beginning to know a little about this work of ours, it is time to
leave it."

This concentration, self-dedication, and entire singleness of purpose made Irving the most influential English actor since Garrick, but it also involved curious correlaries which cannot be summed up in a word. Joseph Jefferson called him "a wonderful man, who lived only for his art." And he added, "There's not a mean bone in him." But Graham Robertson suggests more complicated considerations when he writes:

> His art was his life—his soul. He had vowed himself to it by a pact as awful as that between Faust and Mephistopheles; like Peter Schlemihl, he had sold his reflection; the mirror of memory gives back a score of counterfeit images, but of the true Irving, the dweller in the innermost, hardly a trace.

And he adds that "far more could be learned of Henry Irving by watching his nightly performance than by talking to him for hours." There is a suggestion of something here which is as repellent as the fanaticism of the crusader who is completely absorbed in his "cause," and it was this element in Irving which caused his great vis-à-vis Ellen Terry, who, whatever faults she may have had, was never in danger of sacrificing life to art, to feel "contempt and affection and admiration" for him, all so craftily commingled that she could hardly tell where one ended and another began. In Henry James's curious story, "The Private Life," there is a writer who stays at home and works at his desk while his other self goes out into society. In Irving's case one is tempted to feel that going to the theater he took the whole man with him. Becoming the perfect actor, he necessarily became also the not-quite-perfect man, or, to put it in another way, the man was swallowed up in the actor to such an extent that one cannot but wonder whether he had any existence at all apart from him. This does not make Irving easier to get hold of in his personal aspect, but before the problem can be explored, some attention must be given to the development of his career, the quality and character of his art, and his own attitude toward it.

II

John Henry Brodribb was born, February 6, 1838, at Keinton Mandeville, of mixed Somersetshire and Cornish background. His father was a small shopkeeper. Because of his parents' poverty, he spent nearly ten years of his childhood with a prosperous, larger-than-life uncle in Cornwall. At the age of eleven he was sent to Dr. Pinches' City Commercial School in London. In 1851 he was employed in a solicitors' office, and from here he passed on to an East India merchants' establishment.

He first acted at Dr. Pinches' School, then in London in a play which an elocution and dramatic class to which he adhered gave at the Soho Theater. When he was about sixteen years old, he saw his first great actor, Samuel Phelps, as Hamlet. He is supposed to have refused an offer from Phelps on the ground that he thought he ought to learn his trade in the provinces rather than in London. In any event, he was tutored by a member of the company, one William Hoskins, and when Hoskins went to Australia, Irving declined to go with him, but accepted instead a letter of introduction to the manager of the Lyceum Theater, Sunderland, where he made his debut in 1856 as the Duke of Orleans in *Richelieu*. He borrowed his stage name from two great objects of his admiration—Edward Irving, the then-famous evangelical preacher, and Washington Irving, author of *The Sketch Book*.

In January, 1857, Irving arrived in Edinburgh, where he remained for two and one-half years at the Theater Royal and the Queen's, and where he acted more than four hundred roles. Once he learned and rehearsed seventeen parts in thirty days, and sometimes he assumed four different characters in a single evening. On September 13, 1859, he played his farewell benefit as Claude Melnotte in *The Lady of Lyons*.

His London debut was made at the Princess' Theater in John Oxenford's *Ivy Hall*, in September, 1859, but when he learned that he had only a few lines and saw no prospect of advancement, he relinquished his engagement. In March, 1860, he went to the Queen's Theater, Dublin, where he was hissed for three weeks by the partisans of an actor whom he had innocently replaced. He returned to Edinburgh, and he played too at the Theater Royal, Manchester, where he had some success as Mr. Dombey in John Brougham's dramatization of *Dombey and Son* and supported Edwin Booth in a special engagement. In 1864, Manchester saw his first Hamlet.

He was in London again, unimportantly, at the St. James's, as Dorincourt in *The Belle's Stratagem* in 1866, followed, more importantly, by Boucicault's *Hunted Down* and other plays. In 1867 he visited Paris with E. A. Sothern and acted in *Our American Cousin* at the Théâtre des Italiens. He first acted with his great partner-to-be, Ellen Terry, at the Queen's Theater, London, as Petruchio, in Garrick's bastard version of *The Taming of the Shrew*, on December 26, 1867; apparently neither player was very greatly impressed with the other. In the summer of 1869 he was at Drury Lane in another Boucicault opus, *Formosa, or The Railroad to Ruin*, and in December he appeared at the Gaiety as Mr. Chevenix in *Uncle Dick's Darling*, by H. J. Byron, which ran until the following April and convinced Dickens that Irving was the coming leader of the English stage. But the first characterization which really took the town captive was that of Digby Grant, "a fidgety, selfish being, self-deluded by social hypocrisy, querulous, scheming and wheedling," in James Albery's play, *Two Roses*, at the Vaudeville, June 4, 1870. At his benefit on the 291st night, Irving proved that he had tragic as well as comic power by adding to the bill an impressive recitation of Thomas Hood's poem, "The Dream of Eugene Aram," which not only looked forward to the play on the same theme by W. G. Wills in which he was later to appear, but also attracted to him the attention of H. L. Bateman.

This entrepreneur's primary interest was not in Irving but in his own daughter Isabel, whom he hoped to make a star, like her sister Kate before her, and to this end he had taken a lease of the somewhat decrepit Lyceum Theater in London. But he needed a leading man, and he thought he saw what he wanted in Irving.

They opened on September 11, 1871, in *Fanchette*, based on a story by George Sand, which was not a success. Since Maggie Mitchell in America was making a lifetime career out of *Fanchon the Cricket*, as it was called over here, it would seem to have been the actress that was wrong rather than the play. Irving's role gave no opportunity for the exercise of his particular gifts. Albery's *Pickwick*, in which he played Jingle, would seem to have done so, but the public was still not greatly interested, and the whole enterprise was in danger of foundering when Bateman, in near-despair, agreed to permit Irving to appear as Mathias in *The Bells*, which was the Erckmann-Chatrian thriller, *Le Juif Polonais*, about a desperate Alsatian innkeeper who murders a traveler for his money and becomes a burgomaster and the first man in his village, only to be hounded to death by his own conscience. It was put on, Saturday evening, November 25, 1871, before a half-filled house, and from that moment Henry Irving was England's leading actor. According to his grandson Laurence Irving, Mathias was his 630th role!

From spine-tingling, macabre tragic melodrama, Irving turned to an almost preternatural, fey, silver-toned majesty in W. G. Wills's play glorifying Charles I, which was followed by another conscience-wracked murderer in *Eugene Aram*. Then (September 27, 1873) he challenged comparison with Macready as Richelieu, and though the reviews were divided, the play ran 120 nights. A year later he was ready for the supreme challenge with his revolutionary Hamlet, which he acted on October 31, 1874, and for 200 nights thereafter. (Bateman died on March 21, 1875, and Mrs. Bateman assumed management of the theater.) *Macbeth* (September 25, 1875) and *Othello* (February 14, 1876) were less successful, running 80 and 49 nights respectively. In April, 1876, he enacted Philip II in Tennyson's *Queen Mary*, and Whistler painted him in the character. *Richard III* (January 29, 1877) gave him a chance to blend Shakespeare with "character" acting, and in May his dual role in *The Lyons Mail* (the fiendish

Dubosc and the noble Lesurques, who nearly goes to the guillo-
tine for the other's crime, as in real life he actually did) was one
of the great "thrillers" of his life. His Louis XI, in the Casimir
Delavigne theatrical contrivance (March 9, 1878), was another
triumph, but his Flying Dutchman in the *Vanderdecken* of Wills
and Percy Fitzgerald (June 8, 1878) was not, though even Bernard Shaw thought him very fine in it. In the summer of 1878,
Mrs. Bateman relinquished management and Irving took over,
reopening the theater on December 30 with a revival of *Hamlet*,
with Ellen Terry replacing Isabel Bateman as his leading lady.

The first great new production in which Irving and Terry appeared together was *The Merchant of Venice* (November 1,
1879), which ran for seven months. On September 18, 1880, he
returned to melodrama with the Boucicault version of *The
Corsican Brothers*, which had been played by both Fechter and
Charles Kean, and which held the boards until the end of the
year. Tennyson's one-act play, *The Cup*, was acted in January,
1881, and in May, Edwin Booth came to the Lyceum as guest
star, alternating with Irving as Othello and Iago. Both actors
were much more admired for the villain in this play than for
the hero.

The year 1882 saw two of Irving's greatest Lyceum productions—*Romeo and Juliet* on March 8, in which neither of the
stars was greatly admired (*Punch* asked Irving, "Wherefore art
thou Romeo?"), and *Much Ado About Nothing* on October 11,
in which both were, Ellen Terry finding in Beatrice what may
well have been her very greatest role. The play ran until June 1,
1883. In October the Lyceum Company sailed for their first
American tour,[1] and when they came home on May 31, 1884,
they opened again in *Much Ado*. The only new production between the first tour and the second, in the fall of 1884, was

---

[1] Irving made eight tours in America; the first opened at the Star Theater,
New York, October 29, 1883, with *The Bells*, and the last closed at the Harlem
Opera House, with *Louis XI*, on March 25, 1904. The total time spent here was
209 weeks, or four years of Irving's life. The receipts were $3,441,321.94, the
profits $579,201.04.

Twelfth Night (July 8), a failure so inexplicably disastrous that
Irving was rudely received when he appeared before the curtain
on the first night and so far lost his aplomb as to wonder audibly
how a company of "earnest comedians—sober, clean and word-
perfect," could have been so rebuffed. (His grandson suggests
plausibly that it may have been the failure of his Malvolio, which
caused him to put the idea of playing Falstaff out of his mind.)
In May, 1885, Irving appeared in his most benevolent aspect as
Dr. Primrose in *Olivia*, Wills's dramatization of *The Vicar of
Wakefield*, which had already been acted by Herman Vezin, and
in December, 1885, he found the most "successful" production
of his life in the same author's somewhat workaday version of
Goethe's *Faust*, a showy and "consummate confection of villainy
and piety, of beauty and fearsome hideousness, of claptrap and
culture,"[2] which achieved 375 performances on its initial run
and earned enormous sums of money both in England and
in America.

During the last years at the Lyceum there were several great
Shakespearean revivals. At the end of 1888, Irving stubbornly
returned to his rejected Macbeth, with Ellen Terry in the magnificent "green beetle" gown immortalized by Sargent, and this
time the production ran 150 nights. His Cardinal Wolsey, in
that supreme invitation to pageantry, *Henry VIII* (January 5,
1892), perhaps the most lavish of all his productions, was considered one of his great successes, but he was less successful in
King Lear, largely because he seems to have been inaudible on
the opening night (November 10, 1892). *Cymbeline* (September 22, 1896), in which he played Iachimo, was less a play for him
than for Ellen Terry, and his last new Shakespearean role was
Coriolanus (April 15, 1901), in a play which neither he nor anybody else has ever been able to make really popular.

Meanwhile, among much else, he had achieved a new production of the Watts Philips melodrama, *The Dead Heart*, with its
startling resemblance to *A Tale of Two Cities*; had produced a

2 Laurence Irving, *Henry Irving, the Actor and His World.*

lavish *King Arthur*, by J. Comyns Carr (January 12, 1895), with Burne-Jones-like settings and music by Sir Arthur Sullivan; and had won a minor triumph in Conan Doyle's one-act play, *A Story of Waterloo*, and a major one in Tennyson's *Becket* (February 6, 1893), which last gave him what must have been, in a sense, the crowning role of his life. He had also won countless honors for himself and for the acting profession in the form of honorary degrees (that from Trinity College, Dublin, was the first ever awarded to an actor); lectures at Cambridge, Harvard, and elsewhere; and (to crown all) the knighthood which, in 1895, removed the old stigma of "rogues and vagabonds" from the acting profession forever.

But he was also to suffer great misfortunes. In 1899 he was forced to permit the Lyceum to become a syndicate, and in 1902 he lost it altogether, his last performance there being a matinee of *The Merchant of Venice* with Ellen Terry on July 19. This was partly because public taste was changing somewhat, partly because production was becoming much more expensive, and partly because of the accumulation of ills that came upon Irving, beginning with an injury to his knee on December 19, 1896, immediately after a successful revival of *Richard III*, which incapacitated him for more than two months, and cost him thousands of pounds, but which also seemed to signalize the beginning of a breakdown in his until now phenomenal health. In February, 1898, fire destroyed £30,000 worth of scenery in storage, thus making the revival of many productions impossible without what, at this stage, would have been a prohibitive fresh expenditure. In 1897 he had produced Sardou's *Madame Sans-Gêne*, with Ellen Terry in the role that had been created by Réjane. Now he turned to a Sardou in decline for the two monstrosities which became his last big productions—*Robespierre* (with more than sixty speaking roles), which was the first of the two productions achieved under the management of Lyceum, Ltd. (April 5, 1899), and *Dante*, at Drury Lane (April 30, 1903). Neither was popular on either side of the Atlantic. The role of

Dante favored Irving physically, like nothing else he had ever played, but Tennyson had been right when, upon Irving's asking him for a play about Dante, years before, he had replied that it would take a Dante to write it.

Irving's last performance was as Becket at Bradford, on October 13, 1905; on reaching his hotel after the performance, he collapsed in the inner hall and died before he could be taken into his room. His body lay in state at the residence of the Baroness Burdett-Coutts, and on October 20 his ashes were buried in the Abbey.

III

That Irving was, in his achievements, influence, and effects the most important English actor since Garrick is a fact, not a matter of opinion. He established the dignity and distinction of the English theater—and of the acting profession in England—more than any of his predecessors, and even Bernhardt and Stanislavsky were influenced by his productions. Yet I know of no other great actor concerning whom there has been so sharp a diversity of opinion. So high an authority as William Winter considered him not only the greatest actor he had ever seen but, so far as he could judge by his extensive study of theatrical history, the greatest actor who ever lived. On the other hand, Bernard Shaw, Henry James, William Archer, and John Ranken Towse must all be enrolled with his detractors, and even the admiring Percy Fitzgerald did not consider that he had ever "passed the line where art ends and genius begins."[3] During most of the years

[3] Shaw, as anybody will discover who takes the trouble to read his reviews of Lyceum productions in *Our Theatres in the Nineties*, being Volumes XXIII–XXV in "The Ayot St. Lawrence Edition The Collected Works of Bernard Shaw" (Wm. H. Wise & Company, 1931), though he excoriated Irving as a butcher of Shakespeare, was much less of an extremist (here, as in other matters) than he is generally considered to have been. Shaw was out to destroy the romantic actor's theater of the nineteenth century with a new playwright's theater, exemplified by Ibsen and himself. Yet he was himself deeply indebted to the nineteenth-century tradition, in fiction and drama alike, and much of his best work derives directly from it; see Julian B. Kaye, *Bernard Shaw and the Nineteenth-Century Tradition* (University of Oklahoma Press, 1955), and Martin Meisel, *Shaw and the Nine-*

of his fame, English society swarmed with persons who not only did not care for him but actively disliked and in some cases almost hated him.

His voice and his walk were the favorite targets. Once, on the train in America, Ellen Terry, observing him in a brown study, offered him a penny for his thoughts. "I was thinking," he replied, "how strange it is that I should have made the reputation I have as an actor, with nothing to help me—with no equipment. My legs, my voice—everything has been against me. For an actor who can't walk, can't talk, and has no face to speak of, I've done pretty well."

"No face to speak of" is not fair; if Irving was not handsome, he certainly was interesting, and he had a face which riveted the attention of everybody he met. "Speaking for myself," wrote Henry A. Clapp, "I should say that Irving's face is without exception the most fascinating I have seen upon the stage." "I have never seen a face change so much," says Menpes: "not for more than a moment did it retain the same expression." It was so far from being a common type of English face that more than one writer has wondered whether he might not have acquired a dash of Spanish blood from some survivor of the Armada. Fitzgerald gives Irving credit for having "made" his face as he made his career. "He wore his features down and refined them: and so his face acquired a spiritual look"—and if one looks at some of the pictures taken of him in his youth, when he wore a droopy

teenth-Century Theater (Princeton University Press, 1963). Shaw gives Irving credit for a "beautiful" and "interesting" face, and (against the usual opinion of his detractors), a "finely cultivated voice and diction." His "best technical work" had "finish, dignity, and grace"; he knew "exactly how far to go" in the matter of *décor;* he made the Lyceum "almost our only refuge" from the "hideous vulgarity of stage speech in general." Shaw admitted that he himself wept copiously over *Olivia,* and he sometimes praised characterizations which others condemned: thus Irving's Macbeth was "fine and genuine," his Vanderdecken "a masterpiece." Shakespeare left Iachimo "a mere *diabolus ex machinâ,*" but Irving offered "a new and independent creation." James, in *The Scenic Art* (Rutgers University Press, 1948), though less appreciative, grants that "it must be said of Mr. Irving that his aberrations are not of a vulgar quality, and that one likes him, somehow, in spite of them." Towse, though finding "no trace" of genius, still called Irving "the most learned and enlightened manager of modern times."

moustache, one sees the force of this, for he looks like a grocer's clerk. Certainly he knew his strong points and his weak ones, and understood just how to stress the first and obscure the second. Mrs. Aria says he had his sleeves made unusually narrow from elbow to wrist to draw attention to the hands whose extraordinary beauty and expressiveness were recognized by everybody. And Martin-Harvey adds that when he had his doctor's robe made, "he insisted, to the horror of the robe-maker, that his gown should be cut long enough to trail upon the ground in defiance of the accepted and customary length," thus adding to his height and making himself inevitably the most conspicuous figure in the procession.

But the voice and the carriage always created problems. William Archer speaks of

the depression of the head and protrusion of the shoulders which accompany any rapid motion, like a survival from the low stage of development exemplified by many savage races, in which butting with the skull is an habitual practice. It seems as though locomotion with Mr. Irving were not a result of volition, but of an involuntary spasm.

And even Edward Russell, one of his greatest admirers, says that in moments of excitement, he "rapidly plods across and across the stage with a gait peculiar to him—a walk somewhat resembling that of a fretful man trying to get very quickly over a plowed field." These mannerisms were not constant, he did not carry them into private life, and they decreased considerably as he grew older, but he does not seem to have had much control over them. When he addressed the Lotos Club, in advance of his first appearance in New York, he slyly told them: "I dare say that you will find many of us very strange and very odd, with peculiarities of speech and with peculiarities of manner and gesture; but it would, perhaps, not be so pleasurable if we were all just alike."

As a speaker he was accused of every sin in the linguistic

decalogue. He mispronounced ("Gud" for "God"; "cut-thrut dug" for "cut-throat dog"; "take the rup from mey nek" for "take the rope from my neck"); he destroyed the rhythm of blank verse; he misplaced emphasis on words and syllables so that he seemed to be inventing a new system of English prosody, based on quantity; he produced ugly sounds; he dragged his words and became slower and slower as tension mounted; and he so lost power in sustained declamation that sometimes only incoherent, frenetic excitement remained. When he addressed his audience on the first night of *King Lear*, a heckler cried, "Why didn't you speak like that before?" and when the amazed actor turned for explanation to Ellen Terry, she told him she had not understood a single word all evening. Arthur Warren, who finally wrote a passionately admiring essay on Irving,[4] admitted that when he first heard him, he could not tell whether he was speaking Yorkshire dialect or Choctaw. Henry Austin Clapp sums up his deficiencies in this aspect as well as anybody: "an alternate swallowing and double-edging of consonants, a frequent lapse into an impure nasal quality, an exclusion of nearly all chest tones, the misdelivery of the vowels by improper prolongation or equally improper abbreviation, an astonishing habit of confusing different vowel sounds. . . ."

The most thoroughgoing defense of Irving in this aspect comes from those queerly-assorted companions, Gordon Craig and Bernard Shaw, according to whom it was Irving who spoke correctly while everybody else was wrong![5] But I am more impressed by such testimony as that of Eden Phillpotts, who admitted that he had heard other actors who spoke much better than Irving, but insisted that they were only "singing birds" compared to "the

[4] In his *London Days* (Little, Brown, 1920).

[5] Craig speaks for both when he says that "this is the old English speech, and Irving brought back to us something of the ripe old sounds, and damme if we didn't object." Craig also defends Irving's movements: "He danced, he did not merely walk—he sang, he by no means merely spoke." For another enthusiastic defense of Irving's elocution, with detailed descriptions which are not really very enlightening, see Edwin Drew, *Henry Irving On and Off the Stage* (Henry Drane, n.d.).

bodeful and pregnant ring of intellect in Irving's stacatto, raven croak," that of Max Beerbohm, who speaks of "a strange, suggestive voice that admirably attuned itself to the subtleties of Irving's conception of whatever part he was playing," and that of the hosts of auditors, known and unknown, who testified that his reading of particular lines thrilled them as he spoke and remained in their memories across a lifetime.

That was the way Irving himself thought great actors functioned: they were remembered for single moments, startling touches of illumination in their performances, and though his "views" about drama do not in general seem very important, this conviction is interesting as obviously having been derived from or determining his own performance. He was never rigid about method or, indeed, very much interested in it; what he *was* passionately concerned about was that the dignity and greatness of the theater, which embraced all noble arts, should be recognized and acknowledged everywhere, and in later life, he was very proud of what he had achieved toward this end. "The maxim is well worn that 'Art is long and life is short,' and there is no art, believe me, which is longer than the actor's, and there is no life which can adequately fill up the measure of its requirements." He admitted that there were "reasons based in the tendencies of art-life" for prejudice against the theater, but he always insisted that "though in reaction the stage may have aggravated the vices of society, it has always been society that has first vitiated the stage." He did not believe it possible for an actor to turn himself into the character he was portraying; instead he tried to turn the character into himself as Garrick is said to have done, and he could not understand how an artist "with an individuality so marked as M. Coquelin's, should imagine that his identity can be entirely lost." He believed the mimetic faculty more important in comedy than in tragedy. He believed in taking advantage of the inspiration of the moment but he never thought it safe to rely upon it. He knew that acting must seem natural but not be natural (he admitted that, even in the moot matter of pronuncia-

166

tion, he sacrificed dictionary correctness to dramatic effect), and he did not think it mattered very much whether or not the actor felt the emotions he expressed, so long as he was able to cause the spectator to feel them.

If it be asked how, with all the faults he so obviously possessed, Irving was able so to enthrall the imagination as he did, the answer must be that, for those who were capable of responding to it, his personality exercised almost a mesmeric effect. "Like Beethoven, Paganini, and Liszt," writes George Sampson, "he belonged to the dæmonic race of men who seem to have a personal aura and bring with them an atmosphere that is not quite that of this world." The hierophantic note that he struck seems to have extended itself to the theater itself, and people did not go to the Lyceum as they did to other theaters; it was almost as if they were assisting at some religious rite. Sampson feels that the only stage artist of recent times to whom he can be compared was Chaliapin. The two personalities were altogether different, but both projected greatness.

Mention has been made of Irving's ability to thrill an audience with a single line. He could do the same thing with a look. Benson says that when he came out of the Bastille after his imprisonment in *The Dead Heart*,

> alive and free, he held his audience spellbound, silent, breathless—without a word, with hardly a movement or a gesture, compelling and saw, for the first time in many years, the light of day, felt the warmth of the sun, and slowly realized what it meant to be a man solely by the power of concentrated thought.

One night, when, after Iachimo's emergence from the chest in Imogen's chamber, one of Irving's auditors made a ribald remark, he saved the scene and stopped dead in their tracks an audience on the verge of tittering by raking them with his eyes, and this quite without stepping out of character. In *Romeo and Juliet* he brought Rosaline into the ballroom scene, and Ellen Terry never forgot the look on his face when, pursuing his old love, he suddenly saw Juliet for the first time. In the apothecary scene his face grew whiter and whiter as he listened to Balthsar telling of Juliet's death. But when he played the lascivious Synorix to Ellen Terry's Camma in *The Cup*, she "flamed with outraged modesty," and one night came close to striking him: "he licked his lips at me—as if I were a bone and he a beast." And Violet Vanbrugh always remembered seeing him enter in *The Corsican Brothers*, "a tall picturesque, vital man coming through vineyards to meet his friend who has unexpectedly arrived in Corsica." It was not until many years later that she learned there had been no vineyards on the stage. He entered an ordinary room through an ordinary door. "He only said . . . that he had come down from the hills through vineyards," and that was enough to create them in her mind for a lifetime.

In his time, Irving was a "new" actor; when they appeared together, he was considered much more "modern" in his technique than Booth. But actually he tried to combine the new with the old; the kind of naturalistic acting that the Bancrofts represented he had no use for. Close observers found in him traces of Samuel Phelps and of the three Charleses—Kean, Mathews, and Fechter. He was deficient in the kind of power possessed by Edmund Kean and Forrest, and though he awakened deafening enthusiasm at times, even Gordon Craig admits that he was never agitated or rushed. "I suppose he was the coolest actor possessing *le diable au corps* that ever came upon this earth." Winter called him a "flute," not a "trumpet," and said that he worked "with a thousand subtle touches, with many a sudden jet of light." For those who did not feel his power he was only a stippler; others found the infinite, tireless accumulation of detail bursting suddenly into illumination. One contemporary observer writes:

In *The Bells*, when Mathias unties the money-bag to count out Annette's dowry, he mechanically puts the string round his neck not to lose it, and then snatches it off again with a shiver; and again, in the scene with Christian, note the apparently mechanical action of carefully putting a coal into the stove, of which he opens the door just as the *gendarme* puts forward the hypothesis that the body of the murdered Jew must have been cast into a lime-kiln and burnt.

Irving himself said of his Iago:

> To me he has also a slight dash of the bull-fighter, and during the brawl between Cassio and Montano, I used to enjoy a mischievous sense of mastery by flicking at them with a red cloak, as though they were bulls in the arena.

In one tense scene he manifested his complete heartlessness and amorality by eating grapes and spitting out the seeds.

Irving's taste—and gift—for melodrama has never been denied. Even as a schoolboy he had to be restrained from reciting a piece called "The Uncle," in which "the uncle tells his little nephew of his unrequited passion for his mother; confesses that, maddened by jealousy, he murdered his own brother, the boy's father; and, turning to an old chest, shows the child the bones of his victim."[6] This was probably the beginning of the last act of *The Bells*, as he presented it. Winter is undoubtedly correct when he writes that "in that field which may be called weird, picturesque, romantic, in the slow vivisection of piteous human misery, his figure stands apart from all others—lonely and alone." Sometimes he was naturalistic, as in the horrible, prolonged death agonies of Louis XI, and sometimes he had a fey quality; as Henry Arthur Jones says, he was always fine in passages which could be spoken "with a second-sight of spiritual intimacy, earth far withdrawn, and as by one standing on the confines of the unseen world, encompassed behind and before with superhuman promptings and solicitings." In *The Lyons Mail* he usually hummed the "Marseillaise" while rifling the body of the guard he had killed, but one night he plumbed new depths of degradation by substituting "Nearer, My God, to Thee."

Of course his unearthliness was not always associated with evil. If the demon lay within his range, so did the saint, and this

[6] Charles Hiatt, *Henry Irving: A Record and Review.*

whether the term be taken literally, as with Becket, or extended
to cover such gently good men as Dr. Primrose or those who can
face tragedy with the nobility of spirit shown by his Charles I.
In between these extremes his competency varied. Clement
Scott thought him a convincing lover only in Hamlet's scene with
Ophelia and in Act II of Hamilton Aidé's *Philip*. Max Beerbohm
said that his suicide as Romeo "could only be regarded as a
merciful release." He lacked the robustness required for Othello
and Coriolanus. Matthew Arnold called his Othello "that gibber-
ing performance," and even Ellen Terry writes that "he screamed
and ranted and raved—lost his voice, was slow where he should
have been swift, incoherent where he should have been strong."
His Macbeth was much criticized also, but if we grant him his
basic conception of the character as "LIAR, TRAITOR, COWARD,"
it may deserve a higher place than has commonly been assigned
to it. He is not generally accounted the best of Lears, though he
himself regarded it as his greatest characterization, but every-
one admits that in the reunion scene his pathos was incompar-
able: " 'Forget and forgive' was said in the sweetest accents of
wistful beseeching insinuation, as by a child who had quarrelled
with his nurse, and naïvely wished to be taken back, without any
questions being asked."[7]

Was Irving, then, a great Shakespearean actor? The answer
seems to depend upon whether or not the role in question fell
within his temperamental range. He was a many-sided man, and
his range was wide, but there were types he could not embrace.
Here and elsewhere he sometimes glorified his materials; thus
all the vulgarity dropped out of his Wolsey, and, as one observer
puts it, "you only thought of a crowd of jackals yapping round a
dying lion." He may very well have glorified Benedick also. But
the prime example was his Shylock, which he himself believed
the greatest ever created, and which thrilled the whole Jewish
community. Irving was not so foolish as to try to make Shylock
an amiable figure. But he did emphasize his patriarchal dignity,

[7] Henry Arthur Jones, *The Shadow of Henry Irving.*

conceived his villainy as the inevitable result of heartless Christian persecution, and importantly influenced not only the stage but the critics through two generations.[8] When all is said and done, however, it remains true that Irving often seemed greatest in the tawdriest plays, where the dramatist had given him the least to work with. This may have been partly, as his enemies insisted, because he did not understand great literature, but it is just as likely to have been due to the fact that such plays set him freer to create on his own, and this, of course, is what Shaw, a guerilla fighter not unaccustomed to participating on both sides of the battle, meant by saying that, like Wagner, Irving should have written his own plays.[9]

Two more charges have been made against Irving—that he subordinated everybody and everything else in the theater to

[8] For a long account of Irving's views on Shylock, see Joseph Hatton, *Henry Irving's Impressions of America*, II, 252ff.

[9] This being the case, it is a little difficult to understand why Shaw wished to woo Irving away from the romantic drama and persuade him to appear in his own plays, for he was the last dramatist to encourage an actor to create independently. Shaw believed that Irving was neglecting to encourage the development of contemporary English drama at the Lyceum; the most brilliant defense of him against this charge is George Sampson's in his *Seven Essays*, 188ff., where there is also a devastating examination of Shaw's charge that Irving kept Ellen Terry away from the roles she ought to have had. The truth is that Irving produced the best new plays he could get and spent a good deal of money on plays that never materialized. It is true that few of the playwrights he encouraged were "forward-looking"; Barrie and Pinero (an actor at the Lyceum) were about the only ones. But Irving did not like or approve of the Ibsen-drama or the "problem-play." "I don't believe that the public wants disgusting things. Anyhow it won't get 'em from me." Opinions may differ as to the wholesomeness of some of the sensationalism which held the board at the Lyceum, but Irving *did* think of the drama as a great ethical force. His Mathias was a very moral exhibition compared to Coquelin's. Irving presented a study in remorse and the tortures of conscience. Coquelin gave a more accurate, but less moving, as well as less melodramatic, study of a criminal type, who never repented at all. Irving, who owned the magazine, *The Theatre*, so as to have a voice of his own in theatrical journalism, was never indifferent to criticism, nor did he pretend to be. He thought John Ranken Towse ought to have been called "Lowse," and he told his son he would have been happy to pay Shaw's funeral expenses. Once he hit Shaw directly in a letter: "You are absolutely wrong in your polite insinuation of the cat out of the bag—as I had not the privilege of reading your criticism—as you call it—of Richard. I never read a criticism of yours in my life. I have read lots of your droll, amusing, irrelevant and sometimes impertinent pages, but criticism containing judgment and sympathy I have never seen by your pen."

himself and that he smothered Shakespeare in extravagant *décor.*

On the first point, a divided verdict must be entered; on the second, Irving can confidently be pronounced not guilty. He was not like the old-fashioned "star" who concerned himself only with his own role and let the rest of the production go to pot. Instead he conceived the play as an entity, seeing everything in relation to everything else. In that sense he was "modern." When the Saxe-Meiningen troupe came to England, he studied their methods of crowd management with care and applied them to his own work in *Romeo and Juliet.* He employed good actors in his regular company and brought in others as guests from time to time, and the *décor* and the music represented the best talent available. He was the soul of courtesy to Edwin Booth, when the two played together, himself omitting the epilepsy scene because Booth did not use it. Augustin Daly even speaks of an American who was disappointed on his visit to the Lyceum "because he had expected to find everything subordinated to Mr. Irving, and found that Mr. Irving was simply a personage in a great play, who had no manner of deference paid to him by the rest of the company, beyond what was due to the character he represented."

On the other hand, Irving was never, in the modern sense, a "producer." He was an "actor-manager," and he built his productions around himself. When he put on *Iolanthe,* W. G. Wills's new version of *King René's Daughter,* late in the initial run of *The Merchant of Venice,* he omitted the *Merchant's* last act to make time for it; it is impossible to conceive of his doing this if Shylock had not finished in Act IV. The spotlight was fixed on him, not others, and if even Ellen Terry prepared a costume which he thought drew attention away from what he wished to wear, out it went. He could be quite frank about these things. All Ellen Terry's admirers were indignant that he never gave her a chance to appear as Rosalind, but when the Bancrofts urged him to produce *As You Like It,* enumerating the various roles and casting them for him, he impatiently inquired, "Good—very good—but where do I come in?" He once criticized Comyns Carr severely because he had reviewed *Iolanthe* favorably but said nothing about Irving, and he astonished Walter Pollock by telling him that he could never see *Faust* as he would like to see it: "I want to see the Red Man there—and, of course, I never shall." When Robert Hichens and H. D. Traill wrote that ill-fated play, *The Medicine Man*, for him, they were astonished at his indifference to Ellen Terry's role, though he would probably have been much more concerned about her during earlier years. Their professional break may have been made inevitable by her growing too old to take the parts she had always played, but Irving does not seem to have treated her with much consideration or to have expressed any real regret. On the other hand, it must be admitted that he had produced a number of plays which afforded her better opportunities than they gave him, and also that he was the big "draw" at the Lyceum, as was shown by her failure to attract the crowds alone when he was incapacitated. Probably no other actress of equal stature has ever so subordinated herself as Ellen Terry did to Irving, yet I am afraid we cannot be sure that she would have had a more important career without him than she had with him.[10]

The pictorial element was important in Irving's theatrical vision from the beginning; he himself thought his ambition was first awakened "on that glorious morning when I saw Van Ambrugh, the famous lion-tamer, drive . . . twenty-four horses down Park Street. . . ." But I can find little to indicate that Henry James was just when he said of Irving's *Romeo and Juliet* that "the play is not acted, it is costumed." Personally I should be glad to take one of Irving's settings in exchange for all the ugly "unit sets," priapic pillars, and silly flights of stairs that modern designers can command put together.[11] His only serious fault in stagecraft

---

[10] Her own feeling on the matter was amusingly and clearly expressed: "Yes, yes—were I to be run over by a steamroller tomorrow, Henry would be deeply grieved; would say quietly, 'What a pity!'—and would add, after two moment's reflection: 'Who is there—er—to go on for her tonight?' "

[11] The many reproductions of Irving's sets given in Laurence Irving's book and elsewhere sufficiently attest Irving's good taste.

seems to have been that when he was in one of his Gothic melo-dramatic moods, he always tended toward too dark a stage. He was extremely cunning: because he was too tall for Napoleon, he had the settings in *Madame Sans-Gêne* built oversize and surrounded himself with enormous men. But there was always the touch to fire the imagination: when Iachimo's chest was carried into Imogen's chamber, he was careful to have a piece of red cloth hanging out of it, "like the introduction of the second theme of a symphony," as one writer says, and when the chest was opened, this was seen to be a part of Iachimo's mantle. It should also be made clear that he was never seduced by antiquarianism for its own sake. It was not enough that a thing should be right; it must look right. And if the wrong thing looked right, and the right thing looked wrong, then it was the wrong thing that he must have.

IV

We are now ready to look at Irving as he was off the stage. It should be understood at the outset that the man had armies of friends who adored him. When he died, Mounet Sully declared that "his nobility of character shone in everything he did, both on the stage and off it," and Coquelin adds: "The man was kindliness incarnate."

So far as money was concerned, the truth of this has never been doubted. "Do you think," he once asked Joseph Hatton, "do you think a fellow ever quite gets over the effects of being starved in his youth?" The answer must surely be no, but, as we all know, the effect on many men is to make them hoard their money, as if they could never be quite sure they might not be hungry again. With Irving it took the form of a passionate endeavor to prevent others from suffering what he had suffered. He needed little for himself, lived simply in chambers, long refused even to keep a brougham. Even after *The Bells* he was getting only £15 a week, and of this £8 went to his estranged wife. Later he declared of himself, "I have lived keeping an army, and I shall die a pauper."

Both statements were true. Mrs. Aria says that when she knew him he was giving away about £50 a week. He was a regular contributor to the Salvation Army; he is even supposed to have helped Whitman after visiting him in 1884. "If he were served at an hotel with a luncheon that pleased him," writes Graham Robertson, "he sent the cook a five-pound note, the waiter's tips were golden; it was magnificent—or ridiculous—as you pleased." Ellen Terry thought it ridiculous; she even tried to convince him that it was vulgar, but though he was impressed for the moment, he did not change his ways. No man ever understood himself better than he did when he said that he had not been sent into the world to collect money.

But charity in the ordinary sense was only the beginning. When endowed theaters were discussed, Irving pointed out that London had an endowed theater—the Lyceum—and that he had endowed it. He was a generous paymaster and an extravagant producer. Nobody was so ready to play benefits. His benefit for Westland Marston took the form of a fresh production of Byron's *Werner*, acted once only. Moreover, he took Marston on permanently, seeing that he wanted nothing for the rest of his life. He was also an extravagant host, as when the theater would be turned into a fairyland for the great parties he gave to celebrate special occasions; the great supper after the one hundredth night of *The Merchant of Venice* cost £600. He could be quixotic also; Martin-Harvey says he refused to accept his share of the proceeds when the Lyceum was sold for a music hall. "The man who hasn't the courage of his convictions is not worth a damn."

When he engaged Jessie Millward away from Geneviève Ward, he asked her what Miss Ward was paying her, and when she replied five pounds a week he said he wouldn't dream of giving her that, and her heart sank, but what he meant was that she would get twelve pounds the first year and sixteen the second, with all dresses and accoutrements "found." Another actor who asked six pounds was asked whether he was married, had children, and could live on six pounds, and after he had

175

answered all these questions in the affirmative, Irving replied that since he couldn't, he would give him ten. He was terribly overstaffed because whenever he found anybody who needed a way of earning a living, he managed to make a place for him, and there is the delightful story about how he once asked to have a place made for an old woman only to be told by his business manager that there was absolutely nothing open that she could do. When he suggested that she might look after the theater cats, he was sternly reminded that he was already paying three old women to look after the cats. This stopped him for a moment but only for a moment, for he soon decided that she might look after the old women who looked after the cats.[12] He himself loved all animals, and everybody who knows anything at all about him has heard of his grief after his fox terrier Fussie, whom others regarded as having been stuffed and pampered out of all reason, was killed by falling through a trap door on the stage. He refused to sign a Pasteur testimonial because, though admiring him and recognizing the importance of his work, he could not bring himself to seem to be approving vivisection.

Nor was Irving's kindness confined altogether to material benefits. When Frank Leslie gave what Irving considered a disrespectful burlesque of him in women's clothes, he wrote a peremptory letter ordering him to stop, but when he learned that Leslie was ambitious to play a legitimate role, he coached him in it. In Cincinnati, in 1900, at her mother's request, he coached an American girl who was a perfect stranger to him in the character of Malvolio for a college production. A poor woman threw a trinket to him from the gallery of the Lyceum, and he wore it thereafter on his watch chain. When the actor William Terris, who had often played at the Lyceum, was stabbed to

[12] Martin Harvey gives an amusing picture of Irving salving the pride of one of his superannuated hangers-on, who was receiving a good salary but was now incapable of really doing anything on the stage: "Now, my boy, what I want you to do is *very* important, humph! very important. This is a critical moment in the play. You come on—come *right* on; you see what is happening; you say (to yourself, of course) 'My God!' you see? *My God!* And then—ah—you go slowly off . . . *most important.*"

death by a madman at the Adelphi stage door, he breathed out his life in the arms of a woman who was not his wife. Irving carried the Queen's greetings to the widow, and on the same day he performed a gallant action which nobody else would have dared, when he escorted the broken-hearted mistress to the funeral!

Yet in spite of all his kindnesses, Irving was a formidable man. "He was always courteous and gracious," says Max Beerbohm, "and everybody was fascinated by him; but I think there were few who did not also fear him," and he speaks of "an air of sardonic reserve behind his cordiality."

> With strangers and distant acquaintances [writes Henry Arthur Jones], he was courteous, condescending, superior, reticent; sometimes sardonic and taciturn, with a spice of more or less veiled malice if the occasion and the person seemed to demand it. But, as Ellen Terry has said, he could be "raffish" and companionable enough at his own private suppers and in a club.

Horace Vachell speaks of "the subacid edge to his tongue," and Mrs. Aria says he seldom addressed anyone by first name or used half a dozen words where three or four would do. According to J. Comyns Carr, his voice often broke and his eyes filled with tears when he spoke of something that moved him, but we have endless testimony that he praised, if at all, sparingly and briefly. Mrs. Aria, again, says that when she told him that his son Laurence did not believe he loved him, he asked, "Does he want me to kiss him?" and even Jessie Millward, who adored him, and thought that there never was a "kindlier, gentler, more generous, or more courtly spirit," was quite effectively put in her place when she came to rehearsal one day in a very pretty dress because she expected to go from there to a luncheon party. "Go at once, my dear," said Irving; "go at once. Don't let the rehearsal detain you. But—tomorrow—come in your working clothes—with your mind full of work." Neither food nor rest mattered to him when he was rehearsing, nor did he permit them to matter to the members of his company, and there are countless stories about the cruel things he said to people—sometimes deservedly and sometimes not—as when Richard Harding Davis came to the Garrick Club with some decorations on his dress coat, and Irving went up and fingered them and innocently inquired, "Ah—swimming?" Henry Arthur Jones speaks again of his "sly impishness" and "latent mockery" and "grim diablerie," and it is not possible to believe that he was not fully aware of these qualities, that he was not performing offstage quite as effectively as on, or that he did not himself thoroughly enjoy his performance. In his early days, he carried the theater into life with broad practical jokes; later he gave this up, but the spirit behind it never changed.

The "raffishness" that Ellen Terry speaks of is undeniable also. Irving was a bohemian by nature; he liked to sit up all night, and it never occurred to him that there were people who did not— and could not—do this, or who could possibly object to being called upon in the middle of the night if he should choose to come at that time. (Here, and here alone, I think, one must feel that his dreadful wife had a legitimate ground for complaint.) He seems to have talked very freely in congenial company, "in a deep, even voice," says Menpes, "slowly, deliberately enunciating each word well, though sometimes mumbling in a dreamy manner, and even repeating sentences." "Sometimes he became so enthusiastic that he walked about the room illustrating attitudes and other tricks of manner." But this is, again, the actor— is it not?—and this, too, is the man whose idea of conversation is pretty much a monologue.[13]

He set his own standards in everything; though he lived until 1905 he never entered a motor car nor talked over the telephone. He ordered what he wanted whenever and wherever he chose and tolerated no failure of service. I think one gathers too that generous as his hospitality was, it could also be tyrannical, as when he expressed his disapproval of what, by his standards, was

[13] W. H. Pollock, *Impressions of Henry Irving*, 133–34, tells how Irving once, at a social gathering, skillfully shifted the focus of attention from Buffalo Bill to himself.

an early departure with "I regret, sir, that you are fatigued by our company." Martin-Harvey admits that there was a barrier between him and the members of his company in the theater, and I think the same existed on the larger stage of the world. When he entertained, he was the gracious and performing host; when he was entertained, he was the visiting lion. Either way the focus of attention was upon him, and I am sure the Bancrofts are just when they say that though many people thought they were intimate with Irving, most of these were mistaken.[14]

If Irving was, to any degree, crippled as a social or emotional being, there was certainly plenty to account for it. He lost the girl he loved in his youth, Nellie Moore, first through estrangement (apparently commingled with some degree of betrayal in which another man was involved), and then through death. She died of scarlet fever in 1869; when he died, thirty-six years afterwards, they found her picture in his wallet, pasted back-to-back with one of himself at the time he had known her.[15] In 1869, too, Florence O'Callaghan made a play for him and caught him, but the marriage went bad from the beginning, and according to his grandson the final break came on the first night of *The Bells*, when the loving wife made her contribution to her husband's

[14] There has been much talk about Irving's ascetic or ecclesiastical look, his best equipment for playing a role like Becket. He had this, but it represented only one side of his personality. In many of his unposed pictures, he looks like a Methodist parson turned bohemian. Bastien-Lepage was the painter who caught this aspect best (see the frontispiece to Laurence Irving's book), but in his picture the parson disappears altogether. Irving disliked this portrait, though evidently not so much as the Sargent, which he destroyed. Since he liked the Millais, which presents him in more idealized, conventionalized aspect, this presumably comes closer to his conception of himself, or at least to his idea of what he *wished* to look like. Gordon Craig says that he once saw Irving intoxicated after eating a small steak and drinking nothing after a nine-hour rehearsal. "It was the only time in many years' experience of him that I ever saw him thus." This may well have been. Certainly Irving was not a drunkard. But many bottles were emptied during his all-night sessions nevertheless, and many more cigars smoked, and this may have played its part in the final breakdown.

[15] The most intimate glimpse of Irving's grief at the time of Nellie Moore's death is in Laura Hain Friswell's *In the Sixties and Seventies* (Herbert B. Turner & Company, 1906), Chapter XII. See also Laurence Irving, *Henry Irving*, where the pictures referred to are reproduced facing page 160.

long-delayed and dearly-bought triumph by considerately asking him if he planned to go on making a fool of himself all his
life, whereupon he stopped the brougham in which they were
returning home and left her to continue without him, while he
sought shelter with the Batemans. It is not necessary to "judge"
Mrs. Irving; we really do not know very much about her. But she
came of a military family, and it seems a pity she could not have
been a sergeant. She brought up her two sons (on the generous
provision which Irving always made for her and them) to hate
their father, and it took him many years to overcome this. On
first nights at the Lyceum she sat in her box like a skeleton at the
feast, and was never really happy unless she could think he had
done badly. After *Romeo and Juliet* she gaily recorded in her
diary before going to bed that it had been "a jolly failure—Irving
awfully funny." When Edwin Booth appeared as a guest star in
her husband's theater, she asked Booth to send her tickets, so
that her children might have the opportunity to see some decent
acting. She outlived her husband, and it is said that only Bernard
Shaw restrained her from protesting his burial in the Abbey.

The insane Victorian attitude toward divorce kept these people who never had achieved a marriage chained to each other
legally until death stepped between them, and England's greatest
actor spent his life alone in his old-curiosity-shop-like chambers
in Grafton Street. Seymour Hicks says that Irving "cared nothing
for the society of women, and spent his entire leisure, when not
alone, with the very few males who were his boon companions."
It may not have been quite so simple as that. He was not wholly
without feminine companionship. In the early Lyceum days,
Isabel Bateman, who had the temperament of a saint, and who
died, an Anglican nun, as recently as 1934, found it convenient to
fall madly in love with him, and though he did not return her
passion at all, a very difficult situation was created. It would not
have been reasonable to expect the actor who had virtually
become the Lyceum to continue forever in a subordinate position under the Batemans, especially since he could not help know-

ing that Isabel was not really a first-rate actress and that sooner or later she would have to be replaced. When the crisis arrived at last in 1878, the Batemans behaved with great generosity, but feelings had been wounded nevertheless, and the inevitable resultant estrangement from the family which had helped him weather his own domestic crisis, though it was nobody's fault, was very painful for all the persons involved in it.

Laurence Irving takes up the position that there never was a liaison between his grandfather and Ellen Terry (though he states that at one time Irving hoped to marry her), but Ellen herself seems to have told Marguerite Steen that there was, and that Irving was not faithful to her. One also gathers that she may finally have been replaced by Mrs. Aria, the witty, sympathetic, handsome and distinguished-looking Jewish lady, to whom and to whose family Irving was certainly very close during his last years, and who were very good to him.[16] But we do not know precisely what Irving's relations to Mrs. Aria were, nor is the matter of very great interest, for it is as clear here as with Ellen Terry herself that the physical relationship, if there was one, was not the important thing.

v

As for the other ties that hold men to life: Irving had no interest in politics except as they touched the theater and the arts. "I do not think artists should mix up in politics. Art is my vocation, and I confine myself to it." (He felt very strongly, for example, that there should be no tariff on works of art.) When he does touch

[16] See my portrait of Ellen Terry, in *Seven Daughters of the Theater* (University of Oklahoma Press, 1964), especially pages 109–10, where the matter is considered from her point of view. In fairness to Irving, however, it should be remembered that none of Ellen Terry's emotional entanglements lasted very long; she may well have been right when she said that she had never really loved any man except Shakespeare! Marguerite Steen's book is *A Pride of Terrys: Family Saga* (Longmans, 1962). Mrs. Aria published *My Sentimental Self* (Chapman & Hall, 1922), which in spite of its silly title and sillier frontispiece, is quite sensible in everything said about Irving. Robert Hichens thought Irving cared for Mrs. Aria and has recorded that the actor once asked him what he thought of her character!

questions of international import, he touches them generously, for the most part: when, in America, the Astor Place Riot was mentioned to him, and Forrest blamed for it, he replied that he thought Forrest had some reason to believe that Macready had behaved hostilely toward him. He was acting *King Arthur* in America when Cleveland sent his sabre-rattling message to Britain about Venezuela. "I thank you for your appreciation of this effort to illustrate our Old World legend," Irving told his audience, and then, after just the right pause, "your Old World legend," and brought down the house.

In the world of beauty, learning, and culture he had much more interest, but even here he approached everything through the stage door. Certainly he was modest enough about his attainments. "I have not had the advantage . . . of an University education," he told the Oxford students, when he spoke there. "The only *Alma Mater* I ever knew was the hard stage of a country theater." In his aunt's house there were only the Bible, a *Don Quixote*, and a collection of ballads, which was perhaps better than some of the much larger collections some young people have access to nowadays, but without any of these. He pursued a course of self-education diligently through his apprentice years, including language study, and finally acquired many books. Percy Fitzgerald says he never really learned how to speak French but that he "acted" speaking it so effectively that he made a few words go far. In later years he was always ready to reread Dickens rather than take on new interests, though he was never too busy to devour detective stories or records of crime. When he finally moved from Grafton Street, it seems his only contribution toward getting his things rearranged in his new quarters was to sit on the floor and bury himself in a book, getting in everybody's way and holding up the work because he could not bear the sound of hammering. He gave considerably more than his name to the "Henry Irving Edition" of Shakespeare, yet he himself says, "I may not know all Shakespeare but of any play of his which I present on the stage I know more than any man in England." There was nothing, not even cooking, that he could not learn to do if a play required it. Yet I am struck by the fact that he wrote or said practically nothing that I am tempted to quote for the interest of his way of saying it, as with Booth, Jefferson, and, to a lesser degree (an actor whom Irving despised), Mansfield.[17] (Since he did not keep a diary, there is no self-dissection, as with Macready.) The only memorable things in his letters and speeches are apt quotations. Even his message of congratulation to Baden-Powell in South Africa during the Boer War was a quotation from *Macbeth*; I hope Baden-Powell understood the application.

It was so, too, with art, music, and even, in a measure, nature. When he saw a spectacular sunset over Niagara, he only thought what a pity it was that Hawes Craven was not present to copy it for the Lyceum. Graham Robertson says he never cared much for pictures in themselves, "but when the artist touched a dramatic chord with mastery he responded to it at once." When Talcott Williams asked him where he got a certain light effect he used in the Brocken scene of *Faust*, he replied that he had seen it in a tiny painting by Dürer that he had glimpsed one day in passing through a gallery. Technically he knew nothing about music, but he could always tell Sir Arthur Sullivan and the other composers who worked for him what effect he wanted in a scene, and though he was so little able to express himself in musical terms that they had to get the message by a kind of osmosis, once they had grasped it, they were always sure that he was right.

In the last analysis, even Irving's religion was a part of his life as an actor. He grew up a devout boy in a devout environment, professing conversion at ten and manifesting all the ecstasy that pronounced Evangelicals favored. Sargent thought he had the head of a saint, and he kept a crucifix on the wall of his bed-

---

[17] This is documented by Jefferson Winter, "As I Remember: Glimpses of Old Actors—Henry Irving," *Saturday Evening Post*, Vol. CXC, October 14, 1922, pp. 46ff.; December 16, 1922, pp. 48ff. Winter prints a number of Irving and Mansfield letters. He also mentions (with documentation) Irving's dislike of of Beerbohm Tree and William Archer.

chamber. "I believe in a God of Mercy." "If ever I prayed in my life, it was the night before I played Hamlet." "I believe in immortality, and my faith is strengthened with advancing years; without faith in things spiritual this life would indeed be a weary waste." But, like Sarah Bernhardt's, his religious experience culminated on the stage, and one of his chief designers, William Telbin, even thought that the kind of man he was depended upon what he was playing.

> Catch him while he is engrossed in, say, the Vicar of Wakefield, and I'll warrant you'll find him amiability itself. . . . But tackle him when the role of Mephistopheles is on his mind, and you'll soon get a reminder that he can be unpleasant—decidedly un- pleasant sometimes.

Certainly his religious experience culminated in *Becket*; when Mrs. Pollock suggested that he had *made* Tennyson's play, he replied: "No, no, the play made me. It changed my whole view of life." Once he actually blessed his friend Sir Merton Russell- Cotes, using the same gestures he employed in the play. Nothing could have been more appropriate than that the last words he spoke on the stage should have been, "Into Thy hands O Lord, into Thy hands."

When, late in life, Ellen Terry asked Henry Irving what he had got out of his living, he pondered and replied, "Let me see. . . . Well, a good cigar, a good glass of wine—good friends," and kissed her hand.

It was a niggling and meager summary. But he had left out one thing:

The Theater.

It may be, as George Sampson says, that Irving was a mono- maniac, his best roles those of monomaniacs, and his productions like symphonic poems. *Hamlet*, for example, was "a long and terrible *crescendo*. This intensity did not at first make its effect; but as scene followed scene it grew more and more piercing till, by the time the last violent scenes were reached, the audience could scarcely endure the strain."

Irving paid a heavy price for such effects, but he paid it gladly and without too much sense of deprivation. To him the theater was everything because all life was comprehended in it, and it permitted him to assume his rightful place as a creator of life.

7

~~~~~~~~~

Joseph Jefferson
(1829–1905)

J OSEPH JEFFERSON'S STAGE CAREER owned the phenomenal span of seventy-one years, and a great many of these were devoted to a single play. I do not know whether he acted *Rip Van Winkle* more often than James O'Neill appeared in *The Count of Monte Cristo*, or Denman Thompson in *The Old Homestead*, or Rose Melville in *Sis Hopkins*, but his was certainly the greatest of these or any other achievement in kind, and it would seem to have sunk deeper into the American consciousness. (*Uncle Tom's Cabin*, of course, ran much longer, but *Uncle Tom's Cabin* belonged to no individual; it was the property of the whole theatrical profession.) Jefferson was married twice and fathered ten children. He painted a large number of very creditable canvases. And his *Autobiography* is universally regarded as a classic among the annals of the stage.

But the most remarkable thing about Jefferson is not what or how he acted but the way he made everybody feel about him. Though no man could possibly have been less like Falstaff, it might have been said of him with equal truth that he had given men medicines to make them love him. Perhaps the easiest way to make him vivid to the readers of today is to say that he some-

186

how combined the characteristics of Will Rogers and Lionel Barrymore, but having said this, one immediately recognizes a residuum which can only be described as pure Jefferson. S. Weir Mitchell found his face strangely like Thomas Jefferson's, but the actor himself considered it "classical"—"not the noble Roman or the simple Grecian, but the pure nut-cracker." However that may be, nobody ever doubted that every wrinkle in it was keen, quizzical, humorous, penetrating, and loving. "He was the most lovable person I . . . ever met either in or out of my profession," wrote the actress Mary Shaw. "With great gentleness he combined tremendous strength, which one felt all the time." And Laurence Hutton adds: "He was one of the gentlest, sweetest, cleanest characters I ever knew. He never did a mean or selfish thing. He never said an unwise or an unkind word."

> *Some element from nature seems withdrawn,*
> *The world we lived in being of his spirit wrought,—*
> *His brightness, sweetness, tender gaiety,*
> *His childlike, wistful, and half-humorous faith*
> *That turned this harsh earth into fairy-land.*
> *He made our world, and now our world is changed.*

Thus, Richard Watson Gilder, when Jefferson died. It was on Easter Sunday, which, in 1905, was also Shakespeare's birthday, and his Cape Cod neighbors and their children went out and gathered a great mound of arbutus as a tribute to him. In the city a photographer draped his picture in crape and placed it in his window, and men removed their hats as they passed by.

Jefferson came of a family of actors which ran back to the eighteenth century. He had English, Scottish, and French ancestors, the French strain having Santo Domingan connections. Born in Philadelphia, February 20, 1829, he was cradled in a theater trunk, and literally grew up back stage; when a baby was needed to be "carried on," he was the baby. When he was four years old, Thomas D. Rice carried him on in a bag in his "Jim Crow" act, dumping him out on the lines:

Ladies and gentlemen, I'd have you for to know
I've got a little darkey here, to jump Jim Crow,

whereupon the tiny child proceeded to mimic everything Rice did and created a tremendous hit, especially when he scrambled knowingly for the coins that the delighted audience proceeded to shower upon the stage.

In 1837 he appeared with his parents at the Franklin Theater, New York, but at the end of the season all the Jeffersons left for frontier Chicago, and "for the next twelve years . . . led the life of the strolling player, wandering through the West and South, and even following the armies of the Republic into Mexico."[1] They heard the guns at Palo Alto and acted in the Spanish theater at Matamoras, two nights after the city fell. Often they played in hotel dining rooms and even in barns, with nothing to separate them from the audience but the row of tallow candles which did duty as footlights.

From Galena to Dubuque they traveled over the crackling ice of the thawing Mississippi; their baggage broke through, after which the costumes had to be strung up to dry through the corridors of the hotel where they stayed and the scenery had to be repainted. At Pekin they put on *Clari; or, The Maid of Milan* in a pork house, where the pigs under the floor squeaked in accompaniment to Mrs. Jefferson's singing of "Home, Sweet Home." At Springfield, they spent all their savings to erect a rude shed of a theater, whereupon the theater-hating city fathers slapped on a ruinous license fee, and they would never have been able to play at all if a rising young lawyer named Abraham Lincoln had not come to them, begging to take their case in the name of justice and get the law repealed, collecting no fee, win or lose. When the theater business failed, the elder Jefferson kept his family from starving by painting license plates for drays, carts, and wagons in Mobile, and there, after he had died of yellow fever in 1842, his widow opened a boarding house for actors, many of whom were never able to pay her anything. At one

[1] William Winter, *Life and Art of Joseph Jefferson.*

time, the Jeffersons even ran a coffee stand in a Mexican gambling hell, "ducking" quickly when the bullets began to fly, but
after they had seen a friend killed before their eyes, they had
had enough of this and gave it up.

Jefferson reappeared in New York, after his long absence, in
Jonathan Bradford, at Chanfrau's New National Theater in 1849.
In 1853 he was stage manager for Henry C. Jarratt at the Baltimore Museum. From time to time, he managed himself and
others in country tours. But the real beginning of his career, as
distinct from his long apprenticeship, dates from his joining
Laura Keene's company shortly after the opening of her theater
in November 1856. His first marked success was as Dr. Pangloss
in Colman's *The Heir at Law*, but the role which really made him
was that of Asa Trenchard in *Our American Cousin*, by Tom
Taylor, on October 18, 1858. In September, 1859, he first appeared at the Winter Garden as Caleb Plummer in *Dot*, Dion
Boucicault's dramatization of *The Cricket on the Hearth*. He
also played Newman Noggs in *Nicholas Nickleby* at this theater,
and in 1860 his own dramatization of *Oliver Twist* was acted,
though he was not in the cast. On December 5, 1859, he played
Salem Scudder in the first production of Boucicault's *The
Octoroon*.

It was Jefferson's opinion that, in its relation to the rising tide
of sectional feeling in America, *The Octoroon* was neither pro-
Northern nor pro-Southern. "The dialogue and characters of the
play made one feel for the South, but the action proclaimed
against slavery, and called loudly for its abolition." Since Boucicault wished to rake in the shekels both north and south of the
line, he probably intended the play to be noncommittal, but
Jefferson's interpretation of its meaning was clearly conditioned
by his own profoundly pacifist temperament and convictions.
Like all intelligent men, he saw the Civil War coming but could
discern no place for himself in it, and his discouragement over
the state of the country was greatly deepened by the death, early
in 1861, of his beloved English wife, Margaret Clements, whom

he had married in 1850, and who had given him six children, two of whom had died in infancy.[2] After Mrs. Jefferson's death, her husband went to San Francisco, where he acted from July to November, and then extended his professional activities to Australia, whence he proceeded, four years later, via South America and Panama, to London.

A number of actors had appeared in a number of dramatic versions of *Rip Van Winkle* before Jefferson, including James H. Hackett, who was celebrated in the role in his time, and Jefferson's own adored half-brother, Charles Burke.[3] Moreover, Jefferson had himself acted the part as early as 1859 but was then greatly dissatisfied with his text. Now, in London, he had it rewritten, according to his own ideas, by Dion Boucicault, and it was this version which, mounted at the Adelphi, on September 14, 1865, ran for 170 nights. On September 3, 1866, he brought it to the Olympic in New York. This was essentially the *Rip Van Winkle* that Jefferson used for the rest of his life, but since Boucicault built upon foundations laid by John Kerr and Charles Burke, and since Jefferson himself altered the text whenever he felt he could improve upon it, it is best to call it *"Rip Van Winkle, as played by Joseph Jefferson,"* as Arthur Hobson Quinn does, in his well-known anthology, *Representative American Plays*.

In 1867, Jefferson took as his second wife a cousin named Sarah Isabel Warren. In 1872 he underwent a successful operation for glaucoma. In 1880 he revived *The Rivals* at the Arch Street Theater, Philadelphia, and in later years, Bob Acres was, after Rip, his most famous role. (In the spring of 1896, he headed and managed a famous "all-star" *Rivals* tour, which embraced, besides

[2] It is interesting to note that though Jefferson was the father of ten children, all his living descendants came from the marriage of his second child, Margaret Jane Jefferson, to the English-Jewish novelist and journalist, Benjamin L. Farjeon, and through two of their five children, Joseph Jefferson Farjeon and Herbert Farjeon. Their sister, Eleanor Farjeon, who, in my judgment, was surpassed as a writer for children, among her contemporaries, only by Walter de la Mare, died in the summer of 1965.

[3] See Arthur Hobson Quinn, *A History of the American Drama from the Beginning to the Civil War*, Second Edition (Crofts, 1943), 325–32.

Mrs. John Drew, who had often played her famous Mrs. Malaprop
on the same stage with his Acres, Julia Marlowe and her husband
Robert Taber, William H. Crane, E. M. Holland, Joseph Holland,
Francis Wilson, Nat C. Goodwin, and Fanny Rice.) In 1888 he
acted the First Gravedigger in *Hamlet* at the Lester Wallack
Testimonial in the Metropolitan Opera House. Yale gave him an
M.A. in 1892, and Harvard followed three years later, when he
also received a loving cup from the actors and actresses of
America. When Edwin Booth died in 1893, there was no doubt in
anybody's mind as to who was his logical successor as president of
The Players. During his later years, Jefferson played short seasons
of from eighteen to twenty weeks, each constituting a fall tour,
followed by another short jaunt in the spring, thus avoiding the
rigors of winter travel. He had a home at Palm Beach, a plantation
in the Evangeline country of Louisiana, and the famous "Crow's
Nest" at Buzzards Bay. Jefferson never *decided* to retire from the
stage; when his time came, he simply made up his mind that he
had retired. He was last seen at Paterson, New Jersey, on May 7,
1904, in *The Cricket on the Hearth*, followed by the farce *Lend
Me Five Shillings*. In the fall his tour had to be called off on
account of illness. He died at Palm Beach, April 23, 1905, and
was buried at Sandwich, Massachusetts.

II

In considering Jefferson as an actor, it should first be established that he loved the theater and believed in it, giving the best
possible proof of this when, unlike many actors, he urged his own
children, sons and daughters alike, to adopt the profession. As I
have already recorded, he said that Booth's Theater was the only
theater he had ever seen that was managed properly, like a count-
ing house before the curtain and a church behind, but when a
sanctimonious clergyman asked him to perform *Rip Van Winkle*
in a church because he himself could never enter a theater, Jefferson replied tartly that since he never entered a church, they would
obviously not be able to get together. When he was told that

Augustine Birrell had judged acting an unworthy art, he was not tempery about it, as most actors would have been. Instead he grew philosophical. "Is *anything* worth while?" he asked. "What, perhaps, does the best or worst any of us can do amount to in this vast conglomeration of revolving worlds? On the other hand, isn't *everything* worth while? Is not the smallest thing of importance?" And then, reassured by the general uncertainty of life itself, he summed up: "Acting not a worthy art? Oh, my, I have devoted all my life to it, and I stand today in awe of its greatness!"

Above all else, he valued freshness and spontaneity—not only in acting but in painting and writing too. He once astonished Frederic Remington by telling him that though he was going to paint today, he did not yet know *what* he was going to paint.[4] In the Preface to his *Autobiography* he declares that "thoughts . . . should be jotted down as quickly as they come, and are more vigorous if shaped by the simple language that usually accompanies them; labored alteration will sometimes rob them of their value, as a master stroke of the brush is often ruined by elaboration." His Rip Van Winkle never lost its spell for his audiences because he created it afresh every time he presented it. "I learn something about my art every night," he said, and he was an old man when he said it. There is probably no better piece of evidence extant to establish the great actor's power to cause his audience to see what he desires them to see than the fact that though Rip's dog Schneider never appeared on the stage, many in Jefferson's audiences "remembered" having seen him. And when Richard Watson Gilder "suped" with him for a lark, he found that his spell was nearly as potent close up as it had been across the footlights.[5]

[4] Frederic Remington, "Jefferson as a Painter," *Harper's Weekly*, Vol. XLIX (1905), 684–85.

[5] "A Few Words about Joseph Jefferson and his Art," *Christian Union*, Vol. XLVII (1893), 410–11. The magic worked quite as well on professional actors (Jefferson Winter says he never saw Jefferson's Caleb Plummer without tears), except for Nat Goodwin, whose mean-minded remarks about Jefferson in *Nat Goodwin's Book* (Richard G. Badger, 1914) must be one of the few petty things ever written about him. Cf., too, the venom Goodwin sprays over Richard Mansfield.

Yet this is the man of whom Otis Skinner said[6] that he had made the acting of comedy a science! When Boucicault told him that he was "shooting over their heads" in *Rip Van Winkle,* he replied, "I am not even shooting at their heads. I am aiming at their hearts." But he knew too that he always acted best when the head was as cool as the heart was warm. Remington thought him very excited when he watched him paint. He was excited on the stage also. His tension showed in his often talking to himself *sotto voce* and even upbraiding himself during a performance, and when a beginner asked him for a cure for stage fright, he replied, "If you find one, I wish you would let me have it!" Once when, as Caleb Plummer, he permitted himself to be overcome by his personal emotion, and to allow this to confuse itself with the emotion of the character, he lost control of the effect altogether, and had to ring down the curtain. When Mrs. Drew asked him why she was not getting the accustomed laughs on Mrs. Malaprop's blunders, he replied, "It's because you read the lines as though *you* thought them funny. Try reading them seriously." In his own performances, as Robert Underwood Johnson says, "everything was calculated art but the effectiveness was of improvisation."[7]

Jefferson was a civilized man with civilized interests and a civilized outlook, but it would be absurd to describe him as a scholar. When he warns the readers of his autobiography that he is reconstructing the conversations recorded in it, since nobody could remember the actual words over a lifetime, he is behaving more like a scholar than many professional nineteenth-century writers did, but from his own point of view, he was merely acting like an honest man. His sensitiveness to beauty and to history shows attractively in his account of a midnight visit to Notre Dame on his first visit to Paris:

> How grandly it stood out against the dark blue sky! We recrossed
> the Seine, and I stopped the cab to get out on the bridge. Straight

[6] *Footlights and Spotlights* (Bobbs-Merrill, 1924).
[7] *Remembered Yesterdays* (Little, Brown, 1933).

before me were the gloomy towers in which Marie Antoinette was confined during the Reign of Terror. I almost fancied that I could see the pale face of the murdered queen gazing with anguish through the iron-grated windows.

But when, later, he tried to study the French language with his family, he soon gave it up as a bad job. The wonders of astronomy stimulated his imagination and appealed to his sense of the glory of God, but he had no real interest in science. He was fond of quoting Shakespeare and Dickens, but much of this must have been heard from the stage; we have his own word for it that he had never read Shakespeare through. He did not care for Thackeray. Indeed, he was no great reader in general, and he admitted that he had read only one or two of his son-in-law Benjamin Farjeon's books. One chronicler says that he admired and often quoted Pope.[8] Once he quotes from *David Harum,* which everybody was quoting at the time, and he has one rather slighting remark on Byron and Cooper.

Yet he had considered "views" on everything connected with the drama. As to Shakespeare, again, he was fond of interpreting the great plays in his lectures, though his remarks are rather simple and not always consistent. He considered Salvini the greatest tragic actor he had ever seen, but felt that he played Othello's death scene too realistically. He considered Sardou the "most ingenious" playwright of his time but disliked his female characters because he could not respect them. As a practical theater man, he was quite clear that literary quality did not come first in the theater, and he thought Laura Keene often erred because of her tendency to mount plays which read well but lacked true theatrical tension. "You may have all the good literature you wish in a play if it does not interfere with the play's action; and at the same time the absence of fine writing in a play will not injure it if the story and construction are right." Certainly he paid little attention to "good literature" in his own choice of plays. When

[8] William E. Bryant, "Joseph Jefferson at Home," *New England Magazine,* N.S., Vol. XII (1895), 192–205.

Edwin Booth as a young man.

Booth as Hamlet.

Sir Henry Irving, about 1896.

Irving as King Lear and as Louis XI, from drawings by J. Bernard Partridge.

Irving as Shylock.

Joseph Jefferson.

Jefferson as Rip Van Winkle.

Richard Mansfield in 1898.

*Mansfield in four characters: Richard III and Shylock (above);
Alceste, in Molière's* The Misanthrope, *and Cyrano de Bergerac
(below).*

Harriet Beecher Stowe acutely suggested that Rip's meeting with Meenie had been modeled on Lear's reunion with Cordelia, he admitted the soft impeachment, but when she went on to suggest that he could act Lear, though he was "sorry to differ with a lady," he told her she was quite wrong.

About acting in the technical sense there was not much that he did not know; it might be a spiritual art, the communication of soul with soul, but unless you knew how to make yourself heard and understood under the practical conditions prevailing at *this* performance, there would be no communication and no art. He agreed with Mrs. Siddons that the secret of good acting lay in the pause, and he knew that, if he would create the illusion of life, an actor must know how to listen as well as speak. Every effect must be carefully prepared for, but it must never be anticipated. Evidently Jefferson was not much of a director, concerning himself largely with his own performance, as so many nineteenth-century "star" actors did,[9] but he himself took the utmost pains. When he first acted Dr. Pangloss, he insisted on learning the meaning of all the Greek and Latin he was required to speak, not being content to rattle it off like so much gibberish, as many others did. And though he admitted he had been guilty of it in his youth, he had nothing but contempt for an actor capable of "guying" his colleagues on the stage, and never tolerated it in any company under his control.

In his notions of "fidelity" toward the dramatist, he seems to have gone along with the free and easy attitude of his time rather than the stricter views which are now in vogue. Once, when, as a

[9] Mary Shaw, "The Stage Wisdom of Joseph Jefferson," *Century*, N.S., Vol. LXI (1912), 731–37, and "The Human Side of Joseph Jefferson," *Century*, N.S., Vol. LXIII (1913), 379–84, shows that, in later years at any rate, early rehearsals for *Rip Van Winkle* were conducted in very hit-or-miss fashion by Jefferson's sons, with Henrik Hudson's crew picked up in the local streets and instructed superficially about a quarter to eight, and that even when Jefferson did finally appear, he gave her very little specific instruction, contenting himself mainly with assuring her that everything would be "all right." According to Charles Edward Russell, *Julia Marlowe, Her Life and Art* (Appleton, 1926), even the all-star *Rivals* was thrown together very carelessly, and Jefferson confused Nat Goodwin by ad libbing very freely in their scenes together.

lecturer, he was questioned about the star system, he replied that when he was in stock, he regarded every star as a tyrant, but that as soon as he had become a star, he began to look upon stock actors as so many conspirators! He tried to justify this attitude, in a measure, by appealing to the mystical notion that even great writers sometimes builded better than they knew, creating a work of which they themselves did not understand all the implications. But actually theory was never very important; it was the practical theater man's effect that he was after, and he declared that if he could get the effect he wanted "by dominating the character, then I should certainly dominate the character, but if I could only reach it by subordinating myself to the character, then I should subordinate myself, for the effect I certainly would have." He once criticized W. H. Crane's proposed make-up for Falstaff on the ground that there was no Crane in it. "They want both Falstaff as Crane and Crane as Falstaff." As everybody knows, Jefferson and E. A. Sothern "arrived" together in *Our American Cousin,* but when Sothern was handed the role which became his greatest hit, he was completely discouraged. "I have no scenes," he said. "I have only about ten lines." "We will have scenes," replied Jefferson; "we will make them."[10]

If he could do that for—and with—Sothern, he certainly was no less inclined to do it for himself. Winter admits that the "amiable and lovable personality" with which he invested Bob Acres was never intended by Sheridan. But "the part admits of it, and is the better for it; and this certainly would have been intended had it been thought of,—for it makes the play doubly interesting and potential." This, of course, is to argue that a role is whatever an actor can read into it, a line of reasoning which finds its best validity when the actor is so much greater than his role that he virtually makes himself a co-author. Jefferson glorified his material in *Rip Van Winkle* also, but here his withers were unwrung, for here he had an ancient, traditional theatrical contraption,

[10] E. H. Sothern, *The Melancholy Tale of "Me": My Remembrances* (Scribners, 1916).

whose integrity nobody respected, retailored to his own needs. Whether it was legitimate to do what he did with Sheridan opinions will differ, but to maintain that it was is surely to assume that Sheridan was not quite a first-rate dramatist. Yet, it must be admitted that, even with Shakespeare, problems arise. Irving's Shylock was probably greater than Shakespeare's, but it was a plain misinterpretation nevertheless, and the younger Sothern made the fall of Malvolio that of a much larger and worthier man than Shakespeare drew, thus enlisting more audience sympathy for him. The key-line became Olivia's "He hath been most notoriously abus'd," and nobody ever heard it spoken without agreeing with her.

That Jefferson's Rip Van Winkle was a great and radiant piece of acting, no competent judge has ever doubted.[11]

> In the mountain scene . . . [wrote William Winter], when the man is encircled with the phantoms, he seemed to become transfigured; he lifted Rip into the realm of the imagination; he diffused the atmosphere of poetry; and he made that episode as weird, mysterious, pathetic and awful as the scene of Hamlet's meeting with the Ghost.

I do not for a moment doubt it. But there are serious moral and

[11] See, for example, John Ranken Towse, *Sixty Years of the Theater* (Funk and Wagnalls, 1916), who is very severe upon Jefferson's capacities in general. Fortunately we are not left entirely to reports. When he appeared before a Biograph camera in 1896, Jefferson became the first actor of stage renown to appear in the movies. The film which resulted may still be seen at George Eastman House in Rochester, but it is not very enlightening. In January, 1940, the Collectors Record Shop of New York issued a ten-inch 78 r.p.m. phonograph record containing selections from the Mountain Scene and the Return Scene, announced as having been re-recorded from old Columbia cylinders. Unfortunately these records are fast and shrill and do Jefferson no justice. But my battered Columbia disc record of the Mountain Scene (A385) is magnificent, both in its tenderness and its overwhelming eerie ghostliness; I feel sure that nobody who has heard it will ever forget the haunting cadence of Rip's praise of the trees: "They keep me from the wind and the rain." Collectors who are earnest enough to search for this record in old junk shops should be warned that it is backed by an additional treasure—the Harry Armstrong Male Quartet singing "You're the Flower of My Heart, Sweet Adeline"!

aesthetic problems involved nevertheless. Nobody has ever had any respect for the play upon the printed page; even the character of Rip is only a bag of theatrical tricks, and a pretty clumsy one at that. The man is a sot and a wastrel—not a "bad" man, as Alice Longworth once immortally remarked of an American President, but just a "slob." Properly speaking, the sympathy ought to go to his wife, but when Mary Shaw tried to play Gretchen sympathetically, Jefferson at once stopped her, insisting that Rip must always remain the moral and dramatic focus of interest. He was justly proud of the stroke of inspiration which decreed that the scene in the mountains must be a monologue for Rip, the ghosts of the old Dutch mariners never being allowed to speak, and he was right too in refusing to use a real dog or to permit Rip to yawn and stretch, as if awaking from an ordinary sleep, or to take food after returning to the village of Falling Water. Yet I do not quite follow his reasoning (especially as coming from a man with his pronounced "temperance" views), when he opposed those who thought that Rip should refuse the drink which Meenie offers him at the very end of the play, on the ground that this would make *Rip Van Winkle* a temperance drama and return it to the atmosphere of every-day life, for I do not understand why it is less realistic to take a drink than to refuse one, and if Rip is to be regarded, at this point, as something larger than human, then surely eating and drinking ought to be handled in the same way. Winter says of Rip's drinking in general that it is "only an expedient, to involve the hero in domestic strife and open the way for his ghostly adventures and his pathetic resuscitation," and I think this true also, but as such it is a theatrical "device" in a play compact of devices. Essentially Jefferson was not asking here for "that willing suspension of disbelief" which all great romantic literature requires; he was claiming a license which we are generally more prone to grant purveyors of farce and melodrama than we are to accord it to high comedy and tragedy. Having made this reservation, one must, however, admit that it was all the more remarkable that, working with such ramshackle materials, he should have been able to create the effects he did.

Robert Frost once remarked that there were two kinds of realist —the kind who furnishes a good deal of dirt with his potato to prove that it is a real potato and the kind who prefers his potato cleaned and washed and stripped to form. He added that he himself favored the second type. So did Jefferson. "The actual farmer," he told Winter, "wears soiled clothes; but there is a day when he has a bath, and is shaved, has his boots brushed, and wears a clean shirt; and *this is that day*. Gretchen was always washing clothes; so Rip's clothes couldn't always have been dirty." Even in *The Rivals* he cut certain lines because he could not bring himself to speak them. In the early days, a colleague scornfully referred to him as "the Sunday School comedian," but he stuck to his guns: "You take an unfair and unmanly advantage of people when you force them to listen to your coarseness. They are, for the time, imprisoned, and have no choice but to hear and see your ill-breeding. You have no better right to be offensive on the stage than you have in the drawing-room." But basically it was something more than his own essential moral fineness and integrity that kept him away from such things; it was his temperament and his aesthetic convictions. He was not a realist at all, nor did he ever pretend to be or desire to be. Perhaps his essential attitude comes out best in connection with his painting. Much as he loved the beauty of nature, he never painted a landscape from life, and when it was suggested to him that he should do so, he replied that he could not attempt to paint the scene until he had forgotten it. He even painted on the train or in an empty freight car when he was on tour, finding that the "jiggling" of the train only helped the "leafy" quality of the picture. "I want to paint the woods," he told Remington, "as you see them when you are not looking at them." He thought Millet's "Sheepfold" one of the world's great pictures because Millet "painted from within,—that is, painted with his soul!" and he admired Corot's picture of St.

Sebastian because, unlike other artists, Corot had not concentrated upon physical horror. "There is a calm, a peacefulness in the wounded man's face, and, indeed, about the whole picture, that tells of the work of the big-souled artist."

> I see and feel something I want to paint,—then I paint what I see— my impressions. Fidelity to fact simply for fact's sake means nothing in painting, and it means nothing in acting. In painting, or in dramatic presentations, what is often intended for truth becomes exactly the opposite—truth to nature can be carried so far as to be untrue. If an illusion gives a natural sentiment better than a reality would, then it is a laudable act to deceive.

The only serious question concerning Jefferson as an actor concerns his lack of versatility. His admirers justly urge that though he confined himself during all the years of his fame to a few, not wholly dissimilar roles, and in the main to one, it is not fair to ignore his vast theatrical background and experience or the fact that, in his time, he appeared on the stage in more than a hundred characters. The criticism, however, was not confined to his few detractors. Nobody admired him more than Laurence Hutton, who considered his Caleb Plummer superior to his Rip. "Why is he content to spend his glorious prime in his unceasing Rippings about the country?" Hutton queried as early as 1875. "Can the voice of no familiar Cricket wake him from the twenty years' sleep into which he has fallen, and in which he seems disposed to dream forever."[12] Jefferson himself was not timid about his defense when Charles Mathews called him "the prince of dramatic carpet-baggers," contrasting the huge pile of trunks his repertory of fifty roles involved his carrying with Jefferson's wardrobe packed in a gripsack. "My dear Charlie," replied Jefferson, "you are confounding wardrobe with talent. What is the value of a long bill of fare if the stuff is badly cooked? You change your hat, and fancy you are playing another character. Believe me, it requires more skill to act one part fifty different ways than to act fifty parts

[12] *Plays and Players* (Hurd and Houghton, 1875).

all the same way." This was clever dialectic, and if intended to be taken seriously, it was also pretty cruel and anything but modest. No doubt it does take more skill to act one part fifty different ways than to act fifty parts all the same way. But the obvious answer is that it would still call for a vastly greater artist to act fifty—or even twenty—parts in as many different ways. Essentially, Jefferson handled Mathews' objection about as unrealistically and as trickily as he treated the character of Rip Van Winkle himself.

III

The great affection which Jefferson awakened in his contemporaries showed that he was a man as well as an actor. It should not be forgotten, of course, that he practiced two arts—acting and painting. Once he told Francis Wilson that he would rather paint than act, and when Wilson asked him what he would do if he couldn't paint, he answered, "Die, I think." On another occasion he said he loved both painting and acting so much that he could not choose between them, which is a sufficiently remarkable statement coming from a man who achieved his fame in one of these arts. As a painter, Jefferson was an American adherent of the Barbizon school. In their own dreamy way, many of his landscapes are certainly very beautiful, and nobody knows how far he might have gone if he had devoted himself to painting instead of acting. A distinguished and forward-looking collector, he bought Maris, Israëls, Mauve, and others long before they were famous, but he also owned paintings by Reynolds, Lawrence, Rembrandt, and many more. The *décor* of his houses was determined by his own ideas: at Buzzards Bay the carved mantelpiece came from India and the Dutch tile surrounding the fireplace from the home of Quentin Matsys. Old Dutch plates were embedded around the central panel of the dining room ceiling, and when there were not enough to go round he painted as many more as were needed to make up the requisite number. He told W. H. Crane that he thought whatever fame he might achieve would be as a painter, and it would not have made him happy to know that after his

death his widow and his sons would go to court over the owner-
ship of his pictures.

In music he was much weaker, taking high rank as a Wagner-
hater. When his daughter took him to *Lohengrin*, he wished they
had gone to Tony Pastor's instead, and in his old age his deafness
was a handicap in the whole musical field, and indeed in the
theater too. "The advantage that the drama has over music," he
said, "is that the drama is both emotional and intellectual. Music
is emotional only." This is about what Milton said. Yet he sufficiently admired Calvé to commission an artist to paint her portrait as Carmen for his house.

He loved human beings as well as art, and he knew how to get
on with them. Both Carlyle and Johnson were, in his eyes, horrible
examples of men who thought their own ways or views the only
acceptable ones. Once he said he thought women had all the
endowments of men except the logical mind. "Women, like music,
are chiefly emotional, and an emotional woman has little chance
against a clever, unscrupulous man," But even this statement
shows how deep his sympathy for women was, and he always
knew that in the theater success means even more to a woman
than it does to a man. "The actress who has made a fortune is not
beholden to some rascal of a husband, or to any of the crowd of
men who hang about actresses' heels." He knew, too, that human
beings are never quite so dear to us as when we can help them.
"My boys sometimes get discouraged, and I say to them: 'Go out
and do something for somebody. Go out and give something to
somebody, if it's only a pair of woollen stockings to a poor old
woman. It will take you away from yourselves and make you
happy.' " He himself performed many charities, though he was
never extravagant with money and never did anything rash. He
had what we call the traditional New England attitude toward
money, and in a sense he took good care of it even when he gave
it away. But in Louisiana his neighbors criticized him for his free
and easy ways with his Negro "help" and also for the fare he gave
them. It is touching to read that once when he was inveighing

against the cruelty of the Old Testament God and developing his conception of God as a loving Father, one of his sons remarked, "You never taught us to be afraid of you, Father." He knew his children's faults too, and his sense of humor did not desert him when he confronted them. Once one of them cabled him from Europe, "Please cable two hundred pounds at once." Jefferson cabled back: "What for?" The reply also consisted of two words: "For Willy." He sent the money.

He called his house on Buzzards Bay "Crow's Nest."

> They are attractive to me. All birds are; but crows are more intelligent than most of the feathered tribe. They are very cute and observant. It matters little if they do forage about my place for food; there is enough for them and me. In the strawberry time I cover my beds with nets, so that the crows shall not get more than their share.

In the early days, he shot as well as fished; later he gave this up because he could no longer find pleasure in killing. Apparently he was less sensitive about the finny tribe, and in any case fishing was better suited to his reflective temperament than hunting. He always had strict rules about it; he would not use a barbed hook, and he would not hook a fish through the tail. It is interesting, though, that his great fishing companion, Grover Cleveland, should have been distressed by his "most exasperating habit of viciously jerking a fish after he was fairly hooked and during his struggling efforts to resist fatal persuasion boatwards." Once when Cleveland asked him by he did it, he replied, "Because he jerked me"! And there is a really shocking passage in the autobiography in which he describes himself as a boy who tied tin cans to dogs' tails and was "the champion executioner of all the stray cats of the neighborhood" which is difficult to reconcile with anything we know of Jefferson the man.

Though one observer credits him with a gift for picturesque profanity, he detested gambling and all forms of vice. His special bête noire was poker, and he was not incapable of tongue-lashing

his sons and the members of his company if he caught them playing it behind his back. "Who ever heard of friends sitting down
together to try to take each other's money away? And at such a
game—a game the essence of which is to deceive and mislead your
adversaries. . . . I wonder you don't try waiting for each other up
dark alleys and do it with clubs." In view of the stock picture of
the gentle Jefferson that has been built up in all our minds, it is
especially interesting that none of these grown men dared to play
in his presence, and that there was always a wild scramble to get
the chips and cards out of the way when anybody heard him
coming.

His inclination toward dyspepsia taught him to watch his diet
very carefully during later years, though he loved ham hocks and
sauerkraut. He always speaks of tobacco as "nicotine" and of wines
and liquors as "alcohol." Though he seems sometimes to have
used strong waters during his early life, in later years he never
went beyond a little claret diluted with water; neither did he
smoke, though he could apparently sit in a smoke-filled room
untroubled. When he heard of the death of an acquaintance, he
seldom missed an occasion to remark, "You see, he was a great
smoker" or "You see, alcohol will get in its work."

Jefferson's strict moral principles were bolstered by his profound (though strictly Jeffersonian) religious sense, cultivated
quite without the aid of churches and creeds. When his grandfather was buried, the officiating clergyman spoke of him as "this
man" because he could not bring himself to call an actor "our
brother," and when Jefferson himself went to a certain clergyman
in New York to try to arrange funeral services for George Holland,
the person in charge bluntly refused to hold services for an actor
under any circumstances, though he did condescend to admit
that there was "a little church around the corner" where that sort
of thing might be done.[13] These were not experiences calculated

---

[13] The Church of the Transfiguration, in East Twenty-ninth Street, which
contains a stained-glass memorial to Jefferson and Rip Van Winkle, has ever
since been popularly known as "The Little Church Around the Corner" and the

to endear the reverend clergy to a sensitive boy and man; neither did they have this effect. But he never made the mistake of confusing God with his bigoted self-appointed representatives. He once spent an ocean voyage "trying to divert Father O'Grady from celibacy; I told him that he would never know what true happiness was till he got a wife by his side and had half a dozen children by his knee."[14] He himself had no difficulty with faith of any sort: "Tell it to Jefferson," Cleveland once remarked; "he'll believe anything." He believed, for one thing, that God had protected him from death and injury all through the perils and vicissitudes of his career. In their family life, the Jeffersons made a cult of happiness, avoiding fear and anger, and boycotting unpleasant topics to such an extent as sometimes to remind the reader of Pollyanna or of the Robert Louis Stevenson who declared that "there is no duty we so much underrate as the duty of being happy," which to many of us seems a sober, uninspiring basis for happiness. This mental bias gave Jefferson a temperamental sympathy with various marginal religious sects and movements in his time: Christian Science, Swedenborgianism, New Thought, theosophy, spiritualism, and much besides. He did not really commit himself to any of them, not even Christian Science, of which his daughter-in-law Eugénie was a devout adherent, but he allowed her to give him a "Christian Science treatment" when he was ill and declared he felt better afterwards and asked for a copy of *Science and Health*. Perhaps he came closest to spiritualism, for, like Tennyson, he was a man to whom assurance of immortality was very important. He inclined to believe in the Fox sisters from the beginning, and he claimed once to have seen the ghost of a relative. In his eyes, this life was only a rehearsal for the performance beyond, and he once said that if he believed the rehearsal to be all there was, he would curse the power that

---

actor's church, a living testimonial against bigotry and a living protest against the tendency to regard human beings as members of groups rather than as themselves.

[14] Oddly enough, Jefferson later learned that O'Grady had given up the priesthood for marriage, though remaining a Catholic.

made him.[15] Perhaps his ever youthful spirit had something to do with this; in his seventies he loved gardening because it was "all expectation" and looked forward to much better painting in the future. Oddly enough, the one note of skepticism is recorded by the devout daughter-in-law, to whom he remarked one day that no man with so beautiful a home as he possessed could be perfectly happy, because he knew he must leave it all behind some day. She asked: "Not even if he believes there may be something better beyond?" and Jefferson replied, "Ah, my dear child, we have no way of knowing that; we have no proof." It tempts one to believe in the validity of the New Testament—or St. Francis of Assisi— attitude toward material possessions—does it not?

IV

Richard Mansfield was once quoted in a newspaper dispatch from Cincinnati as having harshly criticized a foreign actor with whom he was known to be on somewhat unfriendly terms. Without waiting to verify the report, William Winter took him to task on the editorial page of the New York *Tribune*. Mansfield was justly indignant, for he had made no statement whatever concerning the gentleman in question or anything else, and Winter and the *Tribune* were obliged to apologize to him, though not without arguing that the mistake they made had been quite natural:

> Reputation affects belief. If, for example, the language ascribed to Mr. Mansfield had been imputed to Mr. Jefferson it would have been discredited at once, as preposterous and absurd. Alleged as the utterance of Mr. Mansfield it seemed credible, because it was harmonious with antecedent publications.

Mansfield replied to Winter:

> You are quite right about Jefferson—nobody would believe that

[15] "When Jefferson Came To Chicago," an item in the Chicago *Record-Herald*, April 30, 1905, has much on Jefferson's interest in spiritualism, including the statement that when he came to Chicago there were always séances at the home of J. H. McVicker.

he had said anything of the kind. But there is this difference—that
I produce four or five plays a year, and have spent thousands on
new and old plays, such as *Richard* and *Nero*—and that I am
striving, striving, studying, and have been starving. Mr. Jefferson
is a dear, lovely fellow, who likes a small company and a jog trot.
Every man to his taste.[16]

As far as it went, this defense was perfectly just. As the flaw in
a tragic hero is often the excess of a quality admirable in itself, so
every man must carry the defects of his virtues. And there is no
denying that Jefferson often does give the impression of being at
ease in Zion. Eugénie Jefferson understood this perfectly when
she wrote:

> Endowed with perfect morality, he has yet no moral enthusiasm.
> The moment after he had seen the serious side of anything he saw
> the comic side of it. Resolute in will, he yet had no aggressive
> impulse. He shrunk from all strife. His province, as he understood
> it, was to dispense humour and kindness. His vocation was the
> ministry of beauty.

This tendency shows in little things as well as great. Jefferson
was a notoriously absent-minded man, and the story is told that
once when he drank with Stephen A. Douglas, Douglas paid for
the drinks with a five-dollar piece, and Jefferson picked up and
pocketed the change! Of course this was a perfectly honest mistake; only I cannot help but wonder whether he would have been
quite so absent-minded if the situation had been reversed. Though
his investments in Florida real estate certainly proved profitable,
Jefferson's moral objection to gambling would probably have kept
him away from the stock market in any event, but what he said
was that he could not accept "being glued to a stock-ticker, and
not being able to get away! . . . I want to fish a little, paint a little,
and then act a little." One day, he encountered Lawrence Barrett
waiting for a street car to take him to a gymnasium where he
planned to exercise. "Why don't you walk?" asked Jefferson. "It's

16 *Life and Art of Richard Mansfield*, I, 203–209.

better exercise, and it'll save you the time and trouble of going."
Here, as so often, his logic seems irresistible, but the easy-going
point of view is evident.

It shows, too, in larger matters involving moral issues. He was
willing to let the theatrical syndicate alone as long as it let him
alone. "The syndicate members never try to interfere with me. If
they did I'd break their hearts by buying the New York Academy
of Music and playing a farewell engagement at triple prices." He
did not stop to consider how the syndicate problem could be
solved by less popular actors who could not, even jocosely, consider such a course. Apparently he never went to the polls until
the time came when he wished to vote for his friend Cleveland
(according to Eugénie, he believed, absurdly, that an actor should
not vote because he must retain the sympathy of his entire audience!), and then he had to have help from those in charge because
he did not know what Presidential electors were! He met the Civil
War crisis in the same way, as we have seen: "I loved my country
so much, I could not bear to see her suffer—some were kind
enough to say that I ran away." And Henry Watterson testified
that he told him: "I cannot bring myself to engage in bloodshed or
to take sides. . . . It may seem unpatriotic, and it is, I know,
unheroic. I am not a hero. I am, I hope, an artist. My world is the
world of art, and I must be true to that; it is my patriotism,
my religion."[17]

Any commentator who would sit in judgment upon Jefferson
for any of this might well be embarrassed to find that his role had
been pre-empted, for Jefferson often sits in judgment upon himself. He never pretended to possess physical courage. Thus he
admits frankly that when he tried exploring the mountains on
muleback, he was scared to death, and that it was a great relief to

[17] Henry Watterson, *"Marse Henry": An Autobiography* (Doran, 1919). The
language is probably more Watterson than Jefferson, but the point of view, I
think, is characteristic. Personally I believe that if we had only had enough people
of Jefferson's reasonableness and humanity in the sixties, the agony of the Civil
War might have been averted. But, however that may be, the point I am trying
to make about his temperament still holds.

him when his wife lost her courage, so that he could spring from his mule and cry, "Gentlemen, this lady can go no farther."

He is quite as frank in theatrical matters, and whoever believes that it must have been dangerous to cross Mansfield because he was a self-centered, ambitious man of violent temper, but quite safe to cross Jefferson because he was mild and amiable and free of ambition and selfless simply knows nothing whereof he speaks. Jefferson made it a rule never publicly to criticize his contemporaries on the stage, but he was frank enough concerning those who had gone. He said bluntly that E. A. Sothern "missed" one of his roles "altogether" because he himself had fun with the character instead of playing him seriously and leaving the fun to the audience. Mrs. Mowatt and James H. Hackett were always amateurs, with "a shyness and uncertainty about everything they do." Charles Mathews failed with Charles Surface because he was too modern. And it would be hard to surpass the complete devastation he achieves with his remark about an actor named Charles Salisbury: "It was said of him that he was generous to a fault; and I think he must have been, for he never paid his washerwoman."

With all his social charm, he could be quite as devastating face to face upon occasion, as with the silly young woman who gushed over the ugliness of his Tilly Slowboy in *The Cricket on the Hearth*, and wondered where he picked up such people: "Oh, that is not such a difficult matter! We do not have to go so far. . . . Tilly Slowboy is my sister." And more characteristically but more crushingly still when he appeared on the same benefit bill with an unnamed star (probably Olga Nethersole in *Sapho*) who was giving a scene from a controversial play, and who objected to the members of Jefferson's company watching her from the wings: "Dear me, is it as bad as that?" In his *Autobiography*, he sometimes remembers and writes down slights that had been put upon him many years before, together with the replies he might have made but refrained from making!

It is true that Jefferson often showed a saintly forbearance when something went wrong during a performance, as when a stage hand inadvertently leaned against a button and brought the curtain down in the middle of a scene, and he contented himself with suggesting that he find some other place to lean tomorrow night. But during his later years he was always deferred to and his temper, consequently, not often tried. It is clear that he was never the kind of man people take liberties with. "A quiet dignity in his manner," writes William E. Bryant, "does not invite a hasty acquaintance. . . . His manner is courteous, his smile is geniality itself; but there is a certain sense of self-protection about him as if he were compelled to be politely on his guard."

Nothing could be more absurd than to assume that he lacked ambition. This awakened in him early through his admiration for John E. Owens; with characteristic frankness he admits that he "had hoped to see something not quite so good" and that he "was a little annoyed to find such a capitol actor." Later he writes of a rival that he "was a good actor, but not too good to be jealous of me, and if our positions had been reversed the chances are that I would have been jealous of him."

He frankly admitted his love of compliments, disliking rehearsals because there was no applause. He found it difficult to understand how a writer could contentedly wait a whole year after he had finished his book for the reader's response to come back to him; he himself missed the audience even when he wrote letters, for he wanted his "hand" as soon as he had made his "point." Yet he welcomed the opportunity to write his *Autobiography* because he hoped that it might help keep his name alive. He disliked imitations of himself because there was always a touch of ridicule present, and he admits that he often read notices of the plays in which he appeared merely to note what was said of his own performance.

He once quarreled with Laura Keene, *on the stage*, in the hearing of the audience, and when she punished him by casting him as Puck instead of Bottom in her production of *A Midsummer Night's Dream*, he refused the assignment until he had convinced himself that he could not play Bottom, whereupon he relinquished the role on condition that Miss Keene release *Our American Cousin* to him for a starring tour. When she meanly left his name out of her announcements of *The Octoroon*, though he was playing one of the leading roles, he forced her hand by resigning from her company as of Saturday, the first night of *The Octoroon* being scheduled for the oncoming Monday.

At the earliest possible reasonable moment he resolved to be a star and thereafter directed his career toward that end. Once he had achieved it, there was never any doubt in his mind nor in that of anybody associated with him that the center of the stage was wherever he happened to be standing. We have already seen this in connection with his Rip and his Bob Acres. Once his colleagues presented him with a special edition of *The Rivals* from which all roles except Bob's had been eliminated. One night, Julia Marlowe dropped a rose on the stage just preceding one of his entrances; he quickly and unobtrusively picked it up before beginning his scene, fearing that its presence might draw the eyes of the spectators away from him. Nor would he permit an orchestra conductor in one theater to turn his back on the stage, arguing that such indifference on his part would make for indifference in the audience also.

He always gave full credit where credit was due, and he insisted on the credit that was owing him. When Francis Wilson asked whether the idea of the silent ghosts in *Rip* was Boucicault's he replied, "No, no, no, no, no, no, no; that was Jefferson, and he is very, very proud of it." Asked whether he had talked nonsense after the fashion of Artemus Ward, he replied, "No, after the fashion of *Jefferson*, which, as I have told you, Ward adopted, and thanked me for when I met him in London." He had no respect for false modesty, arguing that "every man that is clever knows it," and that "vanity does not consist in knowing you have knowledge, but in parading it." Complimented on the good taste of one of his sons, he replied, "Oh, he has splendid taste. He paints very well, too,—while he lacks in detail, his sky and water are as good as mine." When Francis Wilson told him he always did the right thing, he replied, "Well, I believe I make fewer mistakes than most men. I think I am tactful rather than politic." And he himself once asked Wilson what in his *Autobiography* had impressed him most, causing Mrs. John Drew to exclaim, "What an awful question to ask the man! Suppose he can't think of anything?" If there is a touch of smugness here, one is inclined to forgive it (as surely Jefferson's friends always did) for the tenderness and craving for human warmth shown in his request to Laurence Hutton: "There are certain things about myself as an actor, that I want said, which I can't say, and which can't be said by anybody *yet!* Will you say them for me when the time comes?" Though perhaps not many would have added, "I'll write them down and send them to you."[18]

But it is not only in professional matters that I feel Jefferson's self-centeredness and his determination to go his own way regardless of everything and anybody. To a certain extent, to be sure, this is true of all artists, who live in a world apart from other people, but I think it was true of Jefferson to an outstanding degree, and I even believe that his famous much-admired serenity resulted in part from it. I have already spoken of his absent-mindedness. Once when a street car conductor came to him for his fare, he put the letter he was carrying into his hand with "Mail this for me, will you, please?" Here, again, I do not doubt that there was an honest mistake, but I suspect that the absent-minded man in general is more interested in himself than he is in those around him, and even if this is not true, Jefferson's action in this instance is still that of a man who is accustomed to have others do what he tells them to do. Jefferson loved to entertain, but he could not learn to carve for his guests, not only because he could not master the technicalities of carving (Francis Wilson says that when he tried to carve a duck, he did everything but take the creature on his lap), but even more because he always got so interested in what he was trying to say that he forgot the carving

[18] See Laurence Hutton, "Recollections of Joseph Jefferson," *Harper's Weekly*, Vol. XLIX (1905), 657, 661, 663.

altogether. But I think the best example of his capacity for absorption in his own affairs comes from the night of Cleveland's second election. Jefferson and Cleveland spent the night together, but when enough returns had come in to assure Cleveland's victory, the actor became so absorbed in watching the sun rise over Buzzards Bay that he completely forgot what he was there for. "Joe," asked Cleveland, "aren't you going to congratulate me?" "Oh," replied Jefferson, "I do—believe me, I do! but—good God!—if I could paint like *that*—you could be Emperor of the world and I wouldn't exchange places with you!"

In later years, when all men spoke well of him, Jefferson once audibly wondered whether he ought not get himself involved in a scandal to keep him human. That would have been as difficult as it was unnecessary. He was thoroughly human always, and his humanity has been insisted upon here not with any view to disparagement or defacement of the lovely image of him which survives in the American consciousness but because even sainthood has no meaning for human beings unless it can be shown that the saint was touched with all the feeling of our infirmities and won his victories in their despite. Jefferson was not a saint but he was a fine artist and a good man. If he sometimes seems too much at ease in the Zion of art, there is not so much ease in this world that one could reasonably wish it removed even here. If he sought —and claimed and held—his own, few have claimed less of that which belonged to other men. All in all, the canny, timid, meanminded, and realistic Australian manager Rolamo summed him up as well as anybody: "I say, mister, I took you for a green un when I first see you; you got a kind o' innocent look about you, but you're sharp, do you know that?" It is Jefferson's innocence that survives in his legend, but it was his sharpness that made it effective.

8

Richard Mansfield

(1854–1907)

After the death of edwin booth, Richard Mansfield would certainly seem to have been the most famous actor in America, since Joseph Jefferson, though everywhere held in the highest affection and regard, was a highly specialized actor, essentially a comedian and, during his later years, largely concerned with a single role and play. Yet Mansfield's conquest was never complete. If such good judges as William Winter, Walter Prichard Eaton, and William Lyon Phelps were solidly in his corner, there were others who persisted in regarding him as hardly more than a sensationalist, a gifted, arrogant, self-dramatizing eccentric, and one well-known reviewer even felt called upon to proclaim far and wide that he was our "worst" actor.[1] At the very end of his career, he was so badgered by the critics of San Francisco, upon his appearance there, that the faculty of the University of California publicly apologized to him and tendered him a dinner at which they might testify to their regard for him.

Richard Mansfield was born in Berlin, on May 24, 1854, the son of Maurice Mansfield, a London wine merchant, and his wife,

[1] Alan Dale, "Who Is Our Worst Actor?" *Cosmopolitan*, Vol. XL (1906), 683–90.

Erminia Rudersdorff, a distinguished prima donna. Madame Rudersdorff was born in the Ukraine and is generally spoken of as Russian, but her father, a musician, went to Russia, for professional reasons, from Amsterdam. During Mansfield's lifetime he was often described as German and even accused, at times, of betraying a German accent on the stage.

Maurice Mansfield died in 1859, leaving his children to be brought up by their mother, and, in Richard's case, at least, at one period, by an aunt who was unkind to him. In England and on the Continent, the boy grew to manhood in a cosmopolitan atmosphere, which early developed in him much interest and competence in the arts, though his formal schooling was somewhat irregular. His most important educational affiliation would seem to have been that with the Derby School in England, largely perhaps because of his relationship to the headmaster, the Reverend Walter Clark, to whom his passionate nature gave the eternal devotion in which he never failed toward any human being who ever showed him kindness or understanding. There was deep love and devotion between Mansfield and his mother, but he inherited all his "difficult" qualities from her, and though he acted his "scenes" on a much larger stage, he would seem to have succeeded far better than she did in keeping himself under control. Mansfield did not live to see his boy grow up, but if he had done so, one cannot possibly imagine him cutting off his son's allowance and leaving him to starve in a foreign land, as his mother did with him, simply because he had displeased her by taking up a line of work of which she did not approve.

Madame Rudersdorff desired her son to go to Oxford or Cambridge, but this did not appeal to the boy. For a time the Indian Civil Service attracted him. In 1872 his mother came to America to sing in the Boston Peace Jubilee, and here she remained as a teacher of singing, with a studio about where the Colonial Theater now stands and a farm at Berlin, Massachusetts, near Fitchburg. Richard tried painting; he worked for the Boston merchant, Eben D. Jordan, of whom he made a lifelong friend;

and he appeared in amateur theatricals, most importantly perhaps in a Buskin Club production of Robertson's *School.* He also shared his mother's contacts with many celebrities of the region, including Longfellow and Julia Ward Howe. He even served a brief stint as dramatic critic on one of the newspapers.

In 1877 he returned alone to London, ostensibly to study painting, but soon turned, amid great hardship, to almost every conceivable type of professional and non-professional entertaining, frequently with music, his most memorable engagement, as seen in retrospect, being probably as Sir Joseph Porter in *Pinafore.* Following his mother's death in 1882, he came back to America at the instigation of Mr. Jordan, and in January, 1883, he scored his first great hit as the loathsome sensualist Baron Chevrial in Octave Feuillet's *A Parisian Romance* at A. M. Palmer's Union Square Theater.

Never disinclined to take the bull by the horns, Mansfield soon bought the rights to the play and undertook a starring tour, which was unsuccessful. In 1885 he appeared with Minnie Maddern (the future Mrs. Fiske) in *In Spite of All,* and in 1886 he first acted in the comedy *Prince Karl,* in which he proved that charm as well as sensation lay within his range, and which he retained in his repertoire until 1899. But the next great milestone was not passed until May 9, 1887, when he appeared at the Boston Museum in Stevenson's *Dr. Jekyll and Mr. Hyde,* which was dramatized for him by Thomas Russell Sullivan.

In 1888 he had a financially disastrous engagement at Sir Henry Irving's Lyceum Theater in London, but, unwilling to accept defeat, produced Shakespeare's *Richard III* at the Globe before returning with it to America in October. On May 19, 1890, he acted for the first time in *Beau Brummell,* which was developed for him, following his own and William Winter's suggestions, by the young Clyde Fitch, then at the very beginning of his short but brilliant career,[2] and which remained as

---

[2] For the subsequent controversy over the authorship of this play, see Winter's "Note on 'Beau Brummel,'" *Life and Art of Richard Mansfield,* II, 301–12. It

a lifesaver to him during all his years on the stage. "Without it," he told Winter, "I should have been lost."

On May 18, 1891, he appeared in New York in his own play, *Don Juan,* and the next year in his and Joseph Hatton's dramatization of *The Scarlet Letter.* On September 15, 1892, he contracted his only, and unusually happy, marriage to his leading woman, Beatrice Cameron, which produced one son, George Gibbs Mansfield, who was born August 3, 1898, and died of illness in an army training camp during World War I.

Mansfield's first appearance in his second Shakespearean role, Shylock in *The Merchant of Venice,* was achieved in New York in 1893. The next year, at the Herald Square Theater, now looking forward rather than backward, he gave Bernard Shaw his first American hearing with *Arms and the Man,* and it was with this play that he chose to reopen Harrigan's Theater, which he had leased and renamed the Garrick, on April 23, 1895. But his managership of the Garrick was short-lived and not financially successful, his last new production there being Charles Henry Meltzer's *The Story of Rodion, the Student,* an early dramatization of *Crime and Punishment,* in December of the same year.

A second Shaw venture, *The Devil's Disciple,* followed at Albany in 1897. Then, on October 3, 1898, at the Garden Theater, New York, he first appeared in Rostand's *Cyrano de Bergerac,* which not only gave him one of his greatest roles but also marked the turning of the tide in the long heroic struggle under a mountain of debt once estimated as high as half a million dollars. Two years later to the day, he unveiled his lavish production of Shakespeare's *Henry V* at the same theater.

In October, 1901, Mansfield appeared in Philadelphia in Booth Tarkington's *Monsieur Beaucaire,* dramatized by the author and Evelyn Greenleaf Sutherland, and a year later he returned to Shakespeare with *Julius Caesar,* first seen at his Chi-

should be remembered that Winter loathed the playwright (whom he was fond of referring to as "Mr. W. C. Fitch"), and that, for all his gifts as a critic, he could not always be trusted to be fair toward persons whom he disliked.

cago home, the Grand Opera House. In 1903 a translation of the German play, *Old Heidelberg*, familiar to later generations as having supplied the book of the Romberg operetta, *The Student Prince*, provided delightful relief from his heavier roles.

In the spring of 1904 he acted in an English version of Alexis Tolstoi's *Ivan the Terrible*; the next year he played Alceste in the first English production of Molière's *The Misanthrope*. In October, 1905, at Toledo, Ohio, he appeared in his own adaptation of Schiller's *Don Carlos*, and in October, 1906, he achieved his last great production—Ibsen's *Peer Gynt*—in Chicago.

In the early autumn of 1905, Mansfield had been obliged to submit to two operations, and by this time he was a dying man. His last New York engagement, which turned out to be his last anywhere, was at the New Amsterdam from February 25 to March 23, 1907, opening of course with *Peer Gynt*. During his last week on the stage he acted *The Scarlet Letter* on Monday, *Beau Brummell* on Tuesday and Friday, *A Parisian Romance* on Wednesday and Saturday, *Dr. Jekyll and Mr. Hyde* on Thursday, and *Peer Gynt* on Saturday afternoon. Following his last performance he made a curtain speech in which he thanked his public for the confidence they had shown in him, lamented the malicious rumors that had always been circulated about him and expressed the hope that they would not be believed, and hinted, though without reference to his illness, that his career was nearing its end. Capricious as ever, he thought he might be more comfortable in England, and was taken there in May, but the weather was bad, and in July he came back to America. When he was dying, his wife tried to hold him by kneeling beside his bed, while she clasped his hand, and repeated "God is life," but he only kissed her, smiled gently, and replied, "God is love." He died, at New London, Connecticut, on August 30, and was buried in Gardner Cemetery.

II

Though Mansfield seems never to have been a distinguished

student, he was emphatically a man of wide and far-from-super-
ficial culture. Through his mother, he early made the acquaintance not only of the great composers but of a wide variety of
distinguished writers, both English and Continental. He was a
gifted linguist; even as a boy, in amateur theatricals at the Derby
School, he acted, on a single evening, in English, German, and
French. He wrote; he sketched; he both composed music and
sang it. He wrote, or he made important contributions to, the
text of a number of the plays in which he appeared, and though
nobody would pretend that he had a distinctive poetic gift, technically his verses are not incompetent.[3] It is interesting that
though he had some trouble with *Henry V*, generally speaking it
was easy for him to memorize Shakespeare, but when he had to
deal with an inferior writer, his mind was always trying, without
his volition, to improve his material. In 1888 he acknowledged
receipt of a volume of Winter's poems. "When I have a moment,"
he says, "I sit down at the piano and try to sing them, to ex-
temporized music." With some actors this might be dismissed as
"side," but not with Mansfield. A good deal of the first part of
his career was as a singing actor. Besides *Pinafore*, he sang in
The Pirates of Penzance, The Sorcerer, Iolanthe, and *The
Mikado,* and he is credited with having improvised the music
which has ever since been used for the Major-General's patter-
song at an English provincial tryout. He composed music for
some of his plays also, and in the early days he did a good deal
of singing in them, sometimes seriously and sometimes doing
virtuoso-type burlesques on various types of singer. Later he was
inclined to shy from such exhibitions, ostensibly on the ground
that he was not a proficient, actually, perhaps, because he did

[3] Though Mansfield's *Blown Away: A Nonsensical Narrative Without Rhyme
or Reason* (L. C. Page, 1897) is full of echoes of *Alice in Wonderland*, and
though it anticipated *The Wizard of Oz* in having a girl (or, rather, two girls)
carried off by a cyclone, I cannot claim to care much for it, and I should think it
would be much too "arty" and too full of literary and musical burlesque to
interest children. There is also, I think, too much sardonicism, and I do not know
quite what to say about the boy who tortures insects or the fly who crawls slowly
up the window minus a leg.

not wish to be regarded as an "entertainer." In 1891 a whole concert was devoted to his compositions in Washington, and in 1892 he published a book of songs, *One Evening*.

Though he was a friend of President Benjamin Harrison, and later admired William Howard Taft and prophesied his election to the presidency, Mansfield seems to have been much less knowing in social and political affairs. For all his sensitiveness to individual want and hardship, I have found no references to any interest in social reform. One of his best-known poems was inspired by the Boer War, another by Dewey's victory at Manila Bay. Though he never became an American citizen, nor gave up the idea of some day establishing a home in England, he was fond, on occasion, of wrapping himself in the American flag: "The ambition of my stage career has been to prove the superiority of the American stage and the American actor, and I maintain that today against all those who pretend the contrary." In the introduction to his acting edition of *Henry V* he says that he produced the play for

> its healthy and virile tone (so diametrically in contrast to many of the performances now current); the nobility of its language, the breadth and power of which is not equaled by any living poet; the lesson it teaches of Godliness, loyalty, courage, cheerfulness and perseverance; its beneficial influence upon young and old. . . .

This can hardly be called a very penetrating view of a play which glorifies an aggressive conqueror.

Apparently Mansfield's critical intelligence did not match his aesthetic sensitiveness. "The natural way for him to consider any matter of importance," wrote Clayton Hamilton, who was closely associated with him, "was to let his mind dartle all around it, now in this mood, now in that, until at last it swooped to a decision. He was utterly illogical in all his processes of thought. He never reasoned consecutively. He arrived at his results, apparently, by intuition." Hamilton adds that he always thought concretely, not abstractly, expressing himself rather in images than in propositions, and there is independent evidence to indicate that he was right about this, but what he says is less a criticism of Mansfield than a description of how the artist's kind of mind works.

Yet if Mansfield could have achieved real distinction in any literary area, I should say it must have been that of the personal essay. His account of his production of *Richard III*[4] deals with more than the play; it is a charming account of his delighted exploration of the English countryside, and it shows the eye of a painter and a cultivated man's response to the charm of the past. Indeed, his writings are always those of a well-read man, and there is no question that he had the mind to have made a scholar of himself; whether he could have mustered the necessary patience is something else again. Winter says that the explanatory notes in Mansfield's published acting edition of *Henry V* were by the actor himself; they may be condemned as a needless parade of scholarship, but the scholarship is there nevertheless. Scholarly, too, is his discussion of *Richard III*, showing his knowledge not merely of the play but of its historical backgrounds also and the problems involved in the interpretation of Richard's character; this makes it seem all the more remarkable that Mansfield's acting version should have made such a hash of the text as it finally did.

That styles in acting change is beyond question; that they improve is more doubtful; it is true that we might laugh at Forrest today, but that would not prove that Forrest was wrong and that we are right; it would merely prove that our taste is different from that of his contemporaries. The future may laugh at Gielgud and Olivier, but this will not cancel out their worth either. Judged by the standards which prevailed in his time, Mansfield was far from being a barnstormer. "The nearer an actor gets to nature," he says, "the greater he is." He was not great when he made his early Shylock spit on the stage to express

[4] "The Story of a Production," *Harper's Weekly*, Vol. XXXIV (1890), 407–408, partly reprinted in Wilstach, *Richard Mansfield*, 168–72.

his loathing of Antonio, and he wisely gave this up. He warns against the eccentricity and personality cult with which others sometimes reproach him; it is more important, he says, to be correct than to be original. "An actor, in portraying various characters diametrically opposite, has no right to offer his own personality in each." He did not believe that a great actor could be "unruffled and calm and benign" after a performance.

> The very centre of his soul has been shaken; he has projected himself by force of will into another being, another sphere,—he has been living, acting, thinking another man's life, and you cannot expect to find him calm and smiling and tolerant of small troubles, dumped back on a dung heap after a flight to the moon.

But he carefully adds that this does not give the actor a right to "deport himself in any other wise than an honest man when he walks abroad. He can refrain from calling attention to himself by means which would be ridiculed if employed by other men."

Yet it cannot be said that Mansfield adhered to the school of repression. "The simulation of suppressed power is very useful and very advisable, but *when the fire-bell rings* the horses have got to come out, and rattle and race down the street, and rouse the town." It always rang in Mansfield's performances, and it rang too, for that matter, in his life, for he was almost as dramatic off the stage as on it. Read the letters he wrote his wife describing in detail how he and his company had turned pirate after being condemned by a Chicago judge to pay royalties to a Chicagoan who was under the impression that Rostand had stolen *Cyrano de Bergerac* from him.[5] Read, again, the account of the perfect Katherine and Petruchio dinner scene which he staged to tease a gourmand.[6] And though he helped to establish the "new" drama by presenting Shaw and Ibsen, neither dramatist furnished him with his ideal of what the theater ought to be.[7]

[5] Wilstach, *Richard Mansfield, the Man and the Actor*, 332–38.

[6] *Ibid.*, 341–43.

[7] It must be remembered that most of the disparaging things Mansfield wrote about Shaw and Ibsen were written to that man of many prejudices, Winter, who

Few actors have ever craved audience sympathy more than Mansfield did, and in such lighter items of his repertoire as *Prince Karl, Monsieur,* and, most of all, *Old Heidelberg,* he showed himself completely capable of commanding it. In *Beau Brummell,* too, his best effects were in the sympathetic, unhistorical passages. Generally and characteristically, however, his emphasis was upon the "strong" effects customarily associated with melodrama and the "character" actor. "A few of the parts that he played are sweet and winning," wrote Winter, "but most of them, and those especially in which he was most effective, contain more of repulsion than of allurement, and it was in the exposition of wicked power more than in the exercise of pacific charm that he found his advantage and gained his renown." John Corbin called him "powerful rather than subtle, passionate rather than spiritual. He is titanic, volcanic, but his fires burn in the element of earth." Granting him "tragic agony" but denying him "true tragedy," Corbin saw Mansfield "at his best when the eccentric and the sardonic blend with propulsive, cosmic passions."

There is probably much justice in this, but it is not wholly just. Mansfield himself once declared that "as long as the actor acts, he will consider the highest form of his art the display of the most powerful passions of men, and that he will strive at all times to choose such subjects as will best afford him opportunity to sway and impress his audience." Like all great actors who flourish in a transitional period, Mansfield was extraordinarily eclectic. He went through endless exercises of voice and gesture. Though he stigmatized the report that he prepared for Chevrial by studying superannuated rakes as nonsense, he was a close careful observer. On the other hand, he got some of his best effects by pure intuition and was pleased and gratified afterwards when authori-

---

detested them both. Once Mansfield even said that he was presenting *Peer Gynt* in the spirit of travesty, thus hoisting the Ibsen craze with its own petard! When writing to Winter, he even mildly disparages *Cyrano.* It seems clear, however, that he cared much less for Ibsen than did Mrs. Mansfield, for whom he mounted *A Doll's House* before their marriage, though he did not act in it himself. She was one of the earliest American Noras and was accounted very fine in the role.

ties told him he had been right. He used a green light on Mr. Hyde, but he performed the transformation scene without make-up and once almost scared the life out of DeWolf Hopper by doing it for him offstage. "The element of terror was made duly prominent," says Winter, "but the element of pathos was made to exceed that of terror," and though he admits that "the love scenes lacked passion," he insists that the exhibition "transcended personal display; that it came home and had a meaning to every mind."

Mansfield complained of the modern tendency to allow the stage carpenter to become more important than Shakespeare's lines, but when he produced *Henry V* he introduced a whole scene of pageantry and pantomime depicting the conqueror's return to London which seems to have come about as close to anticipating the motion picture with living actors as even Steele MacKaye could have come in his time. Yet Norman Hapgood, who probably stood alone among the critics in finding Mansfield "mental rather than passionate," and convinced "that heroics are naïve and foolish," thought that the actor had "decorated the play with such skill that the sweetness and majesty of it, the poetry which is its whole nature, instead of being crowded aside, seemed to be only appropriately clothed." James O'Donnell Bennett considered his Brutus a figure "of psychological poetry, not a booming rhetorician or a smug elocutionist," and Winter could find in his Richard III not "the faintest reminiscence of the ranting, mouthing, flannel-jawed king of clubs who has so generally strutted and bellowed as Shakespeare's *Glo'ster*." He did not "enter" in his first scene of *Julius Caesar*, but was "discovered" on stage, mingling with the crowd, and many auditors did not realize his presence until he spoke his first line. In *The Misanthrope* he was seated when the curtain rose, with the back of his chair to the audience.

There can be no question that, like Bernhardt, Mansfield was profoundly "theatrical," but I cannot but wonder whether those who cannot read this word without a pejorative accent have any qualifications for considering the problems of stagecraft. Of course a great romantic actor flaunts his ego, but does he not, at the same time, perform the same function for every sympathetic auditor? "In romantic drama," says Walter Prichard Eaton, "a goodly share of the pleasure an audience finds comes from the style of the thing, the sweeping grace of it." The intelligent theatergoer enjoys the play, but he also enjoys the player, and if he enjoys the performance as a performance, this only enhances his delight in what the playwright has created. Whatever validity, if any, "slice of life" theories may have in other branches of art, they have no place here. Mansfield, to quote Eaton again, "never forgot the theater," but the critic cleverly turns the tables on those who would dismiss him with another cliché, "old fashioned," when he adds that in a sense he "foreshadowed the revolt from naturalism of a later generation." Moreover, it is clear that, again like Bernhardt, he created some of his greatest effects by his imagination alone; like all great actors, he had the power of causing his audiences to see what he wanted them to see. When Brutus called Cassius "slight man," the spectator wanted to crawl under his chair, and when Peer Gynt's mother died, "the reindeer bells rang in the air [of the imagination], the roof disappeared, and through happy tears you saw the poor old mother reach the gates of Paradise."

There seems to be general agreement, however, that Mansfield was an uneven actor, who was at his very best only in climaxes, and who unleashed his full power only when he deeply "felt" his role. He was of average height and somewhat stocky build—I once heard Clayton Hamilton say that when he talked to a man who was taller than he was, he always tried to stand on an elevation—but though he was not exactly a handsome man, he was certainly distinguished looking. He had the advantage of a countenance of extraordinary mobility which could assume any aspect he desired with little or no makeup. Yet he could be awkward in posture and stiff and jerky in his movements, and his tempo was often wrong. He had a magnificent natural voice, but his use of it was sometimes as eccentric as Irving's, though some auditors insist that even the wrong things he did contributed to the impression of electric vitality which was one of his most exciting qualities.

If he was like Sarah Bernhardt in his "theatrical" quality, he was like her again in that neither of them ever got over stage fright.

> The excitement of a first night is actual suffering; the nervousness absolute torture. Yet as I walk down the Strand on my way to the theatre . . . and note the impassive, imperturbable faces of the passers-by, I must confess to myself that I would not change places with them—no, not for worlds. I have something that is filling my life brimful of interest; every nerve is dancing, every muscle quivering.

In both players, this was partly just plain shyness, strangely coexisting with the tendency toward exhibitionism, and Mansfield agonized over his lectures as well as his plays. He went to the theater to get himself into the part hours in advance, and while the performance was on, he remained in character on stage and off. Even a dressing room too far from the stage could break the spell for him.

Mansfield was a curious combination of complete self-confidence in his own powers and of no confidence at all. "I am exceedingly ambitious," he wrote Augustin Daly in 1892, "and I confess it. I desire to produce great plays and to play them greatly, and with God's aid I shall accomplish this." The letters to Winter are full of this kind of thing: "If America wants a new actor—new enterprise—new work, and a man who will spend freely all that is given to him, they may encourage me." The fact that he produced his plays with his own money and made himself responsible not only for acting but for staging, directing, lighting, and everything else that goes into a production must always be taken into account in weighing the strain under which he labored. Even in the hour of his greatest triumphs there was no rest for him. Like John Barrymore, he could not bear the thought of settling down to a long "run"; unlike Barrymore, he was a completely disciplined man and artist, carrying a repertoire and envisaging a great career in terms of progress from one mountain peak to another, each ascent being carefully planned for in advance. No wonder he was hurt when, upon Booth's death, Winter hailed him as the last great actor:

> I sympathize with you greatly, in the loss of your friend—but you should not say he is *the last*. What—I—I—*I*, am I—nothing? Do you bite your thumb at *me?* There is much drivel being written about *the last actor*. If there is demand there will be supply. For my part, let me cultivate oranges and not opinions.

He frequently urged the establishment of a National Theater, not only to set theatrical standards but to serve some of the functions of an academy. No doubt he was entirely sincere in this, though I confess I find it as difficult to picture him operating in it as it is to see him living comfortably under the monarchical system which he also advocated for America, should some other than King Richard have been crowned.

Yet he was far from thinking well of all his efforts. He believed his Brummell irreproachable, but he considered his Jekyll and Hyde overrated, and he bluntly declared that in one scene of *Don Carlos* he was "rotten." Before he could bring himself to act Cyrano, he had to steal over to Paris to see how Coquelin was doing it, and he expected *Peer Gynt* to be his worst failure. For that matter, he hardly ever came to a first night without at some point having thought it was going to be necessary to junk the whole enterprise. In some moods he could vaunt himself as Irving's superior, but he could also shrink from playing in competition to him. "I *am* a DAMNED bad actor, and somehow I realize it more every day." And again: "The most severe critic can never tell me more, or scold me more than I scold myself. I have never left the stage satisfied with myself." Sometimes he extended his condemnation to the whole theater:

227

Actors see only the pretense of it all. . . . The silvery moon is tin
and calcium, the swaying trees present nothing but drab canvas
and cut pine from our side of the woodland; fountains are as
dishonest as local elections, and beauties are painted into frights.
It is wigs, it is powder, it is mockery.

And again he cries: "I am sick to death of the sawdust that the
doll is stuffed with."

Sometimes he thought of his audience as a great beast, waiting
out there, the other side of the footlights, for a chance to devour
him, and sometimes he was so much *en rapport* with it that he
could recharacter a whole performance in response to its prompt-
ing. But from audience, from friends, and from critics he needed
constant reassurance of his worth. He never learned how to avoid
being hurt even by those whom he knew in his heart to be worthy
only of contempt. "I have been bitterly and cruelly attacked—so
much so that for some days I trod the stage with almost shame."
"It is futile to do good work . . . in this country. The conditions
are such that every effort is belittled and every ambition de-
rided." "I am disgruntled and I have one of my 'throw everything
away' moods upon me." "I am working because it is preferable
to being idle; but I have very little to work for. I do not care for
money, and *the recognition I hoped for is denied me.*" "No one
comes near me. I am entirely alone." "I do not suppose anybody
realizes how much I long for that friendship and regard which is
denied me." Sometimes he even developed a persecution complex, in which Irving, Frohman, Daly, Barrett, and Booth were
all, at one time or another, involved. Mansfield is not winning in
this aspect. He could be almost childishly petulant. As late as
1905, when John Drew was elected president of the Players'
Club, succeeding Jefferson, he wrote, "I have never been deferred to upon any occasion whatever, and my advice or opinion
is not wanted. No college has ever bestowed any degree upon
me, unless it be that of A.S.S. There is no artistic society or atmosphere, and I evolve everything out of myself and am utterly
alone." On the other hand, it must in fairness be remembered

that his worst enemy never ventured to suggest that he ever stooped to any manner of intrigue or in any way took advantage of a fellow actor, or, for that matter, of any human being. When he was hurt, or fancied he was, he screamed until the welkin rang, but treachery and fainaiguing were outside his range. And his considered exhortation to the critics is no less reasonable today than it was when he formulated it:

> Separate the man from his art. If you dislike the man, you have no right to condemn his art. Your sense of honor must make you just. Personal abuse is not criticism. Never. . . . Criticise with dignity if you criticise at all. What is worthy of criticism is worthy of respect.

Mansfield's uncertainty nowhere shows better than in his wariness toward Shakespeare. All English-speaking actors regard the role of Hamlet as the supreme challenge. Mansfield unquestioningly accepted William Winter's opinion that he was not qualified to play it, and he never tried. As has already appeared, he essayed only four Shakespearean roles—Richard III, Henry V, Shylock, and Brutus—none of them among the greatest. According to Otis Skinner, he thought Brutus "an old fool" and himself "an old fool" in the part, and declared that he produced the play only because he had bought the Alma Tadema settings cheap from Sir Henry Irving and had to mount a Roman play to make use of them! In a long letter published in the Chicago *Inter-Ocean* in 1893,[8] he went so far as to declare that he believed himself unsuited to either tragic or heroic roles, and even that he thought Shakespeare, nowadays, better accommodated in the study than on the stage. Winter urged Falstaff upon him, but Mrs. Mansfield said, "If you ever appear as that disgusting old man, and speak those horrid lines, I will never look at you again!" and from her husband's point of view, this left nothing to be said. Shylock, as Wilstach remarks, he acted, in the course of his career, from every conceivable point of view, but his waverings do honor to his humanity. Intellectually he was clear enough.

[8] Reprinted in Wilstach, *Richard Mansfield*, 243–48.

Shylock is really the only natural person in most unnatural surroundings. The play itself, if written to-day, would be either instantly condemned or put down as a farcical comedy. The noble
Antonio . . . cannot find anybody to lend him three thousand
ducats, but the man he everlastingly abused, kicked, and spat
upon. Bassanio is confessedly a fortune-hunter, Gratiano a lickspittle and time server, Lorenzo is a thief or *particeps criminis*,
Jessica is unspeakable, and the Duke condemns Shylock in open
court before the trial. It is difficult for a sincere actor to play Shylock according to modern requirements with sincerity. I should
like some day, just for fun, to put Shylock and the whole interpretation of the play back where it belongs—in the realm of poetic
farce. . . . However, when all is said, to-day Shylock must be either
a monumental type of the hating and revengeful and much-
abused Jew—or a joke. Anything else is begging the question.

Only, he was too decent a man to enjoy playing the role in either
of these ways, and he was forever trying to inject elements of
nobility into it, though nothing could have been more ill-advised
than his introduction of "business" suggesting suicide at the close
of the Court Scene.

Though Mansfield understood the value of money, and sometimes proclaimed that he acted only to secure it, his record belies
him. Actually, money and the desire for money were not very
important elements in his aesthetic motivation. He produced the
plays he wished to produce, which he regarded as worth producing, and as affording the maximum favorable opportunity for
the public exhibition of his art and his progress in it. For that
matter, there was no economy in him in any aspect. What with
private cars and private trains, yachts, town houses and country
houses, crowded with valuable *objets d'art*, he lived almost as
much like a prince when he was poor as when he was rich, and
his charities and his kindnesses were on the same fantastic scale.
Once, in California, literally on the impulse of the moment, he
bought a ranch, at a highly inflated price, because he "felt sorry"
for the poor people who owned it, and forthwith his mind set to

work to conjure up dreams of a great market trade for oranges, lemons, olives, and figs. If a young lady said she liked flowers, he would give a dinner for her on a table hidden under a blanket of buds; if friends in another city wished to see him act, he would send his private car to bring them where he was playing. For private performances there were engraved invitations and programs printed on silk. His capriciousness and his intuitional methods often added notably to the cost of his productions also, and he could never bear to collect the fees to which he was legally entitled if he knew the local manager was going into the red.[9]

I should not call Mansfield a religious man, but he did live and think habitually against a religious frame of reference. His letters contain frequent references to Deity, statements of dependence upon God and submission to His will—all thoroughly conventional but apparently sincere. "Things have taken a turn and we are playing to crowded houses for which I thank God! . . . it did seem as if the good God had quite forgotten me—or was angry with me—so bad . . . have affairs been with me of late." And again: "I am doing an awful lot of hard praying these days, for Beatrice and my boy are on the sea." Once he speaks of Jesus Christ as "our Lord." Twice he seems to have had psychic experiences, at least one of which involved seeing what is commonly called an apparition. "My favorite stage motto," he once wrote, "is: '*Il faut excuser l'auteur*'—by this I mean that, no matter how great the author, the actor must often disguise him and in a manner excuse him to his audience." He applies this to Henry V's prayer, reminding God of what he has done for Him, and demanding His help in return, which he apparently recognized as shocking to modern religious feeling.

[9] Mansfield's opposition to the Klaw and Erlanger theatrical syndicate in the nineties was defiant; then, very suddenly, he backed down. From the point of view of Mrs. Fiske, virtually the only star who remained permanently irreconcilable, this was treason, but Mansfield himself seems to have been convinced that there was no sense in continuing a fight which could not be won. For the Fiske view, see Archie Binns and Olive Kooken, *Mrs. Fiske and the American Theatre* (Crown, 1955), especially pages 81, 82–85. Wilstach's account, 288–89, is more friendly to Mansfield.

What is certain is that Mansfield saw and used the stage consistently as a powerful ethical force.

> The stage should not be for temptation, from the deliverance of which we pray in the morning; it should not be for the idiotic laugh and the imbecile applause; it is not for the drunkard and the wanton; it is not to be shrieked at to-day and to be ashamed of to-morrow; it is not for gymnastics; it is for the gracious, the graceful, the thoughtful, the gentle; it is to send us home with better thoughts and better feelings, with a lesson learned by example and with food for pleasant reflection. It is for wholesome mirth or for such stirring tragedy as will fire us to nobler deeds, or for such potent example as will sicken us of evil doing. That is the stage as I understand it and as I would strive for it.

He disliked the "problem plays" that were coming more and more into vogue toward the close of his career, for much the same reasons that Julia Marlowe did.

> We may at once confess that there are sewers and some bad sewers. That is the truth. But because it is the truth there is no need to exhibit them upon the stage. There are other means of eradicating such evils.

He rejected *Candida* as "just two and one-half hours of preaching," but probably the basic reason was that he thought Marchbanks unsuited to him. In *The Devil's Disciple* he defied Shaw by changing Essie from a young woman in whom the hero was sentimentally interested to a child who merely aroused his chivalry. He idealized his Don Juan. Peer Gynt touched Beatrice Cameron's lover as a man who was "at last brought to his knees and to a knowledge and recognition of God by a pure woman."[10] Even *Jekyll and Hyde*, for all its sensationalism, was for him primarily a parable. "It seems to me that if there ever was a moral powerfully taught, it is here. I wish I could act it as well as I feel it."

[10] Wilstach's phrase, *Richard Mansfield*, 459.

Mansfield liked to take his final curtain calls without make-up, appearing before his audience as himself rather than the character he had been portraying. The action is symptomatic of the close identification of actor and man. His contemporaries were never able to decide whether he was more dramatic on or off the stage. He vaunted himself, he made scenes, he scolded his audiences, and when the newspapers had reported all the things he said and did, and a great many others which he never thought of saying or doing at all, he often looked more like an ogre than a man. When he turned down *The Man of Destiny*, Shaw was hurt, "not because I think it one of my masterpieces, but because Napoleon is nobody else but Richard Mansfield himself. I studied the character from you, and then read up Napoleon and found that I had got him exactly right."

There is no indication that Mansfield deliberately cultivated his "peculiarities" for their publicity value, as some actors and other public figures have done. He was easy to rouse and easy to placate, and all his outbursts were perfectly genuine. In one sense he was too introverted to play to the gallery; in another he was too innocent. It is as easy to be self-centered in self-deprecation as in self-vaunting; Mark Twain often achieved it, and so did Mansfield. When he wrote, "Look with a gentle eye upon this wretch," or burlesqued the incredibly smug photograph of Augustin Daly reading a play to the members of his company, all of whom listen with rapt attention, with a photograph of Richard Mansfield reading his own play to *his* company, all of whom are asleep, he was still, as Stendhal said of Byron, "the unique object of his own attention." He has been praised for his modesty in naming his New York theater the Garrick rather than the Mansfield, but what he told Winter was that should the theater fail (as it did), "I don't want *Mansfield* to suffer any more than I can help." Now Mansfield was not in the least Napoleonic if this implies victimizing others for your own advantage, for he was incapable of inflicting a deliberate injury upon any human being. He had to believe in what he was doing; he could not have lived with himself if he had not been perfectly convinced that he was serving the public welfare. But it must be *he himself* who served it, and it was not only after the curtain went up that he must occupy the center of the stage. A fantastically kind and generous host, he was an uneasy guest, and he could not associate on easy terms with any enterprise that he did not control.

If he was not, in the ordinary sense, Napoleonic, he certainly was not Byronic, for he is nowhere more winning than in his family life. When he was sixteen years old, he filled out a questionnaire in which he declared that "grace, wit, and modesty" were the qualities he most admired in a woman. He never changed his mind, and in Mrs. Mansfield he found the perfect embodiment of all these. "Beatrice and I are,—or at least *I* am, with her,—completely happy. She is more beautiful every day. She is completely and absolutely good. I can find (and I am a severe critic) in her not one fault. She is the soul of goodness, and appears to possess every virtue. I am lost in wonderment that any human being can be so." She was probably the only human being who ever completely understood him, and who was completely successful in managing him, though without dominating him, but though she was a fine actress who gave up her career to devote herself to his, she had a mind and views of her own, and she never made the mistake of trying to make her mind a carbon copy of his; neither would he ever have wished her to do so. There can be no question that he made her completely happy, for she outlived him by more than a generation and mourned him and worshiped his memory to the day of her death. He was no less winning with their only child, with whom he played by the hour when they were together, and to whom, when they were separated, he wrote immensely long letters, into which he poured as much of his imagination as he put into his roles, yet he was never the foolishly doting father, nor did he ever forget that

234

children must be trained as well as loved. For that matter, Mansfield was always charming with children, all children. "They do not prattle of yesterdays," he said. "Their interest is all in today and tomorrow. So is mine." This seems to me to suggest an interesting limitation in his famous egotism, since most egotists find children too demanding. It may no doubt be replied that Mansfield was a child himself, but this does not get us far. Really spoiled children do not generally like other children; instead they turn to weak adults who will pamper them and be victimized by them.

In any case, the childlike quality was there, and he himself recognized it clearly. "I have never been able to overcome certain traits of my childhood [a lump in the throat and a trembling underlip]. I am as eagerly moved to laughter and tears, to anger and sympathy as I was then, and beyond a certain amount of added knowledge, I feel just as I did then. I run, jump, eat, sleep, and comport myself in most ways as I did when I was a boy." The child quality shows in the frequently exaggerated gratitude toward those who had been kind to him, and though there may be a certain amount of egotism involved even in gratitude (since there is an unspoken assumption that we ourselves are worth being kind to), it is certainly a more amiable quality than its opposite. Mansfield's gratitude could embrace a whole community, as notably Chicago, the one city which seems never to have failed him, and where he maintained an apartment in later years, while the petulance flared up notably in Boston in 1906. He had not expected *The Misanthrope* to do well in general, but he looked forward with confidence to his engagement at the Hub; surely the center of American culture would not let him— and Molière—down. Alas! she half-filled the theater for *one* performance, and Mansfield stormed that he would never play in Boston again, which, unhappily, he would have had no chance to do in any event.

He claimed that he generally knew what people were going to say to him as soon as they began to speak and consequently found it very tedious to continue to listen to them, but, he said, "I always do." He seems to have expected the same prescience when he communicated with others, and when he did not find it he became impatient: "The most surprising thing about him," says Clayton Hamilton, "was the swift and lightning-dartle of his moods. His mind shifted with unusual vivacity of variation. He alternated moments of sudden and incalculable enthusiasm with moments of apparent dulness and uninterest of mind. . . . You could never be certain that what appealed to him to-day would also appeal to him to-morrow."

His own considered defense of himself was clearly formulated: "I am hasty and quick-tempered—but I harm only myself. I would rather be so, than cold, calculating, and insincere." Though I do not know that this always made it easier for those against whom he hurled the thunderbolts, there can be no doubt of its accuracy. "He was by nature kindly," said Hamilton, "by habit courteous, by disposition generous, and though I often saw him impatient I never knew him to be angry. He had a nervous temperament, but he did not have a bad temper." And Paul Wilstach, who also worked with him, agrees: "Anger came from sore nerves, not from the heart. It was from the lips out. He cherished no animosity." One day he caught Arch and Edgar Selwyn imitating him. They expected to be discharged on the spot, but he thought the performance so good that he advised them to go on the stage. It is not surprising to learn that he mellowed considerably during his later years, when his professional life had become less of a struggle. But he did not need to wait for prosperity to reveal his kindness of heart. From the beginning of his career, his charities were innumerable, and he set up his own social security and job insurance plans long before the state ever dreamed of such things. Even when money was hardest to come by and he was deepest in debt, he never dreamed of discharging a sick actor; not only was his place held for him but all the expenses of his illness were paid. He could ask forgiveness when he knew he had been wrong, as in his letter to Winter: "*Don't* be mad with me. I only cried out to you, and against you, as to a father or brother who wouldn't understand." And he could forgive others when they fell upon evil days. He disliked A. M. Palmer, who, rightly or wrongly, he thought had mistreated him in his Union Square Theater days, but when, in 1897, Palmer was broken in health and spirit, he employed him as a manager, as his peculiar means of wreaking "vengeance" upon him. It is true that even here he was the autocrat, as when he forbade the members of his troupe from subscribing to a fund for one of their number: "No collections in my company. Never. Return every cent. Pay all the bills and charge them to my account."

Mansfield's motto *"Maintenant"* has a little of the defiant ring of Bernhardt's *"Quand même."* Both, in a sense, constitute a defiance of life. But from another point of view they indicate an acceptance of life, and if any artist has the right to such a motto, it is the actor, for if he does not get his reward now, he will never get it at all. Nobody worked harder or longer for it than Mansfield, but basically he was not thinking of his reward at all; it was a matter of self-expression and of life itself. "What I take from the public with one hand," he cried, "I will give back with the other," and nobody has ever doubted that he did this.

The public, apparently, always needs to have some actor to love, and certain sub-areas of it seem to have an even greater need of some actor to hate; occasionally, even, the same person may serve in both capacities. In Mansfield's time, as we have seen, they had their object of adoration in Joseph Jefferson, and when, in 1895, Mansfield was recovering from a very dangerous attack of typhoid fever, he received an anonymous letter from a creature presumably human who regretted that he had not died. A certain kind of nobody always hates a somebody, and a man in whom energy flares up several sizes larger than life always antagonizes slugs. For such venom the actor is the ideal target, for his is incomparably the most personal of all the arts, and to hate actors is to hate humanity, for the actor is like everybody else, only more so. Even without his "temperament" and his "arrogance" Mansfield would have been fair game, but the existence of these tendencies in him furnished an excellent excuse. Fortunately there were also those (they are nearly all gone now) who also responded to his vitality, his idealism, and his passion for beauty, and who found their lives permanently enriched and excited for the labors that used him up while he was still in his prime.

One day, when we still had a theater in this country, E. H. Sothern was moving in to an engagement in Louisville just as John Drew was closing his. As they stood chatting in the corridor of a hotel, a dignified elderly Kentucky gentleman approached, bowed, and addressed Sothern.

"Mr. Mansfield," he said, "I am very glad to see you here, and I'm going to be delighted to attend every performance of yours during your all too brief sojourn. I have watched your career, Mr. Mansfield."

With this, he bowed again, shook hands, and walked away. Sothern had not spoken a word.

"Why, in heaven's name, didn't you say something?" asked Drew.

"What," asked Sothern, "was there to say?"

"He doesn't know that Dick Mansfield is dead," said Drew.

"Well," said Sothern, "that doesn't hurt me so much. He doesn't know that I'm alive."

Half of the actor's triumph and tragedy is wrapped up in that story.

Bibliography

1. David Garrick (1717–1779)

A full Garrick bibliography might well fill a book the size of this one. Mrs. Clement Parsons says rightly: "Unauthentic information concerning Garrick is scattered broadcast throughout eighteenth-century memoirs, theatrical and otherwise. He is as much a centre of legend as King Arthur." But to a lesser extent this is true of authentic information also, and the reader who desires a list of the eighteenth-century memoirs and biographies of eighteenth-century figures, from Boswell's *Johnson* on down, in which Garrick figures must be referred to Mrs. Parsons' own biography and to those given by Margaret Barton and Carola Oman in the books listed hereinafter. Fortunately the eighteenth-century material has by now been pretty well mined by Garrick's own biographers.

In using this and the following bibliographies, it should be understood that much valuable material on specialized subjects listed in the footnotes is *not* repeated in the bibliography section.

The two pioneering biographies of Garrick, each in two volumes, are by Thomas Davies, *Life of Garrick*, published by himself (1780), and by Arthur Murphy, *Life of David Garrick* (J.

Wright, 1801). In 1886, Percy Fitzgerald brought out a very extensive *Life of David Garrick* (2 vols., Tinsley Brothers), and in 1894 came Joseph Knight, *David Garrick* (Kegan Paul).

Twentieth-century writing about Garrick reaches a higher scholarly level than the books about any other actor with whom I am acquainted. Margaret Barton, *Garrick* (Macmillan, 1949) and Carola Oman, *David Garrick* (Hodder and Stoughton, 1958) are excellent general studies. The Barton seems particularly right to me—I could not ask for a better biography of anybody—but the Oman gives far more detail. Mrs. Clement Parsons, *Garrick and His Circle* (Putnam, 1906) and Frank A. Hedgcock, *David Garrick and his French Friends* (Duffield, 1912) are more specialized, but both writers were well informed on Garrick in many aspects. There is an extensive German study by Christian Gaehde, *David Garrick als Shakespeare-darsteller und seine Bedeutung für die heutige Schauspielskunst* (G. Reimer, 1904) and another in Swedish by Edla af Klercker, *David Garrick och hans Medspelare i livet och på scenen* (Hugo Gerbers Forlag, 1928). Anne Bird Stewart's *Enter David Garrick*, charmingly illustrated by Ernest H. Shepard (Lippincott, 1951), is a "story"-type of biography for young readers, but it is based on careful study and considerable knowledge.

Garrick study was placed on a new and firmer basis with the publication of *The Letters of David Garrick*, meticulously edited by David M. Little and George M. Kahrl, with Phoebe deK. Wilson as associate editor (3 vols., Belknap Press of Harvard University Press, 1963). Mr. Kahrl's introduction to Volume I is likewise important. This work supersedes all previous collections of Garrick's letters, except for *Letters of David Garrick and Georgiana Countess Spencer, 1759–79*, ed. by Earl Spencer and Christopher Dobson (The Roxburghe Club, 1960). This material is not reproduced in the Little-Kahrl collection, its owners having unfortunately seen fit to take up a dog-in-the-manger attitude. James Boaden's extensive memoir, prefixed to Volume I of *The Private Correspondence of David Garrick* (2 vols., Henry Colburn and Richard Bentley, 1831–32) is still of interest, however, as is George Pierce Baker's commentary in *Some Unpublished Correspondence of David Garrick* (Houghton Mifflin, 1907).

The Diary of David Garrick, Being a Record of his Memorable Trip to Paris in 1751 was edited by Ryllis Clair Alexander and published by Oxford University Press (1928). For *The Journal of David Garrick, Describing his Visit to France and Italy in 1763,* see the edition of George Winchester Stone, Jr. (Modern Language Association of America, 1939).

Under the title "Garrick and His Contemporaries," Harvard Theatre Collection has much manuscript and printed material brought together by Justin Winsor, who apparently at one time intended to write a book about Garrick. Under the title "Shakespeare and Garrick" are a number of articles by Winsor, clipped from *Round Table,* 1864. See also Winsor's "Stage-Struck," *Atlantic Monthly,* Vol. XXII (1868), 79–88.

Brief studies of Garrick, of varying value and significance, will be found in Henry Barton Baker, *English Actors from Shakespeare to Macready,* I (Holt, 1879); Donald Brook, *A Pageant of English Actors* (Rockliff, 1950); W. A. Darlington, *The Actor and his Audience* (Phoenix House, 1949); Austin Dobson, in Brander Matthews and Laurence Hutton, eds., *Actors and Actresses of Great Britain and the United States,* I (Cassell, c.1886); Evert A. Duyckinck, *Portrait Gallery of Eminent Men and Women of Europe and America . . .,* I (Johnson, Wilson and Company, 1873); J. A. Hammerton, ed., *The Actor's Art* (George Redway, 1897); Francis Hitchman, *Eighteenth Century Studies* (Sampson Low, 1881); James Laver, in Bonamy Dobrée, ed., *From Anne to Victoria* (Scribners, 1937); Sir Theodore Martin, *Monographs . . .* (Dutton, 1906); Edward Robins, *Twelve Great Actors* (Putnam, 1900).

A number of these books and others will be cited in connection with other actors treated in this volume, but information about publishers and dates is given only with the first citation. Information concerning the Shakespearean productions of all the actors included will be found in Arthur Colby Sprague, *Shakespeare and the Actors: The Stage Business in His Plays* (*1660–1905*) (Harvard University Press, 1944); this work will not be listed again.

Biographical data of interest concerning Garrick are given in Kalman A. Burnim, "The Significance of Garrick's Letters to Hayman," *Shakespeare Quarterly*, Vol. IX (1958), 149–52; Donald Cross Bryant, *Edmund Burke and his Literary Friends*, being *Washington University Studies*, N.S., Language and Literature, No. 9 (1939); Ernest Clarke, "David Garrick and Junius," *Nineteenth Century*, Vol. LXXV (1914), 180–85; Charles Haywood, "William Boyce's 'Solemn Dirge' in Garrick's *Romeo and Juliet* Production of 1750," *Shakespeare Quarterly*, Vol. XI (1960), 173–87; *Portraits by Sir Joshua Reynolds*, ed. by Frederick W. Hilles (McGraw-Hill, 1952); John Jennings, "David Garrick and Nicholas Nipclose," *Educational Theatre Journal*, Vol. XVI (1964), 270–75; Lewis M. Knapp, "Smollett and Garrick," in *Elizabethan Studies and Other Essays in Honor of George F. Reynolds* (*University of Colorado Studies*, Series B, Vol. II, No. 4 [1945]); Mary E. Knapp, "Garrick's Last Command Performance," in *The Age of Johnson: Essays Presented to Chauncey Brewster Tinker* (Yale University Press, 1949); Louis L. Martz and Edwine M. Martz, "Notes on Some Manuscripts Relating to David Garrick," *Review of English Studies*, Vol. XIX (1943), 186–200; T. H. Vail Motter, "Garrick and the Private Theatres," *ELH*, Vol. XI (1944), 63–75; Cecil Price, "David Garrick and Evan Lloyd," *Review of English Studies*, N.S., Vol. III (1952), 28–38; Dixon Wecter, "David Garrick and the Burkes," *Philological Quarterly*, Vol. XVIII (1939), 367–80; Sybil Rosenfeld, "David Garrick and Private Theatricals," *Notes and Queries*, Vol. CLXXXI (1941), 230–31; Senex, "Recollections of Garrick," *Blackwood's Edinburgh Magazine*, Vol. XVII (1825), 488–93.

The following are of critical interest: Hon. Robert Lytton, "Old Criticisms of Old Plays and Actors," *Living Age*, Vol. CIX (1871), 67–78, 236–39; Walter Herries Pollock, "Garrick's Acting as Seen in his Own Time," *Longman's Magazine*, Vol. VI (1885), 371–84; Sir Edward Russell, *Garrick: A Lecture* (*Liverpool Daily Post* and *Echo* Offices, n.d.). H. D. Traill included a dialogue between Garrick and George Henry Lewes in his *The New Lucian; Being a Series of Dialogues of the Dead* (Chapman and Hall, 1884). Stark Young's "David Garrick to John Barrymore" in the "Letters from Dead Actors" section of *Glamour* (Scribners, 1925) contains a good deal about the Hamlet performances of both actors. A learned indexer entered it as Garrick's composition in the *Essay and General Literature Index*!

2. *Edmund Kean (1787?–1833)*

The earliest memoir of any length seems to be Francis Phippen, *Authentic Memoirs of Edmund Kean* ... (J. Roach, 1814), which runs to 111 small pages. But the first real biography was B. W. Procter (Barry Cornwall), *The Life of Edmund Kean* (2 vols., Edward Moxon, 1835). It was followed by two other nineteenth-century biographies, each in two volumes: F. W. Hawkins, *The Life of Edmund Kean* ... (Tinsley Brothers, 1869); J. Fitzgerald Molloy, *The Life and Adventures of Edmund Kean, Tragedian, 1787–1833* (Ward and Downey, 1888).

W. J. Lawrence, "A New Chapter in the Life of Edmund Kean," *English Illustrated Magazine*, Vol. XXV (1910), 348–57, is an independent piece of research, filling in the years 1804–1805, which had been neglected by the nineteenth-century biographers.

What is now the standard biography, and the only really scholarly book on Kean, is Harold Newcomb Hillebrand, *Edmund Kean* (Columbia University Press, 1933). Giles Playfair, *Kean* (Dutton, 1939) tells the story in absorbing fashion. Maurice Willson Disher's *Mad Genius* ... (Hutchinson, 1950), though the work of a man who has written other respected books about the theater, is nearly worthless. Written in the form of a novel, it necessarily sacrifices some of the advantages of biography without at any point achieving the values of good fiction.

There is a somewhat better novel by a German writer named Julius Berstl, in which Kean is made to tell his own story. This was published in 1946, in an English translation, by Hammond, Hammond & Co. in London under the title, *The Sun's Bright Child*; in 1962, Orion Press brought out an American edition called *Kean: The Imaginary Memoirs of an Actor*.

William Hazlitt's criticisms of Kean may be consulted conveniently in William Archer and Robert Lowe, eds., *Hazlitt on Theatre* (Hill and Wang, n.d.) and Leigh Hunt's in Lawrence Huston Houtchens and Carolyn Washburn Houtchens, eds., *Leigh Hunt's Dramatic Criticism, 1808–1831* (Columbia University Press, 1949).

First-hand data concerning Kean may be found in William W. Clapp, Jr., *A Record of the Boston Stage* (James Munroe and Company, 1853); William Cotton, *The Story of the Drama in Exeter, During its Best Period, 1787 to 1823, with Reminiscences of Edmund Kean* (Hamilton, Adams and Company, 1887); William Donaldson, *Recollections of an Actor* (John Maxwell and Company, 1865); T. C. Grattan, "My Acquaintance with the Late Edmund Kean," *New Monthly Magazine*, 1833, Part the Third, 7–16, 143–51; Sir Theodore Martin, "An Eyewitness of John Kemble," *Nineteenth Century*, Vol. VII (1880), 276–96; Laman Rede, "The Early Days of Edmund Kean," *New Monthly Magazine*, 1834, Part the First, 434–43, and "Recollections of Kean," Part the Second, 51–62; George Vandenhoff, *Dramatic Reminiscences . . .* (Thomas H. Cooper & Co., 1860); William B. Wood, *Personal Recollections of the Stage* (Henry Carey Baird, 1855). Theodore Norton, *Kean: A Poem* (W. Kenneth, 1835) is followed by a collection of anecdotes illustrating Kean's virtue. Raymond Mander and Joe Mitchenson, "Kean minus Make-up," *Theatre Arts*, Vol. XXXIX (1955), 74–76, 85–86, gives an appallingly dissipated picture of Kean in later life by reprinting a hitherto unnoted interview of 1828. There is an analysis of Kean in Henry T. Tuckerman, *Essays Biographical and Critical . . .* (Phillips, Sampson and Company, 1857).

John Doran, *"Their Majesties' Servants": Annals of the English Stage*, (3 vols., John C. Nimmo, 1887) devotes its last two chapters to Kean. The following books and articles contain sketches of Kean, none of which add anything in particular to what the biographies have recorded: Anon., "Edmund Kean," *Temple Bar*, Vol. XLIX (1877), 180–95; Henry Barton Baker, *English Actors from Shakespeare to Macready*, II; Frederick S. Boas, *From Richardson to Pinero: Some Innovators and Idealists* (John Murray, 1936); Donald Brook, *A Pageant of English Actors*; Emily H. Buckingham, " 'Found! An Actor!' " *Cornhill*, N.S., Vol. XXXIV (1913), 78–86; W. A. Darlington, *The Actor and his Audience* (Phoenix House, 1949); St. John Ervine, "Edmund Kean," London *Observer*, May 4, 1933; Daniel Frohman, *Encore* (Lee Furman, 1937); J. A. Hammerton, *The Actor's Art*; Helen Ormsbee, *Backstage with Actors* (Crowell, 1938); Edward Robins, *Twelve Great Actors*; Otis Skinner, *Mad Folk of the Theatre* (Bobbs-Merrill, 1928); A. E. Snodgrass, "The Storm and Stress of Edmund Kean," *Cornhill*, Vol. LXXIV (1933), 513–20. Of these I should say Brook gives the best brief account of Kean's career available.

Edwin Booth's sketch in Brander Matthews and Laurence Hutton, eds., *Actors and Actresses . . .*, III, is interesting for the light it sheds on his and his father's attitude toward Kean. Stanley Kauffman's article, "The Trail of the Splendid Gypsy," *Horizon*, Vol. IV, March, 1962, pp. 12–13, 114–19, was occasioned by the Peter Stone–Robert Wright–George Forrest musical *Kean*, in which Alfred Drake starred. It adds nothing to the reader's knowledge of Kean, but it gives a good account of the various plays that have been written about him.

3. *William Charles Macready (1793–1873)*

Sir Frederick Pollock published *Macready's Reminiscences, and Selections from his Diaries and Letters*, (2 vols., Macmillan, 1875). The section devoted to the Diaries was superseded in 1912 by William Toynbee's much more extensive selection in *The*

Diaries of William Charles Macready, (2 vols., Chapman and Hall). Unfortunately, however, Toynbee did not reprint all the diary materials which Pollock used.

Lady Pollock's *Macready As I Knew Him* (Remington, 1884) supplements her husband's edition of the *Reminiscences, etc.* and provides the most charming portrait of Macready available. William Archer published a brief but reliable biography, *William Charles Macready* (Kegan Paul) in 1890. In 1890 the actor found an American biographer in W. T. Price, *A Life of William Charles Macready* (Brentano's). There is a good modern biography by J. C. Trewin, *Mr. Macready: A Nineteenth-Century Tragedian and his Theater* (Harrap, 1955). This will surely be superseded by Alan S. Downer's *The Eminent Tragedian, William Charles Macready* (Harvard University Press, 1966), which is not being published early enough to permit me to use it, though I have used Downer's article, "The Making of a Great Actor—William Charles Macready," *Theater Annual*, Vol. VII (1948–49), 59–83, where he gives a more elaborate analysis of Macready's acting than I can offer here, where my principal concern is with his personality.

Important contemporary recollections and evaluations of Macready (in addition to those referred to in the notes) will be found in George T. Curtis, Jr., "William Charles Macready," *Appleton's Journal*, May 24, 1873 (see, also, an unidentified newspaper article by the same writer, "Macready the Actor," in the extra-illustrated copy of Matthews and Hutton in the Harvard Theater Collection); George Henry Lewes, *On Actors and the Art of Acting* (Smith, Elder, 1875); Westland Marston, *Our Recent Actors* . . . (Sampson Low, 1888); Sir Theodore Martin, *Monographs* . . .; and James E. Murdoch, *The Stage* . . . (J. M. Stoddart & Co., 1880).

There are sketches of Macready by Henry Barton Baker, *English Actors from Shakespeare to Macready*, II; by Lawrence Barrett, in Brander Matthews and Laurence Hutton, eds., *Actors and Actresses of Great Britain and the United States*, IV; by

Donald Brook, in *A Pageant of English Actors*; and by J. A. Hammerton, in *The Actor's Art*.

Finally there are a number of miscellaneous magazine articles: Gyles Isham, "William Charles Macready, 1793–1873," *Cornhill Magazine*, Vol. CLII (1935), 483–97; S. R. Littlewood, "Intellect and the Actor," *Fortnightly Review*, N.S., Vol. XCIV (1913), 111–21; James F. Marshall, "Alfred de Vigny and William Charles Macready," *PMLA*, Vol. LXXIV (1959), 98–101; Betty Miller, " 'This Happy Evening': The Story of *Ion*," *Twentieth Century*, Vol. CLIV (1953), 53–61; H. Schütz Wilson, "Rachel and Macready," *London Society*, Vol. XXV (1874), 222–30.

4. Edwin Forrest (1806–1872)

The authorized biography is William Rounseville Alger, *Life of Edwin Forrest, The American Tragedian* (Lippincott, 1877). The two huge volumes look almost like the Furness Shakespeare, and the work is often described as sycophantic. It is not, for though Alger is very sympathetic, he admits all Forrest's faults and limitations freely. Alger's worst fault is that he writes about five sentences of commentary to every sentence of fact. Nevertheless his work is still indispensable for the wealth of material contained in it and for the detailed descriptions of what Forrest did on the stage.

The three other nineteenth-century books were all written from personal knowledge also: James Rees ("Colley Cibber"), *The Life of Edwin Forrest, with Reminiscences and Personal Recollections* (T. B. Peterson, 1874); Lawrence Barrett, *Edwin Forrest* (James R. Osgood and Company, 1881); Gabriel Harrison, *Edwin Forrest: the Actor and the Man* (Privately printed, 1889). See also Barrett's article on Forrest, *Galaxy*, Vol. XXIV (1877), 526–34, and his contribution to Brander Matthews and Laurence Hutton, eds., *Actors and Actresses of Great Britain and the United States*, V. Harrison's monograph is almost completely devoted to Forrest's acting.

Montrose J. Moses, *The Fabulous Forrest: The Record of an*

American Actor (Little, Brown, 1929) is able but extremely un-
sympathetic; the author snaps at his subject in almost every
paragraph. Much the best book that has ever been written about
Forrest (or presumably ever will be) is Richard Moody, *Edwin
Forrest, First Star of the American Stage* (Knopf, 1960). See,
also, the same author's *The Astor Place Riot* (Indiana University
Press, 1958).

There are excellent bibliographies in both Moses and Moody,
Edwin Forrest. Among the older writings I have found the fol-
lowing most useful and suggestive: Adam Badeau, *The Vaga-
bond* (Rudd & Carleton, 1859); John Coleman, *Players and
Playwrights I Have Known* (Chatto & Windus, 1888); James
Henry Hackett, *Notes, Criticisms, and Correspondence upon
Shakespeare's Plays and Actors* (Carleton, 1863); John Foster
Kirk, "Shakespeare's Tragedies on the Stage," *Lippincott's Maga-
zine,* Vol. XXXIII (1884), 604–16; James E. Murdoch, *The
Stage* . . .; Francis Courtney Wemyss, *Twenty-Six Years of the
Life of an Actor and Manager* (Burgess, Stringer and Company,
1847); Henry Wikoff, *The Reminiscences of an Idler* (Fords,
Howard & Hulbert, 1880).

There is a good modern "portrait" by Walter Prichard Eaton,
"Edwin Forrest," *Atlantic Monthly,* Vol. CLXII (1938), 238–47;
see, also, Edward Robins, *Twelve Great Actors.* A. Edward Newton's *Edwin Forrest and His Noble Creation* is a pamphlet published by The Managers of the Edwin Forrest Home in 1928.

5. Edwin Booth (1833–1893)

The basic biography is William Winter, *Life and Art of Edwin
Booth* (Macmillan, 1893), but by all means the best for modern
readers is Eleanor Ruggles, *Prince of Players* (Norton, 1953).
Asia Booth Clarke's *The Elder and the Younger Booth* (James
R. Osgood, 1882) has little or nothing about Edwin which has
not now been taken up into more extensive biographies. Stanley
Kimmel, *The Mad Booths of Maryland* (Bobbs-Merrill, 1940)
gives important background material, and information about the

Booth homestead also appears in Ella V. Mahoney, *Sketches of Tudor Hall and the Booth Family* (Tudor Hall, 1925). *Behind the Scenes with Edwin Booth*, by Katherine Goodale (Kitty Molony) (Houghton Mifflin, 1931) gives intimate, personal glimpses of Booth in the theater and on tour nowhere else available. Other biographical works, all of value, are Laurence Hutton, *Edwin Booth* (Harper, 1893); Charles T. Copeland, *Edwin Booth* (Small, Maynard, 1901); and the much more extensive Richard Lockridge, *Darling of Misfortune* ... (Century, 1932).

The best collections of letters in book form are in Edwina Booth Grossmann, *Edwin Booth, Recollections by his Daughter, and Letters to Her and to his Friends* (Century, 1894) and in Otis Skinner, *The Last Tragedian: Booth Tells His Own Story* (Dodd, Mead, 1939). See also Dolores Marbourg Bacon's article listed in n. 18; William Bispham, "Memories and Letters of Edwin Booth," *Century*, N.S., Vol. XXV (1893–94), 132–39, 240–50; Edward L. Patridge, "Edwin Booth to John E. Russell," *Outlook*, Vol. CXXVII (1921), 637–39; Charlotte F. Bates Rogé, "A Memorable Letter of Edwin Booth's" *Century*, N.S., Vol. XLV (1903–1904), 414.

Booth's papers on Edmund Kean and Junius Brutus Booth are in Volume III of Brander Matthews and Laurence Hutton, eds., *Actors and Actresses of Great Britain and the United States*, and Hutton's on Booth is in Volume V.

References to Edwin Booth will be found in almost all of William Winter's theater books, notably in *Shadows of the Stage* (Macmillan, 1893) and *Shadows of the Stage*, Third Series (Macmillan, 1895); *Shakespeare on the Stage* (Moffat, Yard, 1911); *Shakespeare on the Stage*, Second Series (Moffat, Yard, 1915); and *Vagrant Memories* (Doran, 1915). Much the best biographical portrait is Gamaliel Bradford's in his *As God Made Them: Portraits of Some Nineteenth-Century Americans* (Houghton Mifflin, 1929).

The following contain personal recollections of Booth: Adam Badeau, "Edwin Booth On and Off the Stage," *McClure's*, Vol.

I (1895), 255–67; John Denison Champlin, "Edwin Booth's 'Becket,'" *The Looker-On*, March 1897, pp. 187–97; R. Ogden Doremus, "Edwin Booth and Ole Bull," *Critic*, Vol. XLVIII (1906), 234–44; "Edwin Booth's Real Life," by an Intimate of Twenty-Five Years, *Theatre*, Vol. XXIV (1916), 360, 400; Florence Marion Howe Hall, "The Friendship of Edwin Booth and Julia Ward Howe," *New England Magazine*, N.S., Vol. IX (1893–94), 315–20; E. H. House, "Edwin Booth in London," *Century*, N.S., Vol. LV (1897–98), 269–79; Brander Matthews, "Memories of Edwin Booth," in *The Principles of Playmaking* (Scribners, 1919); John Malone, "An Actor's Memory of Edwin Booth," *Forum*, Vol. XV (1893), 594–603; Emma Pressay, "Edwin Booth and the Bouquet," *Ladies' Home Journal*, Vol. XX, July 1903, 24; Edwin Milton Royle, "Edwin Booth As I Knew Him," *Harper's Magazine*, Vol. CXXXII (1916), 840–49—also published in book form, in a limited edition, by The Players, 1933; Jefferson Winter, "As I Remember—Glimpses of Old Actors —Edwin Booth," *Saturday Evening Post*, Vol. CXCIII, Oct. 30, 1920, pp. 34ff.

The following are mainly, though not exclusively, concerned with critical evaluation: Lyman Abbott, *Silhouettes of My Contemporaries* (Doubleday, 1922); Adam Badeau, *The Vagabond*; David Belasco, "Edwin Booth, The Actor," *Century*, N.S., Vol. LXXIII (1917–18), 196–210; Lucia Gilbert Calhoun, "Edwin Booth," *Galaxy*, Vol. VII (1869), 77–87; Henry A. Clapp, in Frederic E. McKay and Charles E. L. Wingate, eds., *Famous American Actors of Today* (Crowell, 1896); Walter Prichard Eaton, "Edwin Booth," *Theatre Arts Monthly*, Vol. XVI (1932), 888–94; Laurence Hutton, "Edwin Booth," *Harper's Magazine*, Vol. XCVI (1898), 196–210; A. D. Kellogg, *The Hamlet of Edwin Booth: A Psychological Study* (Appleton, 1872); Montrose J. Moses, *Famous Actor Families in America* (Crowell, 1906); Henry C. Pedder, "Edwin Booth," *The Manhattan*, Vol. III (1884), 295–310; Edward Robins, *Twelve Great Actors*; E. C. Stedman, "Edwin Booth," *Atlantic Monthly*, Vol. XVII (1866),

585–93—reprinted in his *Genius and Other Essays* (Moffat, Yard, 1911).

Innumerable books of reminiscences, theatrical and otherwise, bearing on the nineteenth-century scene, contain references to Booth. These are some of the most important: Mrs. Thomas Bailey Aldrich, *Crowding Memories* (Houghton Mifflin, 1920); Daniel Frohman, *Encore*; Henry Holt, *Garrulities of an Octogenarian Editor* (Houghton Mifflin, 1923); Helena Modjeska, *Memories and Impressions* (Macmillan, 1910); Clara Morris, *Life on the Stage* (McClure, Phillips, 1901); Augustus Pitou, *Masters of the Show* (Neale Publishing Co., 1914); Otis Skinner, *Footlights and Spotlights* (Bobbs-Merrill, 1924); E. H. Sothern, *The Melancholy Tale of "Me": My Remembrances* (Scribners, 1916).

6. *Sir Henry Irving (1838–1905)*

There are two elaborate biographies: Austin Brereton, *The Life of Henry Irving*, (2 vols., Longmans, 1908) and *Henry Irving, The Actor and His World*, by his grandson Laurence Irving (Macmillan, 1952). Brereton adds background material in *The Lyceum and Henry Irving* (McClure, Phillips, 1903). Considering its bulk, Bram Stoker's *Personal Recollections of Henry Irving*, (2 vols., Macmillan, 1906) has surprisingly little in it.

Gordon Craig's *Henry Irving* (Dent, 1930) is an impassioned tribute. See, also, his *Ellen Terry and Her Secret Self* (Dutton, 1932); *Henry Irving, Ellen Terry: A Book of Portraits* (Herbert S. Stone & Co., 1899); and the following articles: "Henry Irving, 1838–1938," *London Mercury*, Vol. XXXVII (1938), 400–405; "Henry Irving, 1838–1938," *Theatre Arts*, Vol. XXII (1938), 31–40; "Irving Seemingly Perplexed," *Drama*, No. 43, Winter 1956, pp. 25–26.

Clement Scott collected his reviews of Lyceum Theater productions in *From "The Bells" to "King Arthur"* (John Macqueen, 1896) and William Winter his reviews of Irving's performances in New York in his *Henry Irving* (George J. Coombes, 1885).

See, also, Winter's *Other Days* (Moffat, Yard, 1908) and *Vagrant Memories* (Doran, 1915). Edward R. Russell published a fairly elaborate study of *Irving as Hamlet* (Henry S. King & Co., 1875); see, also, "Mr. Irving's Interpretations of Shakespeare," *Fortnightly*, N.S., Vol. XXXIV (1883), 466–81, and "Irving's *King Lear*: A New Tradition," *Nineteenth Century*, Vol. XXXIII (1893), 44–51. Max Beerbohm's criticism is in *Around Theatres*, (2 vols., Knopf, 1930). But the book which brings Irving closest to the modern reader and gives him his best chance to judge what it must have been like to see him on the stage is *We Saw Him Act: A Symposium on the Art of Henry Irving*, ed. by H. A. Saintsbury and Cecil Palmer (Hurst & Blackett, 1939).

Irving's articles and addresses were largely ghostwritten, but they no doubt represent his views with a fair degree of accuracy. Some of them may be found in *The Stage* (Ridgway, 1878); Preface to Diderot's *The Paradox of Acting*, translated by W. H. Pollock (Chatto & Windus, 1883); *The Drama: Addresses* (Tait, Sons and Company, 1893); *The Theatre in its Relation to the State* (Richard G. Badger, 1898); Introduction to Talma's *Reflexions on the Actor's Art* (Columbia University Press, 1915); *The Art of Acting: A Discussion*, by Constant Coquelin, Henry Irving, and Dion Boucicault (Columbia, 1926). See, also, "The Works of William Shakespeare," ed. by Henry Irving and Frank A. Marshall, (8 vols., Scribner & Welford, 1888–90).

Articles published over Irving's by-line include "My Four Favorite Parts," *Forum*, Vol. XVI (1893), 33–37. In *The Nineteenth Century* he published "Actor-Managers," Vol. XXVII (1890), 1052–53, and "Some Misconceptions about the Stage," Vol. XXXII (1892), 670–76, as well as three notes on Shakespearean items: Vol. I (1877), 327–30, 524–30, and Vol. V (1879), 260–63. There are reports of addresses in "Henry Irving on Marlowe," *Critic*, N.S., Vol. XVI (1891), 72, and "Henry Irving's Harvard Address," N.S., Vol. XXI (1894), 204–205. There are extracts from various addresses in J. A. Hammerton, ed., *The Actor's Art*.

Though it has some interest as a kind of travelogue of Irving's American tours, Joseph Hatton's *Henry Irving's Impressions of America* (2 vols., Sampson Low, 1884) is thin and stilted, with everything arranged as if on dress parade. In "A Chapter in the Life of Henry Irving" in his *Old Lamps and New* (Hutchinson, n.d.), Hatton supplements the larger work by describing Irving on the Continent. His "Sir Henry Irving: His Romantic Career On and Off the Stage" was serialized in *The Grand Magazine*, Volumes II and III, beginning with the issue for January 1906.

Other books on Irving are: William Archer, *Henry Irving, Actor and Manager* (Field & Tuer, 1883); Hall Caine, *"Richard III" and "Macbeth": The Spirit of Romantic Play in Relationship to the Principles of Greek and Gothic Art, and to the Picturesque Interpretations of Henry Irving* (Simpkin, Marshall, 1877); Frederic Daly (pseud. of Louis Frederic Austin), *Henry Irving in England and America, 1838–1884* (T. Fisher Unwin, 1884); Percy Fitzgerald, *Sir Henry Irving: A Biography* (George W. Jacobs & Co., 1906); Charles Hiatt, *Henry Irving: A Record and Review* (George Bell and Sons, 1899); Henry Arthur Jones, *The Shadow of Henry Irving* (Morrow, 1931); Haldane Macfall, *Sir Henry Irving* (John W. Luce & Company, 1906); Mortimer Menpes, *Henry Irving* (Adam and Charles Black, 1906); Walter Herries Pollock, *Impressions of Henry Irving* (Longmans, 1908). There is also a modern Italian study: Gigi Lunari, *Henry Irving e il teatro borghese dell'800* (Cappelli, 1961).

Reminiscences of Irving may be found in many books, notably Marie Bancroft and Squire Bancroft, *The Bancrofts: Recollections of Sixty Years* (Dutton, 1909); Sir Johnston Forbes-Robertson, *A Player Under Three Reigns* (Little, Brown, 1925); Joseph Harker, *Studio and Stage* (Nisbet, 1924); *The Autobiography of Sir John Martin-Harvey* (Sampson Low, 1934); Jessie Millward, *Myself and Others* (Hutchinson, 1923); Howard Paul, *Dinners with Celebrities* (Newton & Eskell, n.d.); W. Graham Robertson, *Time Was* (Hamish Hamilton, 1931); Seymour Hicks, *Between Ourselves* (Cassell, 1930); Sir Merton Russell-Cotes, *Home and*

Abroad, II (privately printed, 1921); and, above all, *Ellen Terry's Memoirs*, ed. by Edith Craig and Christopher St. John (Putnam, 1932). See, also, Robert Hichens, "Sir Henry Irving," *Fortnightly*, Vol. CLXVIII (1947), 455–60; The Dean of Winchester, "The Irvings—Some Memories," *Cornhill Magazine*, N.S., Vol. LIV (1923), 30–38.

There are sketches of Irving in Donald Brook, *A Pageant of English Actors*; J. Comyns Carr, *Some Eminent Victorians* (Duckworth, 1908); Arthur Goddard, *Players of the Period* (Dean & Son, 1891); Lewis C. Strang, *Players and Plays of the Last Quarter Century*, II (L. C. Page, 1902); John Ranken Towse, in Brander Matthews and Laurence Hutton, eds., *Actors and Actresses of Great Britain and the United States . . .*, V; Geoffrey Trease, *Seven Stages* (Vanguard, 1965). Edward J. West's "Henry Irving, 1870–1890," in *Studies in Speech and Drama in Honor of Alexander M. Drummond* (Cornell University Press, 1944) is a thorough, well-balanced, systematic consideration of Irving's acting. See, further, the same author's "Irving in Shakespeare: Interpretation or Creation?" *Shakespeare Quarterly*, Vol. VI (1955), 415–22.

To the foregoing the following articles may be added: L. F. Austin, "Sir Henry Irving," *North American Review*, Vol. CLXXXI (1905), 767–76, and in his *Points of View* (John Lane, 1906); William T. W. Ball, "Henry Irving's Influence on the American Stage," *New England Magazine*, N.S., Vol. X (1894), 173–83; Henry Austin Clapp, *Reminiscences of a Dramatic Critic* (Houghton Mifflin, 1902); Harry Furniss, "Henry Irving: An Artist's Sketch of an Actor," *Strand Magazine*, February 1906, pp. 32–38; Tighe Hopkins, "On Some Portraits of Henry Irving, with Certain Reminiscences," *Cassell's Magazine*, Vol. XXIV (1906), 417–26; Augustin Lewis, "Henry Irving," *Dublin University Magazine*, Vol. XC (1887), 284–307; E. S. Nadal, "An Impression of Henry Irving," *Scribner's Magazine*, Vol. XXXIX (1906), 120–23; Ouida, "Mr. Irving on the Art of Acting," *Nineteenth Century*, Vol. XXXVII (1895), 786–97; George Sampson,

Seven Essays (Cambridge University Press, 1947); H. M. Walbrook, "Henry Irving," *Fortnightly*, N.S., Vol. CXLIII (1938), 203–11; Talcott Williams, "Sir Henry Irving," *Atlantic Monthly*, Vol. XCVI (1905), 826–33; Sir Charles Wyndham, "Sir Henry Irving" and Percy Burton, "Anecdotes, Reminiscences, and an Appreciation," *Pearson's Magazine*, December, 1905, pp. 619–24.

7. Joseph Jefferson (1829–1905)

The Autobiography of Joseph Jefferson was first published by The Century Company in 1890. The two most important reprints have been those by Reinhardt & Evans, 1949, with an introduction by Eleanor Farjeon, and by The Belknap Press of Harvard University Press, in "The John Harvard Library," with an introduction by Alan S. Downer, 1964.

This, the most important source for knowledge of Jefferson, is importantly supplemented by Francis Wilson, *Joseph Jefferson: Reminiscences of a Fellow Player* (Scribners, 1906) and by Eugénie Paul Jefferson, *Intimate Recollections of Joseph Jefferson* (Dodd, Mead, 1909), and less importantly by Nathan Haskell Dole, *Joseph Jefferson at Home* (Estes and Lauriat, 1898). William Winter's *Life and Art of Joseph Jefferson* (Macmillan, 1894) is a scholarly and authoritative work, especially on Jefferson's family background; among Winter's numerous papers on Jefferson, the most important is the one in *Other Days* (Moffat, Yard, 1908). Gladys Malvern's *Good Troupers All* (Macrae Smith, 1954) is a readable, semi-fictional, but conscientious account of Jefferson's life, addressed primarily to young readers. There is a psychograph of Jefferson in Gamaliel Bradford, *American Portraits, 1875–1900* (Houghton Mifflin, 1922). See, also, the references to him in Rosamond Gilder, ed., *Letters of Richard Watson Gilder* (Houghton Mifflin, 1916).

Among the numerous articles that have been published about Jefferson, the following are, for various reasons, of special interest: William Hosea Ballou, "Joseph Jefferson at Home," *Cosmopolitan*, Vol. VII (1899), 121–27; Rosamond Gilder, "Joseph

Jefferson," *Theatre Arts*, Vol. XXVII (1943), 375–84; Muriel G. Henshaw, "Joseph Jefferson, A Memory of Louisiana," *Bohemian Magazine*, Vol. XVI (1909), 737–47; James Huneker, "Joseph Jefferson," *World's Work*, Vol. X (1905), 6317–20; Edward King, in McKay and Wingate, eds., *Famous American Actors of Today*; James S. Metcalfe, "Goin' Fishin' with Joseph Jefferson," *Ladies Home Journal*, Vol. XVIII, July, 1901, pp. 2–3; Gilbert A. Pierce, "A Good-by to Rip Van Winkle," *Atlantic Monthly*, Vol. LII (1883), 695–703; James B. Runnion, "Joseph Jefferson," *Lippincott's Magazine*, Vol. IV (1869), 167–76; E. H. Sothern, "Joseph Jefferson," *Frank Leslie's Popular Monthly*, February 1903, pp. 422–24; Jefferson Winter, "As I Remember," *Saturday Evening Post*, Vol. CXCIII, August 7, 1920, pp. 38, 40, 42, 44; September 4, 1920, pp. 22–23, 85–86.

8. *Richard Mansfield (1854–1907)*

The principal sources of information are Paul Wilstach, *Richard Mansfield, the Man and the Actor* (Scribners, 1908) and William Winter, *Life and Art of Richard Mansfield, With Selections from his Letters*, (2 vols., Moffat, Yard, 1910).

For Mansfield's own writings, see the bibliographies included in the above-mentioned works. His play, *Don Juan*, was published for the author by J. W. Bouton in 1891. *The Richard Mansfield Acting Version of King Henry V* (McClure, Phillips, 1901) has interesting introduction and notes. "As You Find It" may most conveniently be read in *One-Act Plays for Stage and Study, Eighth Series* (Samuel French, 1934). Among Mansfield's magazine articles, the following are notable: "A Plain Talk on the Drama," *North American Review*, Vol. CLV (1892), 308–14; "Concerning Acting," *North American Review*, Vol. CLIX (1894), 337–42; "My Audience—and Myself," *Collier's*, Vol. XXVI, Oct. 6, 1900, p. 13; "Man and the Actor," *Atlantic Monthly*, Vol. XCVII (1906), 577–85.

Mansfield figured contemporaneously in William Henry Frost, in F. E. McKay and Charles E. L. Wingate, eds., *Famous Ameri-*

can Actors of Today; Margherita Arlina Hamm, *Eminent Actors in Their Homes* (James Pott & Company, 1902); Gustav Kobbé, *Famous Actors and Their Homes* (Little, Brown, 1905); Amy Leslie, *Some Players: Personal Sketches* (Herbert S. Stone & Company, 1899); Lewis C. Strang, *Famous Actors of the Day in America* (L. C. Page, 1900). Contemporaneous and near-contemporaneous articles include: Anon., "How I Became the Private Secretary of Richard Mansfield," *Young Men's Home Journal*, Vol. I (1904), 109–12; James O'Donnell Bennett, "Richard Mansfield," *Munsey's Magazine*, Vol. XXXVI (1907), 772–76; John Corbin, "The Greatest English Actor," *Appleton's Magazine*, Vol. IX (1907), 287–94; Joseph H. Dillon, "The Richard Mansfield I Knew," Boston *Sunday Herald Magazine*, May 17, 1914; Lyman B. Glover, "Richard Mansfield." *The World Today*, Vol. XIII (1907), 973–76; Clayton Hamilton, "Richard Mansfield, The Man," *North American Review*, Vol. CLXXXVII (1908), 60–69; Henry P. Mawson, "Richard Mansfield's True Rank as an Actor," *Theatre* [New York], Vol. VII (1907), 282–84, ix–x; Harry Wandmacher, "Was Mansfield a Genius?" *Arena*, Vol. XXXIX (1908), 166–76; Kenyon West, "Richard Mansfield," *Arena*, Vol. XXXV (1906), 3–15. See also the references to him in Norman Hapgood, *The Stage in America, 1897–1900* (Macmillan, 1901) and John Ranken Towse, *Sixty Years of the Theater* (Funk and Wagnalls, 1916). The most important articles of later years are probably Walter Prichard Eaton, "Richard Mansfield," *Theatre Arts Monthly*, Vol. XI (1927), 111–16; W. A. Stanley, "Richard Mansfield's Real Self," *Theatre* [New York], Vol. XXVI (1912), 126, 162, 200, 256; Garff B. Wilson, "Richard Mansfield: Actor of the Transition," *Educational Theatre Journal*, Vol. XIV (1962), 38–43.

Index

(In the main entry for each, the names of the eight actors considered in this book are spelled out; elsewhere in the index, initials are employed.)

Abbe, Charles S.: 142
Abington, Frances: 20
Alanienonideh, EK's Indian name: 53
Albery, James: 157
Alcott, Louisa May, on EB: 140
Aldrich, Thomas Bailey: 129, 141, 153
Alger, Horatio Jr.: 105
Alger, William R., on EF: 93, 100, 104, 117
Alma Tadema, Sir Laurence: 229
Anderson, David: 142
Archer, William: 58, 162, 164, 183
Aria, Eliza, and HI: 164, 175, 177, 181
Arnold, Matthew, on HI's Othello: 170
Arnold, Samuel: 34, 50
Astor Place Opera House Riot, The: 79, 93, 96, 105, 105–109, 182
Austen, Jane: 77
Ayres, Alfred, on EB: 123

Badeau, Adam: 134, 135, 139, 141, 150
Baden-Powell, B. F. S.: 183
Baker, Mrs.: 33
Balfe, Michael William: 61

Bashkirtseff, Marie: 139
Bancroft, Squire and Marie: 168, 172, 179
Bannister, Charles: 13–14
Barrett, Lawrence: 206–207, 228; on EF, 104; partnership with EB, 129, 134, 137, 138–39
Barrie, Sir James M.: 171
Barry, Spranger: 7, 11
Barrymore, John: 46, 227
Barrymore, Lionel: 187
Barton, Margaret: 7
Bastien-Lepage, Jules: 179
Bateman, Hezekiah Linthicum: 157–58
Bateman, Isabel: 158–59, 180–81
Bateman, Kate: 158
Bateman, Sidney Frances (Mrs. H. L.): 158, 159, 180–81
Beaumont and Fletcher: 26
Beerbohm, Sir Max, on HI: 166, 170, 177
Belasco, David, on EB's voice: 131
Bellamy, George Ann: 7
Benjamin, Ophelia: 52
Bennett, James O'Donnell, on RM: 224
Benson, Sir Frank, on HI: 167
Bernhardt, Sarah: 22, 134, 144, 151, 162, 184, 224, 225, 226, 237